Women and Revivalism in the West

Women's Studies at York Series

General Editors: **Haleh Afshar** and **Mary Maynard**

Haleh Afshar
ISLAM AND FEMINISMS
An Iranian Case-Study
WOMEN AND EMPOWERMENT
Illustrations from the Third World (*editor*)
WOMEN IN THE MIDDLE EAST
Perceptions, Realities and Struggles for Liberation (*editor*)

Haleh Afshar and Stephanie Barrientos (*editors*)
WOMEN, GLOBALIZATION AND FRAGMENTATION IN THE DEVELOPING WORLD

Haleh Afshar and Carolyne Dennis (*editors*)
WOMEN AND ADJUSTMENT POLICIES IN THE THIRD WORLD

Myfanwy Franks
WOMEN AND REVIVALISM IN THE WEST
Choosing 'Fundamentalism' in a Liberal Democracy

Judy Giles
WOMEN, IDENTITY AND PRIVATE LIFE IN BRITAIN, 1900–50

Mary Maynard and Joanna de Groot (*editors*)
WOMEN'S STUDIES IN THE 1990s
Doing Things Differently?

Haideh Moghissi
POPULISM AND FEMINISM IN IRAN
Women's Struggle in a Male-Defined Revolutionary Movement

Shirin M. Rai (*editor*)
INTERNATIONAL PERSPECTIVES ON GENDER AND DEMOCRATIZATION

Carmel Roulston and Celia Davies (*editors*)
GENDER, DEMOCRACY AND INCLUSION IN NORTHERN IRELAND

Women's Studies at York
Series Standing Order ISBN 0–333–71512–8
(*outside North America only*)

You can receive future titles in this series as they are published by placing a standing order. Please contact your bookseller or, in case of difficulty, write to us at the address below with your name and address, the title of the series and the ISBN quoted above.

Customer Services Department, Macmillan Distribution Ltd, Houndmills, Basingstoke, Hampshire RG21 6XS, England

Women and Revivalism in the West

Choosing 'Fundamentalism' in a Liberal Democracy

Myfanwy Franks
Research Fellow
Department of Social Policy and Social Work
University of York

First published 2001 by
PALGRAVE
Houndmills, Basingstoke, Hampshire RG21 6XS and
175 Fifth Avenue, New York, N. Y. 10010
Companies and representatives throughout the world

PALGRAVE is the new global academic imprint of
St. Martin's Press LLC Scholarly and Reference Division and
Palgrave Publishers Ltd (formerly Macmillan Press Ltd).

ISBN 0–333–92287–5

This book is printed on paper suitable for recycling and made from fully managed and sustained forest sources.

A catalogue record for this book is available from the British Library.

Library of Congress Cataloging-in-Publication Data
Franks, Myfanwy, 1947–
    Women and revivalism in the West : choosing "fundamentalism" in a liberal democracy / Myfanwy Franks.
        p. cm. — (Women's studies at York series)
    Includes bibliographical references (p.) and index.
    ISBN 0–333–92287–5
    1. Religious fundamentalism. 2. Women and religion.
    3. Feminism—Religious aspects. I. Title. II. Women's studies at York series (Houndmills, Basingstoke, England)
    BL238 .F73 2001
    305.48'6—dc21
                                                                2001021258

10   9   8   7   6   5   4   3   2   1
10   09   08   07   06   05   04   03   02   01

Printed and bound in Great Britain by
Antony Rowe Ltd, Chippenham, Wiltshire

In memory of Alice Mary Franks

Contents

Acknowledgements   xi

Introduction   1
A shared voice   1
Postmodernism: women and politics   2
Right-wing women   5

1. **Revivalisms and Feminisms**   9
   'Fundamentalism' and the construction of a
       fanatical 'Other'   9
   Revivalisms – Christian and Islamic   11
   Millennialism, pessimism and Christian revival   13
   Islamic and Christian revivalist groups in the West   14
   Christian revival: 'signs and wonders' in
       Britain and the United States   17
   Islamic revival: science and 'naturalness' versus
       postmodernism   20
   Protestantism and women   22
   Protestant fundamentalism and gender: the recipe
       for feminine submission   23
   Feminisms within religious traditions   25
   Muslim and Islamic or 'Islamist' feminist scholars
       of Islam   25
   Islamic feminists   26
   Muslim feminists   28
   Progressive readings of Islam   28
   Feminist theology and biblical feminism   29
   Why revivalisms?   34

2. **Reflexive Methodology**   37
   Introduction   37
   Feminist methodology and epistemology   38
   Method   48
   Questionnaires   61
   Power   67

Difficult issues – caught in the crossfire: reframing 72
Mixed methods 74

3. **Marriage, Obedience and Feminine Submission** 77
Feminine submission 77
The concept of submission 79
The question 81
Muslim responses 82
Christian responses 84
Submission in evangelical Christian marriage 85
Leadership and submission 90
Responses that disrupt the stereotypical image 95
Submission is a complex issue 99

4. **Rights and Responsibilities** 103
Rights 104
Pre-Islamic and pre-Christian conditions 108
Respondents to the snowball questionnaire and
 rights under British law today 112
Rights and religious affiliation 114
Marriage, motherhood and divorce 117
Islamic feminist approaches to claiming Islamic rights 118
Women's *tafsir* 122
Feminist and non-feminist strategies 123

5. **Modesty Codes and the Veil** 127
Modesty and head covering in Islam and Islamic revival 127
Hajib and *hijab* 128
Hijab: criticisms and counter-arguments 129
Modesty and head covering in Christianity and the new
 Christian churches 145
Christian responses: modesty 148
Covering in Christianity 150
Modesty and everyday life 153
Head covering and modesty in two traditions 156

6. **Empowerment through Revivalisms:
Some Gains and Losses** 159
Empowerment 159
Rational choice theory 163
The Christian respondents 164

The Muslim respondents	168
Converts: family and friends	169
The gains	170
Kinds of empowerment	183
Conclusion	**185**
Notes	189
Bibliography	195
Index	207

Acknowledgements

I am grateful to the ESRC for providing me with a scholarship with-out which the research, which forms the basis of this book, could never have been carried out. I wish sincerely to thank all the partici-pants in this study for their generosity in sharing their knowledge and experiences and, frequently, their hospitality. To protect their anonymity, all names used in the text are fictitious. I am indebted to religious scholars, both Muslim and Christian, who have offered their advice, help and guidance and to religious leaders for their invaluable time and help. Special thanks are due to Neal Robinson for igniting my interest in Islam and for encouraging me to go on to do research. I am grateful to Mary Maynard, Anne Ackroyd and Kim Knott for their help and suggestions. I am indebted to Julie Reichert and Kristin Aune for their input. Unrivalled gratitude goes to Haleh Afshar for her unstinting advice and support and for being there during the difficult times. Any inaccuracies or misrepresentations are attribut-able to none of these persons but to me.

A special thank you to Non Franks and to Phil Cutler for their encouragement at all stages of this study and for their belief in me.

Introduction

A shared voice

Written at a time when an emphasis on difference has largely eclipsed any shared feminist voice, this project began as a quest for shared views among disparate groups of women. It is a study about why some Western women choose to negotiate a path to empowerment within the limits of particular forms of revivalist Protestantism and Islam. It touches on many areas of women's lives where there are indeed shared anxieties and concerns. These include finance, exploitation through the beauty myth, the avoidance of sexual objectification, marriage, mothering and family life, justice in the workplace and how to balance the difficult juxtaposition of work outside the home with concerns about child care. Although these issues manifest themselves differently for different women who are from diverse social and ethnic backgrounds, they remain matters of importance for many women. Despite earlier feminist struggles and the progress that has been made, these problem areas of women's lives have never gone away nor found a final resolution.

Women in a liberal democracy who join revivalist groups by *choice* represent a counter-culture. My intention has therefore been to put the stereotypes – such as the belief that women who choose Islamic and Christian revivalist faith communities are compliant, submissive and oppressed – to the test. In reality, many women take this path as a matter of informed choice and there is evidence that some women who are high achievers affiliate themselves to revivalist movements.

1

Data collected through fieldwork in Britain as well as material from interviews with Muslim and Christian participants from the United States are included in this account. The aims are to compare the position of women in revivalism in two faith traditions; to understand the attractions revivalism holds for Western women who do not find a solution in Western feminisms; and to examine the notion that some women who involve themselves in revivalism have an overt feminist (Afshar 1998) or closet feminist (Faludi 1991) agenda and to see how this compares across the two faith traditions.

Revivalist or restorationist groups look to early Islam or Christianity and aim to reproduce a pristine form of their faith traditions in the present day. In this respect revivalisms may be located in the postmodern longing for authenticity that is so prevalent in Western society today. Revivalist movements have a reputation for policing gender boundaries and reinforcing binary gender roles. Yet, by taking what is often called a biologically and culturally 'essentialist' position on what it is to be a women, they share with some radical feminists the confidence that what it means to be a woman can be defined. By reinforcing binary gender roles revivalists reject both postmodern formulations of gender fluidity and relativism which have come to dominate postmodern Western feminisms and post-femininism. Nevertheless, the culturally essentialist position is not universal among the Christians, some of whom reject the 'equal but different' (complementarian) model of gender relations and accept a more androgynous model of gender equality.

The consequence of 'gender skepticism' (Bordo 1990) has been that for many Western feminists motherhood has been abandoned as an issue of feminist concern. This study attempts to trace the degree to which revivalist women represent a repository of an embodied species of feminism or activism for women's rights which, based on holy texts, relates to the lived bodily experience of women at different stages of their lives.

Postmodernism: women and politics

Postmodern analysis (a heading under which I include poststructuralism) has become mainstream across a broad range of academic disciplines and it is unavoidable that this study should utilize postmodern and poststructuralist tools of analysis to some degree.

Poststructuralist analysis has enabled us to make a nuanced analysis of power relations, and previous assumptions that power relations were generally one-way now seem crude. Yet the institutionalization of postmodern discourse is something of a two-edged sword: the post-modern discrediting of grand narratives (Lyotard 1984) includes not only an agenda of the deconstruction of feminism as a metanarrative, but also incredulity of the category 'woman' itself (Kristeva 1974; Butler 1990). This gender scepticism has widened the dichotomy which already existed in feminist discourse between an essentialist view of womanhood and a view of gender as the result of encultur-ation. This bifurcation of feminisms in relation to the political posi-tion of women in current thought emerges as a core concern of this study.

Models of womanhood that view femininity as a social construc-tion, liberating as they may be, also have their limitations (Gram-Hanssen 1996). Postmodern constructions of 'woman' as a production of discourses, who does not exist *per se*, lead swiftly to the conclusion that if the category 'woman' does not exist, then women cannot be oppressed. This does not reflect the lived and embodied experiences of many women in the developed and the developing worlds when it comes to pregnancy, childbirth, ageing and the constrained choices which they face. Poststructuralism, gender fluidity and 'play' do not take account of the global feminization of poverty (Pateman 1992) and the double and triple burden of nurturing, child care and work-ing outside the home which is the lot of so many women, nor the lack of rights which women face in many parts of the world. As Fatmagul Berktay has pointed out, the emphasis on difference has '[p]aradoxically... given rise to an increasing perception of many differences between women, and has shattered "woman" as a notion. It is no longer easy to believe in the cosy and comforting concept of sisterhood' (Berktay 1993: 110).

Yet poststructuralist analysis has afforded us a greater understanding of how it is that oppressed people learn to internalize their oppres-sion. Sandra Bartky makes a Foucauldian analysis to show how, within the institution of heterosexuality, women internalize the patriarchal view: 'In contemporary patriarchal culture, a panoptical male connoisseur resides within the consciousness of most women: they stand perpetually before his gaze and under his judgement' (Bartky 1988: 72). The problem is not merely external; it is installed in the feminine consciousness. Throughout their lives women are exposed to texts and images that render violence against them unexceptional to the point of invisibility. Religious images from the Old Testament, such as the portrayal of Jerusalem as a whore (Ezekiel 16) and more ancient mythologies, such as the Sumerian creation myth in which the Goddess Tiamat is split like a fish by the God Marduk to provide heaven and earth (Dalley 1989: 254–5), provide an inheritance which normalizes violence against women. Nor is Islam blameless in this respect. Surah 4:34 of the Qur'an is often cited, especially by Christian evangelizers, as an example of Muslim permission to beat women: 'As for those [women] from whom ye fear rebellion, admonish them and banish them to beds apart, and scourge them'. Here the Arabic word *daraba* is translated by Marmaduke Pickthall as 'scourge'. A 'reformist' translation will deny that *daraba* means to beat: Ahmad Ali, in his translation of the Qur'an, cites examples of pre-Islamic use of the word *daraba* to indicate sexual relations. But surely, this could be as bad. The idea that sexual intercourse can subdue the wayward wife has affinities with the pornographic fantasy that women enjoy being raped.

Yet, though religions may be used to justify violent conduct, it is not particular religions which are the cause of violence against women: the problem is that the majority of religions continue to reinforce and reproduce patriarchal relations. Some religious groups in the developed world, for instance, try to persuade women to relinquish their hard-won rights and support male supremacy, which they justify in the name of religion. One such group is the Council on Biblical Manhood and Womenhood (CBMW), which currently operates in the United States and is active on the Internet, where its message is translated into languages ranging from Arabic to Pidgin. Although patriarchal relations can no longer be viewed as monolithic but as situated within cultures, they nevertheless remain dominant as power structures. The idea of post-patriarchal religion (Cooey et al. 1991) may be optimistic at this juncture.

Postmodern Western feminisms' concern with difference asserts that women's problems are not universal across class and ethnic differences. This means that women no longer have a shared voice (Berktay 1993: 110–31). This is the very voice that we need if we are to make a stand against crimes committed against women in the name of religion and no religion, across cultures, throughout history and across the globe. Nancy Hartsock has indicated with irony that at the very point when women and non-Western peoples gained a voice, postmodernism, poststructuralism and semiotics, by deconstructing discourses, led to the devaluation of that voice (Hartsock 1987: 187–206). Although there is a situatedness to all women's issues, and feminisms must be a response to located forms of patriarchal relations, there must nevertheless be some shared concerns. This study attempts to establish what these might be.

Right-wing women

Women who are apparently non-feminist or anti-feminist have not occupied a great deal of feminist theory, yet there have been some important works on the subject which have been influential in my choice of topic and in my thinking. The first was Andrea Dworkin's groundbreaking *Right-Wing Women* (1979) in which she examines why some American women associate themselves with the New Right. She concluded, amongst other things, that new reproductive technologies are a threat as women will no longer be valued as mothers and she sees women as hiding behind theology in order to keep a sacred place for motherhood. The second was Susan Faludi's *Backlash* (1991). Faludi also looked at why some women identify themselves with the New Right, in Britain as well as the United States. She concluded that many of the women she interviewed were exhibiting a closet feminism because, by taking the role of spokeswomen against feminism, they were able to claim many of the things for which feminists were fighting. These included the right to work and have a family, a personal income, status and a voice. For some this included a jet-set life-style. The third influential writer was Haleh Afshar (1991, 1995, 1995a, 1998), who has written in a similar, but more generous vein, in relation to why women identify with 'fundamentalism' in Islam. She concluded that it was in response to the double and treble burdens of which Islamists complained: that women are obliged to be responsible for child care as well as compete in the labour market. Women who work outside the home return to another one or two jobs in the home. Since then a number of writers, including, Gerami (1996), Karam (1998) and Brasher (1998), have begun to explore why some women freely join movements that apparently restrict their freedom. It appears to be a subject which is gaining momentum.

In the process of working on this study I came to the conclusion that being a revivalist is not necessarily synonymous with being 'right-wing'. Donna Luff (1999), in a recent study involving 'anti-feminist-women', felt uneasy with moments of rapport she experienced with her participants. But it may be that these moments point to the possibility of shared agendas between women of disparate beliefs, a kind of postmodern feminist politics (Roseneil 1999) that is issues-based. If patriarchy and feminism have been dismantled and can no longer be viewed as monoliths, then neither can anti-feminism. Indeed what anti-feminist might mean becomes increasingly difficult to define.

In women's studies, the theme of women and religion (as opposed to 'women and spirituality') is still not popular in some quarters. Yet because women continue to affiliate themselves with faith communities and are largely, through their influence in the home, the transmitters of religious tradition, it is an important area of study. Even though the majority of religions are patriarchal, women make up the majority of believers (Cornwall 1989; Batson et al. 1993).

Contrary to the popular image, there are strands of feminism within revivalisms. For instance, the work of biblical feminists, such as those in the organisation Men Women and God, is gaining influence in the house church fellowships with their egalitarian message which is based on the biblical text. Similarly, Islamic feminists are changing the way in which the rights and responsibilities of women, set out in the Qur'an, are viewed. Unlike the secularist stereotype of second wave feminism, there never has been a generation of feminists who were *all* secular. There were, in the 1970s and later, feminists who sought new kinds of spirituality for women as well as a tradition of feminists who linked themselves with various religious groups. Among the multiplicity of feminists today, there are many who work *within* religions and some have participated in this study. It pleases me to imagine all these feminists working in their own ways and within their own traditions but joined by the fact that they are all chiselling away at patriarchal relations. This kind of tailored response to local conditions is beautifully illustrated by Um Zhivago, a woman activist in a Palestinian refugee camp, who said: 'a revolution is like cooking; before you begin, you have to look in the cupboard to see what ingredients you have at hand to work with'

(Warnock Fernea 1998: 415). Her statement exemplifies not only the reflexivity and practicality of feminist struggle in responding to located conditions, but also the degree to which it reflects the lived experience of women.

1
Revivalisms and Feminisms

Even though traditional religions are patriarchal and engage in the policing of gender boundaries and roles, it is revivalist religious groups that are popularly perceived to be hotbeds of female oppression. Women who affiliate themselves with revivalist Islamic or Christian groups are often regarded as embracing their own oppression and as being anti-feminists who actively promote the interests of patriarchal relations. The findings of this study suggest that the choices revivalist women make in the context of Western societies are more complex and varied than often supposed. This comparative study is a means of contextualizing the position of women within a variety of revivalist groups. There are clearly similarities as well as differences between Islamic and Christian revivalist movements in terms of gender relations and there are also differences between groups, in this respect, *within* the faith communities. Where gender relations are concerned, the differences between revivalists and secularists are not always as significant as popularly perceived.

'Fundamentalism' and the construction of a fanatical 'Other'

Despite the criticism that anyone who writes about 'fundamentalism' ends up writing about why this originally Protestant term is inappropriate to Islam (Moghissi 1999), I feel the necessity to mention briefly its inappropriateness, not only to Islam, but also as a universally applicable term with which to describe house church fellowships and other Christian revivalist groups. At the outset of this study

I had intended to use the term 'fundamentalist' to describe modern movements within the traditional religions, which hark back to a 'pristine' tradition and which, on the surface at least, appear to place an emphasis on the masculinity of God and the submission of women (Barr 1977; Hawley 1994). It soon became apparent though that 'fundamentalism' is inappropriate in this comparative study for four reasons: (1) It arose as an adopted, rather than an ascribed term, in the first quarter of the twentieth century, from a Protestant movement of conservative evangelicals in the United States. They were militantly opposed to modernism in culture and theology, including higher biblical criticism and Darwinism, and held the Bible to be inerrant. It is therefore an historically incorrect term to apply to Islam, which has its own tradition of renewal (*tajdid*).[1] Revitalization movements in Islam are not a new phenomenon (Rahman 1979: 196). (2) The term does not fit the modern charismatic house church fellowships within Christianity, which owe much to the Pentecostal tradition and have ecstatic elements in their practice. (3) The term 'fundamentalism' is unhelpful for it polarizes debate and is used pejoratively to construct a rational self vis-à-vis a fanatical 'Other'. (4), what is termed 'fundamentalism' is considered by many feminists to be irreconcilably anti-woman (Connolly 1991), yet some revivalists in both the Islamic and Christian traditions are activists for women's rights or feminists seeking gender equality within their faith communities and beyond.

In short, women participants in revivalist movements, who find the experience positive, are unlikely to call themselves 'fundamentalists'. Overall, the term 'fundamentalist' tends to be adopted by white, secularized Westerners and used to describe zealous believers with whom they cannot agree. The term 'fundamentalist' encapsulates the problem in someone 'Other' and avoids the necessity of examining the implicit Western insistence that liberal, secular thought is 'inerrant'. As a by-product, it constructs a rational/reasonable self via an 'irrational' Other.

For these various reasons I decided to use the term 'revival' in the case of both Islamic and Christian renewals because it has roots in both traditions. Nevertheless 'revival' has a different meaning in each case and there were those among my Christian informants who were critical of my use of the word. Specifically, the four members of the organization Men Women and God who are conservative evangelicals associate the term with events referred to as 'revivals' which happen in various places and times. Nevertheless 'revival' seems a useful working definition and it is a word used frequently by members of the house church movement itself.

Revivalisms – Christian and Islamic

By a 'revivalist' way I mean the modern-day path of a total commitment to Islam or Christianity. In the case of Islam this may follow the classic revivalist pattern, described by Yvonne Haddad, of an initial love affair with Westernization and secularism quickly followed by disenchantment and an impassioned return to Islam (Haddad 1983). By 'revivalist movements' I refer to those seeking a 'pristine' tradition of Islam or Christianity stripped of all accretions. Present-day revivalist movements in Christianity and Islam share this longing for an authenticity which they perceive in the early Christian and Islamic communities. But this authenticity tends to be constructed in the likeness of dominant discourses of the time from which believers and scholars attempt to discern it.

The reconstruction of a 'flawless' past in the likeness of the present has become very much a turn of the century experience. Nevertheless, the Islam and Christianity that revivalist women choose is something more than nostalgia for a 'pristine' past. It is also a modern appropriation and reconstruction of the faith in terms of their present needs and experiences.

As in Christianity or within any major religious tradition, there are divisions within the vast heritage of Islam, which is divided not only into Sunni and Shi'i Islam but also into groups of various kinds of Shi'i and Sunni Muslims (Enayat 1982: 18–51). Sunni groups tend to be led by laity and Shi'is to have clerical leadership. (Interestingly, this difference parallels a difference between early Protestantism and Catholicism). In terms of Christian revival I am dealing mainly with new churches within the Protestant tradition. But in both the Islamic and Christian cases, revivalists tend to see themselves as above division and as representing the 'true' tradition, whilst those who disagree are represented as sectarian.

In all mainstream religious traditions the problem for women is the fact that the holy texts have been interpreted by men. In Islam the interpretation of the Qur'an by men has prevented women from

gaining their Islamic rights. The revivalist call for *ijtihad* (independent reasoning) in Sunni Islam,[2] which would allow the Qur'anic
teachings to be interpreted and applied in a way that would facilitate
the liberation of women, is taken up by Anisa Abd El Fattah, chairwoman of the National Association of Muslim Women in North
America. In an interview with *Q-News*, a journal for Muslims published in Britain, she suggests the need, in a new situation (that is, in
a non-Muslim environment), for *ijtihad*. El Fattah mentions in the
same interview that their monthly newsletter includes *tafsir* (interpretation of the Qur'an) by a woman.[3]

In the Christian revivalist case, a degree of ecstatic practice in
worship is frequently present. Islam and Christianity, however, both
have ecstatic traditions. But because the Islamic tradition of *tajdid*
(renewal) has, at various points in Islamic history, aimed to purify
Islam of its accretions, Islamic revivalists historically have rejected
the more intoxicated (ecstatic) forms of Sufism (sometimes called
'mystical Islam') as *bida* (innovation). Historically, some revivalists
have, however, been members of the more sober Sufi orders. A recent
issue of *Q-News* noted a shift to a pride in the Sufi tradition as integral
to Islam; the inside cover of the April 1998 issue featured an enrap-
tured dervish dancer.

In Protestantism, the Pentecostal movement represents an ecstatic
form of religious practice in which the extraordinary events in Acts of
the Apostles become lived realities. Some contend that its roots are in
black religion, and some black writers now see Pentecostalism as
having been hijacked by the white church (MacRobert 1988: 81).
More recent writers suggest that the ecstatic quality of Pentecostal
religion offers women a voice which may be used subversively as a
means of transgressing the 'feminine' role (McClintock Fulkerson
1996: 131–41). Because the phenomenon of glossolalia is just as likely
to give women a voice as men, it may be that it breaks down gender
barriers to some degree.

Chevreau (1994) and others involved in the 'Toronto Blessing'
movement – the phenomenon that had people rolling in the aisles
in the mid-1990s – and the charismatic movement use the term
'anointed' to signify 'anointed in the Holy Spirit' which may lead to
ecstatic occurrences such as emotional release, speaking in tongues,
receipt of spiritual gifts such as prophecy, and other phenomena. The
'Toronto Blessing' proved, according to Chevreau, to be remarkably

transferable from one recipient to the next, around the world: hence the title of his book, *Catch the Fire*. But this phenomenon is not new, as can be seen from descriptions of the Azuza Mission, the Welsh Revivals, the Shakers and the early Methodists.

The media emphasis on the Toronto Blessing has since waned, and insiders no longer refer to it as such, but may use a term such as 'The Father's Blessing' instead. An interview with Roger Forster, leader of Ichthus Christian Fellowship, in *Jesus Life* (1998) suggests there is now less emphasis on Toronto-type phenomena of falling to the ground. Forster says: 'I'm not happy that people collapse under the Spirit and don't speak in tongues. I'd much rather they spoke in tongues and didn't collapse.'[4]

Millennialism, pessimism and Christian revival

As with Islamic revivalism, the view that decline has taken place in religious tradition is at the heart of Christian revival. Christians who are millennialists tend to the opinion that things can only get worse (before they get better), understanding history as a downward spiral which ends, ultimately, in Apocalypse. Depending on whether they are pre- or post-millennialists, they will envisage 1,000 years of peace either pre- or post-cataclysm. It may be that the millennialist view is in one sense summed up in the idea that 'the worse things are, the better'. This is because the Second Coming will take place only after the Beast 666 has held sway over the world as described in Revelation 13: 16–18:

> He [the Beast] compelled everyone – small and great, rich and poor, slave and citizen – to be branded on the right hand or on the forehead, and made it illegal for anyone to buy or sell anything unless he had been branded with the name of the beast or with the number of its name.[5]

Will this revivalist fervour subside now that the dawn of the new millennium has passed? Perhaps not. Leon Festinger, Henry W. Riecken and Stanley Schachter discerned an 'increase of proselytising following unequivocal disconfirmation of a belief'. Writing of the Millerites, a millenarian sect in the United States at the beginning of the twentieth century, who in waiting for the end times failed to cultivate their crops and gave their possessions away, the researchers pointed out that it took three disconfirmations of successive projected dates for the tragedy of their situation to dawn on them. Prior to that they had increased in fervour (Festinger et al. 1956: 216).

Islamic and Christian revivalist groups in the West

The revivalist movements I shall discuss, although anti-modern in their perception of the moral decay of a secularized society, are very much present-day movements, at home with technology and well represented on the Internet. Shahin Gerami (1996), who has compared Islamic 'fundamentalism' in Iran and Egypt with Protestant fundamentalism in the United States, argues that the apparent contradiction arises in their being 'modern in the public domain and traditional in the private domain' (Gerami 1996: 152). Many Christian revivalist groups use the Internet as a means of proselytization: the, Jesus Fellowship have a colourful website which includes an e-mail prayer service where one is invited to 'E-mail your "troubles" to our e-prayer mail-box and we will pray for you'.[6] Young Muslims UK also have a home page on the World Wide Web where they set out their purpose: 'The aim of YMUK is to invite the youth of the UK to the pristine message of Islaam.'[7]

In Britain Islam is popularly associated with the British South Asian communities. Although much of the detailed studies on the British Muslim migrant community has been conducted in Bradford (Saifullah Khan 1977; Barton 1986; Mirza and Nielson 1989; Lewis 1994), one should be wary of any form of generalization or exoticization of Muslims and of Bradford. Even in Bradford Muslims are diverse in terms of their origin, class, occupation, political and social aspiration and the degree of intensity of their commitment to their faith. The situation becomes far more complex once we take a wider perspective which could, for example, include London with the input of Muslims from around the globe. Fuad Nahdi, the editor of *Q-News*, has reported on some research he carried out on behalf of the An-Nisa Society[8] regarding Muslims and drug use. He writes of the diversity (and poverty) of Muslims living on an estate in Harlesdon where there are 'Muslims from all parts of the world including: the Caribbean, Africa (Ghana, Nigeria, Morocco, Egypt, Somalia, the Sudan and Kenya), the Middle East and others from Afghan, Kurdish, Malay, English and Irish communities'.[9]

It is also necessary to note the important divergence of view among the different generations of Muslims. According to Paul Vallely and Andrew Brown in their *Independent* cover story:

> The English education system has encouraged young Asians to analyse and to argue... . The impact of external events – from Iran and the Salman Rushdie affair, Saddam and the Gulf War, to the persecution of Muslims in Bosnia – has prompted an emotional identification with the idea of what it means to be a Muslim. Many of those so aroused have begun a more serious exploration of the faith and have begun to practise. The result is an Islamic revival. But this is not a 'descent into some kind of fundamentalism...'. It is something altogether different. A new type of Islam is beginning to manifest itself: a British form of Islam.[10]

I am not sure that these Islamic revivalists would like the description of 'a British form of Islam' especially if it is the case, as Ron Geaves states and Fuad Nahdi implies, that young British Muslims have shifted from a reliance on models such as Jamaat i-Islami in Pakistan (Nielson 1992: 136) and now look to a world Islam (Geaves 1995). Geaves has pointed out that the internationalist flavour of the organization Young Muslims UK derives from the world-wide associations formed in universities. Young Muslims UK, a group at home in, yet rejecting of, many facets of Western culture, have numerous members who are among the children of these migrant peoples. Some of them will be third generation and some, of course, are not from South Asian British communities at all, as their group includes members from the Yemen and Somalia as well as non-Asian British converts to Islam (Geaves 1995: 204). Islamic revival differs from traditional forms of Islam in that students and young converts universalize the *ummah* (Muslim community) in their aim to rise above sectarianism, and tend to write in those terms (Ahmad 1983: 223).

Reports of the Americanization of young Muslims emanate from the United States where Islam is one of the fastest growing religions.[11] About 25 per cent of American Muslims are of South Asian descent, 12 per cent are Arabs and nearly half are converts, mainly

African-Americans[12] and male. A *Newsweek* report suggests that as young Muslim people draw on the richness of their hybridity American society allows them 'to strip away the cultural influences and superstitions that have crept into Islam during the past 1400 years. By going back to the basic texts, they're rediscovering an Islam founded on tolerance, social justice and human rights.'[13]

Philip Lewis, an adviser to the Church of England on Islamic matters, sees monolingual, English-speaking Muslims as debasing Islam (Lewis 1994: 206). This viewpoint seems somewhat purist in an age and condition where so many of us are in a state of 'cultural hybridity' (Werbner and Modood 1997) and unable to return to our roots (Puar 1996). Lewis points to the fact that South Asian Muslim youth in Bradford who are unable to speak Urdu (the main means of transmission of Islam there) 'by-pass the *ulama*' (religious leaders). According to Lewis their Islam is assembled from pamphlets translated into English which contain 'polemic and diatribe against the West' and 'discount 1500 years of scholarship' (Lewis 1994: 206). I find this view limiting, especially when one considers that the majority of English-speaking Christians can read neither Hebrew nor Greek. It may be that Lewis inadvertently highlights the essence of present-day revivalist movements and their refreshing appeal to the young. They are movements which free themselves from old Islam and old Christianity, adapting religion to meet the needs of present times.

The separation of faith and culture is a strategy used by modernists and revivalists alike in both Christianity and Islam. For instance, an example from Islam is given by Wenonah Lyon in relation to her research among young British Islamic revivalist women in Manchester. Lyon mentions the separation of Islam and South Asian custom as being important to the young women she interviewed, who attend the West Didsbury Mosque which was described as 'the Middle Eastern Mosque' (Lyon 1995: 51). By 'customs' I mean the cultural and social customs of the various South Asian communities which were brought to, and have been modified or intensified in, Britain. One such custom is that in South Asia women pray at home but at West Didsbury women attend and listen to a sermon in Arabic (Lyon 1995: 51). Lyon writes: 'The young women in this group that I interviewed are concerned with separating religion, Islamic, from culture, Pakistani. Islam is very important to them; Pakistan is not' (Lyon 1995:

51–2). This distinction is important to these young women because it is custom which oppresses them and Islam which is seen as liberating.

But in spite of the specificities and the generalities of the 'new' and 'old' forms of Islam and the different practices within their particular associations of the various groupings within both, they all claim a generalized, universal form of Islam. What is of interest amongst the new revivalists is that they do not scrutinize the denomination of the participants in the way that the older generations did. There is a sense of solidarity created by the universal context represented by the global presence in major cities and Internet communications.

Christian revival: 'signs and wonders' in Britain and the United States

For Islamic revivalists (who, as already discussed, generally reject the more ecstatic forms of Sufism) there is no celebration of inexplicable healings, no requirement for a euphoric state and no expectation of miraculous intervention. They unite in a form of solidarity and adhere to the correct path, pursuing their revivalist way with the intention of overcoming an inferior world image which has been projected onto them. There are differences amongst the Christian revivalists, but many currently go for the miracle option, a kind of immediate salvation which may improve their lot in this world as well as in the next. The Muslims have their miracle too; it was the Qur'an. Now they just have to understand it.

In terms of Christian revival in Britain, it is clear that the growing churches are the charismatic ones, the ones that choose the miracle option. The UK Christian Handbook (1994/95) estimates that membership of this kind of church has grown from 12,000 in 1975 to 140,000. Ian Cotton, writing in the growth of the British house church movement, notes these new Christians are charismatics who 'really do believe that God intervenes on a daily basis, heals the sick, helps out believers, raises the dead' (Cotton 1995: 1). Cotton claims that, today, there are 400 million charismatics in the world (the number has doubled in a decade) and that they now represent 25 per cent of the world's Christians. In Britain the evangelical/charismatic meeting 'Spring Harvest' attracted 2,700 in 1978, and 80,000 in 1993. Since then the numbers have remained fairly constant, though the number of new churches increased by 49 per cent between 1990 and 1998 (Brierley 1999: 2.16). Church attendance is greater than membership. Brierley (ibid.) estimates that 263,000 attend such churches on Sunday.

Similarly, the house church movement numbered 100 house churches in 1970 but was estimated by Cotton to stand at 120,000 in 1995, with the expectation of a rise to 200,000 by the year 2000. A series of new church groups have sprung out of them, especially in prosperous areas of the South East (Cotton 1995: 3). Sometimes, new church communities are 'planted'[14] by bigger fellowships and at other times small churches affiliate themselves with larger churches such as Ichthus and Pioneer, or the transatlantic Vineyard Fellowship.

In terms of Christianity I have, for my study, concentrated largely on 'restorationist' groups, many of which have this charismatic style (Walker 1985) and have grown out of the house church movement. House churches started as ad hoc prayer groups, formed by 'denominationally dissatisfied Christians' which usually begin by meeting in members' homes and who later rent halls (Cotton 1995: 1). Martyn Percy (1996: 140–1) suggests that rapid church growth is promoted by 'miracles and rumours of miracles'. Malise Ruthven (1995) describes the extent of belief some charismatics in present-day Britain hold in the miraculous in the following terms: 'The revival of supernaturalism – the belief that God intervenes routinely in the mundane affairs of the individual, that diabolic powers can dominate, even control physical spaces like problem housing estates, to be exorcised by prayer – is the hallmark of Nineties populist religion'.[15] Frightening indeed is this idea that prayer not policy is the answer to all problems caused by poverty and alienation.

Percy, I think rightly, points out that these new Christian movements tend towards dualist interpretations of the Gospels which desist from concentrating on the suffering involved in the crucifixion and the imitation of Christ and instead emphasize superhuman experience. Percy insists on calling all 'anti-liberal' movements 'fundamentalist'. Yet many of the groups he describes as 'fundamentalist' are shot through with liberalism, which itself has an innate tendency towards a conservative position because of its emphasis on individualism. The emphasis on 'signs and wonders' and on the continuing revelation of the Holy Spirit links these fellowships to the tradition of Pentecostalism.

Much of Christian renewal in the 1990s appeared to be connected not only with the expectation of urban and suburban miracles but also with the millennium. Ruthven (1995) describes new Christian revivalism, which looks for signs and portents of end times in world events and attempts to match them up with revelation in Scripture, as a 'Manichean, do-it-yourself faith'. He suggests that ideas like 'the Beast mentioned in the Book of Revelation is to be found in supermarket bar-codes belong to pre-millennialist ideas directly imported from the US'.[16] In a less extreme example, Bryn Jones, of Covenant Ministries, stated in an interview with Noel Stanton of the Jesus Fellowship in 1993:

> My present conviction is that we're in the end times. I look at what Jesus and Paul describe as the characteristic trends of the end times. The trends in world economics, in international relations, in the social conditions of every nation. There's clearly a divine arrangement of these trends. They all indicate the collapse and passing away of our present age; they all point to the end of the end times.[17]

These thoughts are echoed by many other revivalists of the time.

British charismatic Christian groups tend to exhibit social concern in various kinds of work with disadvantaged people. Cotton praises the achievements of new Christian groups such as the London-based Ichthus, whose projects include nurseries and primary schools, and Pecan, which provides training schemes for the young unemployed and claims a 40 per cent placement rate in training schemes or work (Cotton 1995: 76–90). I find myself wondering if and how the fact that Ichthus and Pecan clearly have an agenda of converting their customers affects the service that is being offered. What happens if someone refuses to convert? Do they continue to receive the same service? What happens if a potential client has a problem related to something which is disapproved of by the group, for instance abortion? What if the client is homosexual? Yet the fact remains that some of these new churches *are* filling gaps in social provision. They provide help and services, friendship, and belief in the ultimate 'redeemability' of service users, the last of these a dimension which may not be offered by the statutory services.

Islamic revival: science and 'naturalness' versus postmodernism

Islamic revival today sometimes exhibits a scientific face. The book *The Bible, the Qur'an and Science* by the surgeon Maurice Bucaille, in which the author claims that modern science proves the veracity of Qur'an as divine revelation, and at the same time, that the Bible is lacking in this respect, is popular with some young Muslims. I attended a talk at the York University Student Islamic Association where the speaker claimed that the Qur'an contained the 'Big Bang' theory[18] as well as an account of human gestation.[19] The tendency to scientism was first evident in the Manar publications (*c.* 1900), in the commentaries of the modernist Rashid Rida (1865–1935), who thought that the technological wonders of the modern age were foretold in the Qur'an. Later, Sayyid Qutb (1906–66), who became the leading theorist of the Muslim Brotherhood in Egypt in the early 1950s, drew on the writings of another French surgeon, Alexis Carrel (1935)[20] (Choueiri 1990). Ibrahim Abusharif, a contributor to *Q-News*, attributes the present tendency to the fact that the majority of Muslim students are taking science degrees.[21] Barr (1977: 94) suggests in the case of Christian 'fundamentalists' that secular education imparts a materialistic and scientific idea of truth and that this is transferred to religion. But in the case of Islam I think the idea of the need for the discoveries of science to be prefigured in the Qur'an is a consequence of the concept of *fitra* (that which is in conformity with natural law) and the idea that the Qur'an and natural law are in harmony. Further, if the Qur'an is the final revelation, which Muslims believe it to be, then for the scientifically minded, it should contain in some way all the discoveries which are to follow.

In modern Islamic revivalism, the idea of *fitra*, which is thought to be accessible to the faculties 'of any right thinking individual', has been accentuated. Islam is considered to be 'the primeval religion *din al-fitra*, a sort of natural religion in conformity with natural law' (Al-Azmeh 1991: 7). The idea that science can prove the veracity of the Qur'an as revelation is a logical step based on this belief. It is thought that the order of the universe reflects the order of the revelation of the Qur'an and that this will be confirmed by the scientific uncovering of 'natural law'. The emphasis on *fitra* can be partly attributable to polemic with Christian missionizing evangelicals, as a counter to

Christian fundamentalist beliefs. Fundamentalist Christians, by resisting science in the form of Darwinism (because this is contrary to the creation story in Genesis), laid themselves, and Christianity, open to ridicule. To be able to point to proofs of how the Qur'an is in harmony with science, and how it indeed contains all science in encapsulated form, could be seen as a proof of Muslim superiority.

The idea of the 'naturalness' of Islamic law has been used to make women's 'biology their destiny' and to define and limit women's role to domestic and nurturing tasks. 'Essentialism', or the unreconstructed view of 'naturalness', held within some religious discourses is a problem because it has previously been the means by which women have been locked into a biological destiny. Yet in the longer run, a recognition of lived realities of the body (however they may be constructed or derived) may contain the 'baby' that the postmodernists throw out with the authorial bathwater.[22] By this I mean that postmodernist discourse, where everything is treated as a 'text', has a peculiarly distancing effect from the body. From a feminist viewpoint it is necessary to interrogate that which is deemed to be 'natural' on the grounds that naturalness is defined by dominant discourse. Nevertheless, following Mellor and Shilling (1994; 1997), I would argue that the opposite extreme, which is represented in poststructuralist analysis and which defines gender relations as *purely* a construction of discourses, results in disembodiment. This in turn denies women the right to any special role or consideration at any time or in any condition of their lives. This is detrimental to women because such an analysis takes place against a backdrop of largely unchanged power relations and dominant discourses. This other extreme to 'naturalness' is, in my view, also disempowering for women because it denies the possibility of collective political struggle and has the potential to strip women of their hard-won rights. From this viewpoint we cease to be women: we are just masquerading as such (Riviere 1986). In employing poststructuralism as a feminist analytical tool it is necessary to re-evaluate its political potential and to find ways of grounding it in a wider discourse which utilizes its possibility for an analysis of power relations but which also acknowledges the lived realities of the body, such as pregnancy, childbirth, ageing, and so on. These are not phantasms but realities with which women have to contend in a society which remains sexist, inconsiderate towards mothers and their children, and ageist in its treatment of older women.

Protestantism and women

In the Christian tradition the dawn of Protestantism did not necessarily improve the lot of women. By removing the option of the convent, the Reformation decreased the possibility of celibacy as a means by which some women could control their fertility. In 1522 Luther, for example, wrote *The Estate of Marriage*, in which he based his directive that all believers should marry and procreate on God's commandment in Genesis to 'reproduce and multiply'. Protestantism thus forged the belief that a woman's place is in the home (Armstrong 1987). Merry Wiesner (1990) discusses the way that the Reformation displaced a sublime model of femininity, largely rejecting the 'two Marys', the Virgin Mary and Mary Magdalene.

Women were no longer socially permitted to live alone, or together as unmarried women; all were expected to come under the authority of a man. Wiesner points out that this prohibition on feminine independence may even have been a contributory cause of witch-hunts. Women who chose to remain celibate were believed to be fighting an insatiable sex drive[23] (Rowbotham 1973: 6). This is interesting, from a comparative viewpoint, because it echoes the description given by Fatna Sabbah of the construction of the 'omnisexual woman' in Muslim discourse and the imperative that she be controlled and made to reflect the inert and silent 'feminine' ideal (Sabbah 1988: 25).

With regard to this question of control, I was struck by the strong similarity between Luther and the early medieval Islamic view, for instance, of Imam Ghazzali (1056–1111) quoted in Sabbah (1984) concerning the role of women: 'she must remain in her private quarters and never neglect her spindle. ... Let her exchange but few words with her neighbours and not visit them' (Sabbah 1984: 3). Reading the book *Heirs Together*, a book about marriage by the Biblical feminist Patricia Gundry (1980), I came across the following: 'The [Christian] Jurist Gratian [1090–1155] said: Woman's authority is nil; let her in all things be subject to the rule of man . . . . And neither can she teach, nor be a witness, nor give a guarantee, nor sit in judgement.'[24] The similarity to some present-day conservative interpretations of the position of women in Islam is striking. Shamsad

Khan (1993) gives over 50 medical citations as to why women are incapable of acting as witnesses throughout their entire lifespan. Although we are dealing here with *different* religious traditions at vastly different times, what these interpreters of their traditions share are patriarchal frameworks which, in some quarters, have remained largely unchanged.

Luther, who saw marriage and childbirth as a woman's sole functions, advised that the way to console women in childbirth was to 'Say, yes, dear lady, if you were not a wife, you would certainly wish to become one, so that you could do God's will by suffering and perhaps dying through these delicious pains' (Wiesner 1990: 127).[25] Some modern Christian groups appear to draw on Luther's model, especially those that aim to develop a new brand of 'muscular Christianity'. The Protestant fundamentalists of the 1920s clearly did.

Interestingly, celibacy as an option is now being reintroduced by some Protestant revivalist groups. Rosemary Radford Ruether (1990) points out that historically there have been millennialist sects that have adopted celibacy because they believed they were living in the last days. Today, for the Jesus Fellowship in Britain, celibacy is regarded as the highest state.[26] But celibacy within Protestantism is unusual. For some it may represent a practical way of dealing with the issue of homosexuality in a situation where sex is not permitted outside marriage and can therefore only be heterosexual. This is also the case in Islam.[27] Generally, in terms of both Protestantism and Islam, the ideal state is the married one. Homosexual activity is proscribed by both Islamic revivalist and Christian revivalist groups. This does not mean that a person cannot recognize that they are lesbian or gay, but because sexual activity outside marriage is prohibited in both cases the only options are to remain celibate or to marry. This opens up an apparently unbridgeable rift between many Western feminists and Christian and Islamic revivalists and frequently makes dialogue between them impossible, even when they share concerns about women's rights.

Protestant fundamentalism and gender: the recipe for feminine submission

It was in the 1920s that Donald Grey Barnhouse proposed feminine submission as a solution to the reversal of the 'feminization' process

(Bendroth 1992: 22). The epitome of the cult of feminine submission dawned in the 1970s in the form of Marabel Morgan's *The Total Woman*. In it Morgan wrote: 'It is only when a woman surrenders her life to her husband, reveres and worships him, and is willing to serve him, that she becomes really beautiful to him' (Morgan 1975: 96).

It often goes unnoticed that women play a *consensual* part and that the return to muscular and masculine religion depends upon the submission of women in order to reinforce masculinity against the threat of erosion. This does not necessarily come easily to men. In the late 1980s, Carl (of the Covenant Community in the US) told Susan Rose: 'my wife is actually better at accounting than I am, but we know that as a man, I should be running the finances . . . . I'm not a natural leader; I've had to work at it.' Marcie, Carl's wife, describes her husband in the vocabulary of the submissive wife: 'He is my spiritual father in the Lord; he brought me to Christ and he is my cover and the head of our household. I sit at his feet in amazement, much as the church sits at the feet of Christ, the bridegroom' (Rose 1988: 66). It seems that women have the role not only of producing 'femininity' by submission, but also, by way of contrast to their enactment of obedience and dependence, the appearance of 'masculinity' in their men as well. But religious submission for women is frequently a double submission – submission to both men and God.

The requirement by some Christian groups that women submit to male authority is drawn selectively from St Paul. The conservative wing of the house church and independent church movement has its dissimilarities from Pentecostalism. These are described by Andrew Walker as being linked in particular to the practice of 'shepherding' whereby a believer has a personal leader who is given authority over his or her private life. This approach has recently been given less emphasis, perhaps because of criticism that it offers the potential for exploitation and abuse. Walker (1985) Davies (1986) and Percy (1996) all see the house church as being unmitigatedly male-led. Domestic arrangements follow a similar pattern, where the husband is head of the household and wives should submit to their husbands' authority.

There follows a discussion of some of the responses that various kinds of feminists or activists for women's rights make to the different kinds of patriarchal interpretations of what it is to lead a religious life.

Feminisms within religious traditions

In order to be able to ascertain the extent to which revivalists from the different traditions have (or have not) taken feminism on board a discussion of the nature of feminist movements within religions is necessary. Although the descriptions are written with a Western readership in mind, I am aware that the term 'feminist' is considered unsatisfactory by some Muslim and Christian women, who nevertheless engage in the struggle for women's rights within their respective traditions. I found this to be the case on a recent visit to Jordan where women's rights are largely fought for under the banner of human rights, and where I met a Christian worker at a women's refuge who was adamant that she was not a 'feminist', a word she associated with 'man-hating'. This was a difficult encounter as I felt that although we shared many concerns, we were divided by a word.

There are basically two types of feminist scholarship of the 'liberal' kind, which have already taken place within the Christian and Muslim traditions. I use the term 'liberal' here in order to differentiate, in the Muslim case, between Muslim feminist scholars who are grounded in Islam but who incorporate some Western values in terms of an Enlightenment view of equality, and Islamic feminists who regard Islam as the source of feminism and who draw solely upon that tradition. The latter are sometimes referred to as 'fundamentalist feminists' (Afshar 1996: 203–4; 1998: 16). In the case of the Christians there is a difference between the theologically conservative evangelical feminists and the more liberal feminist theologians, a difference discussed below.

Muslim and Islamic or 'Islamist' feminist scholars of Islam

In order to understand some of the difficulties it is necessary to take account of the historical development of colonial feminism in the Middle East. Leila Ahmed has traced the history of feminism in Egypt and has described how colonials tried to import the very feminism they were aiming to suppress in Britain as a means of disrupting Muslim society (Ahmed 1992: 175–83). The British occupation of Egypt, which began in 1882, accentuated Egyptian class divisions. The beneficiaries of British reform and involvement in European capitalism were the European residents and the Egyptian upper and

the new middle classes. Islamic practices in relation to women were
viewed through Western eyes as inferior to Western customs. Ahmed
points to how, threatened in Britain by an increase in feminism, the
colonial establishment in Egypt, while opposing British feminism,
appropriated the emancipatory politics and language of feminism
'and redirected it, in the service of colonialism, towards Other men
and the cultures of Other men' (Ahmed 1992: 151). However, Ahmed
undervalues the vigour of the Egyptian women's movement of the
time. She goes along with the idea that Qassim Amin, a modernist
and upper-class Egyptian servant of colonialism, through his book
The Liberation of Women (1899),[28] was the source of Egyptian feminism. Amin admired civilization founded upon science and perceived
European culture as pointing the way to progress. He re-expressed the
colonial belief in the inferiority of Muslim culture. The outcome of
the history of colonial feminism in the Middle East has been the
association of feminism, by many Muslims, with imperialism, a
view which is still current for some.

Ahmed has made a distinction between two kinds of feminism
based in Islam and with their roots in early twentieth-century
Egypt. These are modernist feminists who were in favour of unveiling
and women's suffrage and who had dialogue with the West, and
'Islamist' feminists who were opposed to Westernization and unveiling (Ahmed 1992: 180). Huda Sha'rawi, founder of the Egyptian
Feminist Union in the 1920s, favoured unveiling and women's suffrage and had many links with Western feminists. Malak Hifni Nassef
was, however, in the first two decades of the twentieth century,
already representative of a form of feminism which was opposed to
Westernization and unveiling (Ahmed 1992: 175–83). Ahmed cites
these two examples as the way feminism in Egypt could go. Neither
was created in a vacuum but in relation to the West.

Islamic feminists

Both modernist and 'Islamist' feminism have influenced the later
forms of Islamic feminism which are now apparent in the West
where there is, among some Islamic revivalist sisters, a desire to
wear the veil and reject Western consumerism at the same time as
claiming their rights. Azza Karam differentiates in present-day Egypt
between 'Muslim feminists' who, she says, use Islamic sources 'but

[whose] aim is to show that the discourse of equality between men and women *is* valid' (Karam 1998: 11) and 'Islamist feminists', who hold the view that 'women are oppressed precisely because they try to be "equal" to men and are therefore being placed in unnatural settings and unfair situations, which denigrate them and take away their integrity and dignity as women' (Karam 1998: 9–10). Because of their belief in natural law and the possibility of conforming with it (*fitra*) (Al-Azmeh 1993: 77), Islamic or Islamist feminists are complementarian in their approach to gender difference. The belief that women and men are counterparts who complement each other differentiates them, not only from Muslim feminists but from the majority of Western feminists as well, who base their notion of equality on a more androgynous model. Both Muslim and Islamic feminists, however, argue for *ijtihad* (independent reasoning) and against 'existing patriarchal formations . . . and the implications of their formations on gender, and both use similar "tools" of analysis and argumentation', that is, they both refer to Islamic texts (Karam 1998: 12). But the difference is in the Muslim feminist's contextualization (like Biblical higher criticism) of Qur'anic and other religious requirements.

The Islamic feminism that does not look to the West as a model and that bases itself upon the provision for women within the Qur'an appears to be growing. Islamic feminist activists who do not reject the *hijab*, feminists who go back to Malak Hifni Nassef of Egypt at the beginning of the twentieth century (Ahmed 1992: 175–83), have been joined by activists not only in the Muslim world, but in the West.

Many women who are activists for women's rights in Islam do not like the term 'feminist' (Kian 1997: 75; Karam 1998: 209) because of its Western connotations and because they argue there are 'no women's issues' within Islam. Karam nevertheless uses the term for two reasons: first to distinguish them from 'non-feminist' Islamists, and second to 'indicate . . . possible points of intersection with other women activists' (Karam 1998: 10). The latter is an important point. It is about shared views and the endeavour to discover if and where interests between women with disparate beliefs intersect and where it might be possible, for a moment, to find a shared voice. This is a necessary response to the postmodern atomization of feminisms into myriad particularities and specificities with no common articulation.

Muslim feminists

Feminist theologians and feminist scholars of Islam who take a pro-gressive approach from within their faith traditions are seeking ways to improve the situation of women by using methodologies which facilitate a progressive reading of the primary sources of their reli-gions. The fact that, over the centuries, men have mainly had control of interpretation of the primary sources of Islam – the Qur'an, the *Hadith* (the sayings of the Prophet), as well as the *Sunnah* (the exam-ple of the Prophet), which is known through the *Hadith*, and the *Fiqh* (jurisprudence), which aims to interpret the *Shariah* (the divine law) – means that Islam has remained in a patriarchal mould (Hassan 1991).

Ghazal Anwar focuses on the Qur'an as the primary source of Islam and describes the various strategies or positions which may facilitate a feminist reading of it (Anwar 1996: 57). She includes: the apolo-getic, the reformist, the transformative, the rationalist and the rejec-tionist (ibid.). These categories may also be used to classify the various kinds of feminist theology in the Christian tradition. For the purpose of this study I would narrow these down to the apolo-getic, which is the revivalist, 'fundamentalist' or 'traditionalist' stance, the 'progress within' position, which includes the reformist, transformative and rationalist standpoints, and the rejectionist posi-tion, which sees progress as possible only from without. The rejec-tionists are those who decide that their tradition is hopelessly patriarchal and leave (Daly 1973; Hampson 1990) and who adopt a post-Christian feminist position.

Progressive readings of Islam

Like Riffat Hassan, scholars who seek to reclaim that which they believe to be liberating within their tradition look to 'elements in scriptures or tradition that have been suppressed, forgotten, or erased by patriarchal power relations and theory' (Cooey, Eakin and McDa-niel 1991: ix). Muslim feminists, such as Leila Ahmed and Fatima Mernissi, attempt to make a progressive reading of the primary sources of Islam, they also make a feminist reading of early Islamic history and both conclude that their religion, especially its legalized aspect, has been appropriated by men. They see the codification, which took place 300 years after the life of Muhammad, as a misrepresentation of an earlier revolutionary Islam which has been influenced by Zoroastrian attitudes to women (Mernissi 1991; Ahmed 1992).

Rana Kabbani (1993) also makes a positive reading of the Qur'an which promised women liberation, money and economic independence and the right to inherit so they would no longer be chattels that were exchanged between men. Islam, which gave women the right to refuse to be married, is now seen through Western eyes as a religion which forces women into arranged marriages. Islam gave women economic independence in seventh-century Arabia. Yet in Britain it was not until the passing of the Married Woman's Property Act in 1870 that married women were able to have control of their money. Kabbani indicates that in the Qur'anic story of the Fall, Adam bears equal responsibility with Eve and she contrasts this with what she sees as the inherent sexism in Christian scriptures with regard to this story (Kabbani 1992: 37). Bouthaina Shaaban is another of the writers who suggest that women were empowered by early Islam to become 'queens, doctors, warriors, poets, and literary critics' (Shaaban 1995: 62).

If one way of assisting women's struggle within Islam is to accentuate the positive teachings in the Qur'an in relation to women, another is to question the validity of the *Hadith*, with regard to those utterances, attributed to Muhammad, which appear to encourage the oppression of women (Mernissi 1991: 49). An extension of this approach, which gives flexibility in an environment hostile to Islam, is to discount the *Hadith* altogether, a method practised by the *Ahl Al-Qur'an* (People of the Qur'an) (Wolffe 1993). This was one of the responses to colonial rule in India, a way of being able to stay Islamic under unIslamic rule. It is a method currently utilized by members of the present-day group the Submitters who are described in the next chapter.

Feminist theology and biblical feminism

Making a feminist reading of Islam or Christianity is still a minority activity which is largely viewed with suspicion by the mainstream. But the more liberal dimensions of feminist theology, like liberal Muslim interpretations which, for example, deny the validity of *hijab*, tend to be dismissed by revivalists as irrelevant to their cause and as playing into the hands of the enemy. In the case of Christian revivalists this is because feminist theology begins with 'a hermeneutic of suspicion, expecting that close study asking the right questions will uncover many levels of patriarchal bias, some in the Bible itself' (Katherine Doob Sakenfeld, in Russell and Clarkson 1996: 27) whereas biblical or evangelical feminists start from a 'hermeneutic of faith' (Kroeger et al.: 1995) which takes a more positive view of the Bible, assuming it to be a book of liberation rather than of oppression. This sums up the difference between biblical feminism and feminist theology and runs parallel to the difference between Islamic feminism and Muslim feminism. Feminist theology starts from women's experience and the promotion of full humanity. Biblical feminism starts with the Bible. Elaine Storkey (1985) is one of the key figures in Britain who take an evangelical feminist position. The emphasis is on gender 'equality to serve' God (Hull: 1989). Organizations which promote biblical feminism are CBE (Christians for Biblical Equality)[29] and in Britain, MW&G (Men Women and God). They work in the very 'jaws of the lion' as it were, conservative evangelicals who insist on gender equality, believing that it is 'God's inspired word which cannot lie that grants both men and women full membership in the priesthood of all believers' (Kroeger et al. 1995: 6).[30]

Biblical feminism is not a new movement. In 1974, Letha Scanzoni and Nancy Hardesty wrote *All We're Meant to Be* in which they call themselves biblical feminists. But biblical feminism follows a long tradition of evangelical feminism: Elizabeth Cady Stanton, for instance, wrote *The Women's Bible* in 1898. Nancy Hardesty (1984) has written a topography of evangelical feminism in the nineteenth century, and Ruth Tucker and Walter Liefeld quote a number of evangelical feminists from the late nineteenth century (Tucker and Liefeld 1987: 402 ff.).

There are methodological overlaps between Islamic feminists and biblical feminists, but one of the main differences, the egalitarian rather than the complementarian approach, is based on Gal 3: 28: 'There is no longer Jew or Greek, there is no longer slave or free, there is no longer male and female; for all of you are one in Christ Jesus.' Biblical feminists understand St Paul's words to mean that gender-based barriers are disappearing and consequently tend to play down gender difference in their approach. Islamic feminists, on the other hand, tend to believe that the roles of women and men are 'equal but different' in the tasks of child-rearing and family life. This does not mean, however, that Islamic revivalist sisters engage only in traditionally 'feminine' kinds of paid employment and are not career-minded. One of my Muslim interviewees, for instance, was an engineer.

Like the hierarchical, non-feminist participants, the biblical feminists in my sample are conservative, being evangelicals, not liberals in their theology. Another similarity between the biblical feminists and the Islamic feminists is their desire to build a better world alongside men. For evangelical feminists this is in the spirit of Acts 2, where Peter quotes Joel: 'your sons and daughters shall prophesy'. Believing in cooperation with men in order to build a better society both biblical and Islamic feminists bear some similarity to the earlier liberal and socialist feminists.

Biblical feminists are at one end of a spectrum of Christian feminists in terms of hermeneutical strategies in that, as evangelicals, they require themselves to follow 'the plain sense of the text on all points. Feminists in this tradition focus their efforts on seeking out an alternative, nonsubordinationist meaning for each text that seems to subordinate women' (Katherine Doob Sakenfeld, in Russell and Clarkson 1996: 29). This they do with enormous creativity. An example of this emerged during my interview with Valerie Griffiths, one of the founder members of Men Women and God. Valerie spoke of St Paul's 1 Cor 11 injunction that when a woman prophesies her head should be covered. It was the first time I had ever heard this explained with the emphasis on the fact that *the woman has permission to prophesy*. Previously I had understood this as a command that women should wear a head covering during *worship*. Valerie pointed out that prophesying was 'not just foretelling, but discerning the message of God to give his people'[31] and that prophecy was linked with encouragement and exhortation (1 Cor 12 and 1 Cor 14: 3) to build up others. In other words, St Paul was recognizing the prophetic ministry of women, a significant role within the church, which allowed them to discern the word of God.

Although women have participated in theological debate, Ann Loades dates feminist theology to Valerie Saiving's (1960) article in which she points to the specific burden women carry in a religion 'where women's realization of full self identity was likely to be characterized as sin or temptation to sin' (Loades 1990: 81). Although feminist theology covers many different positions it implies a reclaiming of Christian history and a feminist reading of the Bible, in interpreting the earliest Christian community as being egalitarian (Fiorenza 1984), in discovering women's story in the Bible story (Trible 1984) and in developing feminist Christologies which are more 'woman-friendly' ways of understanding the person and message of Christ (Ruether 1990).

In the 1990s, theologies taking a feminist position multiplied along lines of difference, a paradigmatic shift to liberation theologies which reflect the 'experiences of women who have endured double or triple burdens'. This is especially the case in the United States where there is Womanist Theology (African-American), a term coined by Alice Walker, Mujerista Theology (Latina), Evangelical Theology (or Biblical Feminism), Queer Theology, Indigenous Women's Theology (Native American) and so on (Russell and Clarkson 1996: 283–300).

All feminist theologies may be considered as part of liberation theology as all theologies of liberation depend on the concept of 'the hermeneutical (epistemological and interpretational) privilege of the poor' (Sölle 1991: 69). This means that in theologies of liberation oppressed peoples are deemed to be better able than the oppressors to understand the Bible: the poor are the teachers. This situation is described in the Magnificat (Luke 1: 50–53). Delores S. Williams, a womanist theologian, finds an illustration of black women's history in Hagar's story (Genesis 16: 1–6), the story of a black slave woman compelled by Sarah, her mistress, to conceive a child by Sarah's husband, Abraham. Williams connects Hagar's plight with poor black American women today who may find themselves forced into the situation of maternal surrogacy in the production of white babies (Williams 1993: 15–33). Williams elsewhere reclaims Christianity for black women, by developing 'a womanist notion of sin informed, in part, by Black female and Black male sources'. Sin has been defined for us by men, largely by white men (Williams 1995: 130–47).

Elisabeth Schussler Fiorenza takes a 'transformative' approach which reconstructs, rethinks and reformulates aspects of the tradition which have legitimized the oppression of women (Cooey, Eakin and McDaniel 1991: x). In *In Memory of Her*, Fiorenza (1984) reconstructs the history of a Jesus movement at the outset of Christianity and describes it as consisting of equals. Fiorenza has four disciples at the end of Mark's Gospel, who are women: 'Mary of Magdela, Mary, the daughter or wife of James the Younger, and the mother of Joses and Salome' (Fiorenza 1984: 320).

As mentioned above, reconstruction may also take the form of feminist Christologies (Hampson 1990: 62–6) and Womanist Christologies (Grant 1989) – ways of understanding the person or message of Christ in a manner which is more accessible and meaningful to women. According to Caroline Walker Bynam, in the late Middle Ages there were feminine images of God which allowed women to be more Christ-like (Bynum 1982), and Ozorak turns the tables on androcentric conceptualizations of Christ by suggesting that women are, in reality, more Christ-like than men: 'women shed their own blood, sacrifice themselves, in the service of new life' (Ozorak 1996: 25).

Some feminist theologians such as Mary Daly (1973; 1978) and Daphne Hampson (1990: 41ff) adopt a rejectionist approach. They have concluded that because the Bible is a patriarchal text they have to depart from the Christian tradition. Hampson (1996), for instance, argues that to be a Christian is to be in a heteronomous position, but that feminism favours autonomy. I would argue that autonomy understood as self-governing freedom is not necessarily a feminist position but more of a masculine ideal. Of course it is the case that choice is a feminist requirement, but in order to be autonomous *per se*, in individualistic societies, women need to be young, healthy, in receipt of a good income and have no dependants. It seems to me that to succeed, the feminist project needs cooperation amongst women, not autonomy. As in feminist theology, where there are those who take a 'post-Christian' route, so also in Islam there are those who argue that Islam is so deeply patriarchal that it is unmitigatedly antagonistic to women's rights. Afsaneh Najmabadi sees the Islamic Republic of Iran as pushing women into that position. She has concluded that 'to have a room of her own, the Iranian woman is now faced with subverting God and state' (Najmabadi 1991: 70). But white feminist theology generally has failed to identify any commonality with non-feminist Christian women, especially those revivalist or Pentecostalist women who self-abnegate. Recently though Mary McClintock Fulkerson (1996) has attempted to extend the boundaries of feminist theology 'to interpret the working of Christian traditions in the lives of non-feminist women' (McClintock Fulkerson 1996: 131) and Sarah Coakley (1996) has attempted to reframe the Christian practice of 'self-emptying' (*kenosis*) as a means of enrichment.

Why revivalisms?

The literature suggests a number of theoretical bases from which it is possible to make an analysis of why some women might choose to associate themselves with radical religious groups which stress gender boundaries and difference. These range from rational choice (Brasher 1998) to models of choice concerned with rationality (Poston 1992) or responses to social or psychological distress (McCrickard 1991; North 1996). There are also explanatory frameworks which relate to feminist issues. These include concerns which relate to the preserva- tion of motherhood (Dworkin [1979] 1988) and assistance with child care; a backlash against feminism or a closet feminist agenda (Faludi 1991); and a shared agenda with feminism (Afshar 1991; Gerami 1996). The last of these is a theory I most favour, but it is problematic because, as already discussed, many secular feminists do not accept religious 'feminists' as being feminist (Karam 1998: 13) and Islamic feminists do not generally wish to use the term 'feminism'. What all the theories do share is a belief that women choose revivalisms for reasons of direct or indirect empowerment.

Also attractive in making an analysis is rational choice theory (Young 1995). Often criticized for assuming that human beings are motivated by greed alone, rational choice theory applies a 'market forces' model to selection. When applied to religion it theorizes the genesis and growth of religious movements in terms of a response to popular demand (Warner 1993). It hypothesizes that when people join religious movements they do so as a rational response after weighing up the material and spiritual gains and losses which they would incur (Becker 1976; Elster 1986). This is a model which is appropriate to those who are able to make 'life-style' choices in Western consumerist society, but it cannot be applicable to societies where people are unable to make religious choices. This theoretical model has its attractions when applied to the religious decisions of Western women. Such a model counters the idea that women join revivalist movements out of passive compliance to male demands or because they are victims, 'brain-washed' into joining movements which may not have media and popular approval. 'Re-enchantment' (renewal in religious interest) in Britain comes at a time of change as we move towards a more American-style welfare culture. It seems possible in this climate that many new churches attract followers, at least in part, because they offer tangible benefits as well as spiritual ones.

The position of women in religious traditions is a variable feast. Location, socio-economic grouping, ethnicity and other forms of difference influence the position of women even within the same group. Revivalist groups do not represent a united front on gender relations. The situation of women is by no means uniform across revivalist movements in the West or elsewhere. This is the case for Christians and Muslims alike. The sense of variety and difference within revivalist groups is, if anything, the message of this chapter. We should be careful not to project an imagined uniformity onto gender relations in revivalist movements in the West, either Christian or Islamic. Reasons for affiliation with such groups must, to some extent, reflect this diversity.

2
Reflexive Methodology

Introduction

The subjects of this study are minority groups who, though strong in belief, are frequently vulnerable as individual believers who are swimming against the prevailing consumerist current. I shall therefore discuss not only the means by which I gained access to informants and the manner in which I collected data, but also how I deliberated on what might be a feminist way to proceed with my research and the conclusions I reached. In the interviewing and follow-up process, like Donna Luff (1999) and Ann Phoenix (1994), I discovered that the interviewer is not always in a position of power and that there were converse issues of power for which the body of feminist theory on interviewing had not prepared me.

This study has entailed contact with Islamic revivalist groups, and house church fellowships and conservative evangelical groups. Frequently, I was offered a warm welcome but this was not universal and there were moments when I felt I should abandon the project, especially when I found myself located in the crossfire between secular feminists and religious revivalists. Like Nilufer Göle (1996) in Turkey, I found there were some members of each group who insisted that I represented the opposing view. In other words, each believed in the stereotype of the other and assumed I embodied it.

My methods of data collection have been qualitative and ethnographic. In this chapter I shall describe the theoretical and practical issues which informed this process and the choice of methods I used in the process of data collection: a snowball questionnaire consisting of open questions, interviews and participant observation. The snow-ball questionnaire and the interviews yielded different profiles of respondents but, overall, while the Christian interviewees were white and lower-middle to upper-middle class, the Muslim interview-ees were from a greater variety of backgrounds. The respondents to the questionnaire were more ethnically diverse, especially the Mus-lims, of whom only five out of 30 described themselves as white British. The majority of the 43 Christian respondents to the ques-tionnaire were white and middle class. Data from e-mail interviews with evangelical feminists in the United States and participant obser-vation on an Islamic forum in cyberspace and follow-up correspond-ence have also been included. These participants, in possession of computers and with access to the Internet in the mid- to late 1990s, are largely middle-class.

Because of the complexity of feminist methodological issues the chapter is divided into two parts: (1) methodology and epistemology; and (2) method. 'Methodology' is concerned with theoretical issues of how the research should proceed, and epistemology the theory of (in this case feminist) knowledge (Edwards 1990: 478). 'Method' relates to the practical details of my own fieldwork – how I gained access to informants and the means of gathering data.

Feminist methodology and epistemology

Postmodernism

Postmodernist theory, in terms of critical theory, deconstructionism and poststructuralist analysis, has profoundly affected the way in which we can look at feminist research, the way in which it 'effect-ively negates the possibility of fruitful political interventions' (de Groot and Maynard 1993: 157), alluded to in the Introduction to this volume. It does this by dismantling gender as well as race and class, for instance by suggesting that women exist only as a 'binary cat-egory in a hierarchical relationship to "Men"' (Stanley and Wise 1993: 204). If this is the case, then women's experience ceases to exist, and becomes a shadow; it puts theory 'in an imperialistic relationship to life' (ibid.). According to Stanley and Wise: 'Deconstructionist, like post-structuralist, approaches imply change at the level of language and texts and categories alone; but, as part of a world-wide political movement, academic feminism necessarily retains a praxis firmly concerned with more than a "linguistic turn"' (ibid.: 205).

An emphasis on 'difference' is also an aspect of the postmodern repertoire. To concentrate on difference *alone* and to ignore any shared interests, such as the dismissal of the category 'woman', also results in the inability to act politically. Fatmagul Berktay writes: 'if women, as a marginalized group, are to be able to transform existing power relations, they have to communicate, to hear each other's voices, to learn about each other, and to forge alliances' (Berktay 1993: 111). Angela Davis points to the shared interests of working-class women and how, like their black sisters, white working-class women in Britain were, until the beginning of the twentieth century, used as beasts of burden, as they were cheaper to produce and keep than a horse (Davis 1982: 10). Davis shows the interests of groups of oppressed women to be linked in that 'Low wages for women of colour establishes [*sic*] a standard which leads to low wages for white women. So that white women are victims in any upsurge in racism' (Bhavnani 1989: 71). To explore afresh where interests may be linked is a way out of the sense of political paralysis which is symptomatic of an overemphasis on difference and postmodern relativism.

As a feminist, based in a Centre for Women's Studies, it seemed clear to me that my research would use feminist methodology. But changes in feminist epistemology have cast doubt on the idea that there can be feminist knowledge and, by implication, feminist research. Formerly it was said that feminist research was 'by women for women' but now, not only has it become clear that there is no unified women's voice, there is even doubt in some postmodern or perhaps post-feminist quarters, following the influence of French feminist, Lacanian and poststructuralist theories, that 'women' can be defined at all.[1] Politically, this is problematic in that it may lead to a denial of oppression (Moi 1985; Hartsock 1987; Berktay 1993; Hoff 1994; Maynard 1994). Theoretically, the inability to define 'women' can be construed as negating not only the idea of feminist methodology, but of feminism itself. So, embarking on a piece of feminist research at this time and in place was not without its problems. One is in danger of being deemed to be 'essentialist' (in its pejorative usage), especially if one is studying groups that not only believe in womanhood, but also in its being a creation of God.

In view of the fragmentation of feminism into a multiplicity of feminisms, where does one start to piece together an appropriate methodology and method? Feminist research has been about praxis, the idea that it should *do* something. It has tended to use qualitative methods and has been regarded as potentially empowering to the participants and as directed towards social change (Kelly et al. 1994). Even though the emphases on deconstructionism and difference have engendered a sense of theoretical unease about the current relevance of feminist methodology, de Groot and Maynard conclude that a woman-centred approach to women's studies, which connects 'the empirical and the analytical... [and] made with a concern for practical interventions', is the way forward (de Groot and Maynard 1993: 174). Feminist scholarship is enriched by adopting the positive insights of poststructuralism, deconstructionism and critical theory in respect of power relations, but such analysis needs to be set within social and historical contexts if it is to be linked to political action. My intention has been that this study should point in the direction of a more inclusive approach to women's studies, a shift to embrace not only secular Western feminists[2] but also feminists who are working within the religious traditions. For although there are many differences, some of which are no doubt irreconcilable, the global picture is one of feminists chipping away at patriarchal power relations within all manner of different religious traditions and in a multiplicity of ways. Surely this is something all feminists can celebrate.

Stanley and Wise (1993) have alluded to a current problem for women's studies, where a shift to 'interdisciplinarity' may actually mean 'literary criticism' where postmodernist feminists from many disciplines look at data merely as a 'text' to be deconstructed. This has a peculiarly distancing effect from the content of the data in that emotional contact is superseded by an intellectual exercise. Treated in this way the 'text' is often divorced from its historical and social context.

Some writers claim – rightly, I think – that postmodernism can potentially be used as a weapon in the backlash against feminism (Harding 1987; Hartsock 1987). Hartsock writes that the postmodern claim that 'verbal constructs do not correspond in a direct way to reality has arisen precisely when women and non-western peoples have begun to speak for themselves and, indeed, to speak about global systems of power differentials' (Hartsock 1987: 187–206). She sees postmodernism as an attempt by dominant culture to subvert oppressed people from obtaining a voice. Introduced to feminist thought systems, it spreads like a virus, turning all research findings into fiction. One way to address the problem of the nonviability of truth-claims is to admit to the biographical nature of research (Foucault [1982], in Gutman and Hutton 1992: 11) and to render the researcher visible in the research process so that the reader can make her own evaluation (Harding 1987: 9). Hartsock (1987) suggests that the postmodern view that truth and knowledge are contextual and multiple can be seen to be a truth-claim in itself. This is an interesting point. It seems we cannot get away from the idea of truth.

Objectivity

Not only postmodernist and poststructuralist theory but also feminist methodology in general has treated the goal of objectivity in research as an unattainable phantasy. This, in the feminist case, is because of the 'masculinist' bias of the notion of objectivity in mainstream studies. In order to combat the distortions of the unconscious male bias Rosalind Edwards has attempted to monitor and reveal her own effect on the research process and makes her reasoning process explicit (Edwards 1990: 479–80). Harding argues that making the presence of the researcher overt helps to avoid the deception of the objectivist stance that veils the researcher's cultural practices and beliefs, but which simultaneously displays the research object's beliefs and practices. Harding suggests that the best feminist analysis positions the enquirer:

> in the same critical plane as the overt subject matter thereby recovering the entire research process for scrutiny in the results of the research. That is, the class, race, culture and gender assumptions, beliefs and behaviours of the researcher her/himself must be placed within the frame of the picture that she/he attempts to paint.
>
> (Harding 1987: 9)

I agree that a representation that allows the reader to analyse the ways in which the tendencies of the researcher may have influenced the research is more genuinely informative than if the researcher has maintained invisibility. But this poses the problem of how much to write about oneself, especially if the act of writing has autobiograph-ical qualities. Why, for instance, did I choose to engage in this particular study? There are connections between my choice and my own background and experiences. My lower-middle-class experience of 1950s, pre-Vatican II Catholicism has left me with a deep interest in the relationship between truth-claiming religious organizations, women and gender roles. This has left me struggling throughout my adult life with the Janus-faced dynamic of oppression/liberation which I have found in organized religion. From a poststructuralist viewpoint, Roman Catholicism has instilled a patriarchal God within my subjectivity. Wrestling with this unwanted personal reality has led me, from a religious viewpoint, to a position that is largely that of post-Christian feminism.[3]

Objectification

It has been regarded as essential that the feminist researcher should not be in the business of objectifying women (Oakley 1981), objecti-fication being regarded as a masculine preoccupation. Feminists should not objectify their sisters because this necessitates a power relation. But the problem is that feminists *are* in hierarchical relation-ships with feminists because of the structures in which we live and move. It is also not possible to conduct any research without objecti-fying the researched: 'The very idea of representing women, even if in the form of "letting them speak", is to constitute women as object. To claim that "they" are subjects is to avert the question of authorship and the constitution of a "feminist self" via an other' (Game 1991: 31). Not only is a degree of objectification integral to the research process but, as Ann Game points out non-feminist women are the means through which the researcher constructs an academic feminist self. Further, because, historically, Western women have been defined as object of the gaze and not the subject, the idea that feminists should not objectify their sisters complies with the dominant ideol-ogy of femininity, which also, by implication, states that women should not be in the business of objectifying other women. So I find myself wondering whether feminist research techniques do indeed challenge Western, middle-class notions of femininity. There is, of course, no universal construction of femininity. Sojourner Truth made this plain in her much quoted 'Ain't I a Woman' speech, that the construction of white women's femininity is different from that of black women (Carby 1982: 214). Further, the construction of white working-class femininity is different from white middle-class femininity (Davis 1982). Therefore, I see the dilemma of objectification as potentially paralysing when carrying out feminist research. In the case of this study I concluded that there could be only a partial solution to this problem and I therefore aimed to be scrupulous in sending transcripts and notes from interviews to informants for comment, as well as requesting permission or otherwise to use their words. But without a degree of objectification there can be no research since my informants' words ultimately become data for my analysis.

Feminist empiricism and standpoint

Sandra Harding sets out two 'transitional epistemologies' on which theories of feminist research methods are based: 'feminist empiricism' and 'feminist standpoint'. She identifies 'feminist empiricism' as a feminist response to the biases and problems of traditional disciplines (Harding 1987). This is largely a response to mainstream methods and is demonstrated by Hilary Graham in the title of an article on women and the survey method: 'Do Her Answers Fit His Questions?' (Graham 1983). Surveys were viewed by many feminists as being appropriate to dominant male culture and inappropriate as a means of gathering women's experience (Finch 1991: 196). Although there may be truth in the fact that few of us fit the questions in questionnaires, my experience of the use of a snowball questionnaire, as part of my data collection process, has been positive. Because the respondent generally chooses a time appropriate to herself in which to answer the questions, has time to ponder on her responses, and is anonymous, many answers have been deeply illuminating. A questionnaire does not have to consist entirely of multiple-choice questions, but can give space for free expression of reactions and ideas. Multiple-choice questions might make for easier data processing, but open questions elicit more richly textured and sometimes surprising answers. In this case, the data collected through the questionnaire were processed through a method suggested by Coffey and Atkinson (1996) whereby similar statements are collected under a general heading. This is a good indicator of the overall response. Later, variant statements were analysed.

Implicit also in the idea of appropriate and inappropriate means of collecting information is a 'feminist standpoint' because 'knowledge based on a feminist standpoint is identified as scientifically preferable since it is more complete and less distorted' (Stanley 1990: 39). So, in a sense, a feminist standpoint still has the goal of objectivity. A feminist standpoint implies a true feminist knowledge and, as Stanley has indicated, this necessitates the acknowledgement of other feminist standpoints as equally valid (Stanley 1990: 27). This equalization of standpoints can present a problem though if it is used to revalorize white, middle-class feminist standpoints, which black feminists have criticized as being dominant.

Moral concerns: feminist piety and the pristine researcher

As a researcher exploring the relationship between women and religion I cannot help but detect traces of religiosity within the Western secular feminist project. This is not to say that the various kinds of secular and religious, feminisms do not overlap at times. Here I use the term 'secular feminist' to describe a feminism that does not directly have its foundation in a religious text, even though it may be argued that modern Western feminism derives from Christian evangelical beginnings (Hardesty 1984; Tucker and Liefeld 1987). The religiosity to which I refer is a kind of moral imperative which makes its imprint throughout all but the most anarchic of Western feminisms.

As already mentioned, it has been thought that feminist research should be by women, for women (Oakley 1981; Stanley and Wise 1983; Finch 1991: 195) and that few feminist researchers would feel at ease with producing work which damaged the interests of other women (Finch 1991: 199). But this implies that a feminist, such as myself, will necessarily know what will and will not harm the interests of other women. In the case of feminisms within religious traditions there is a division between these and some of the Western secular feminisms. Some religious activists for women's rights wish to dissociate themselves from secular feminisms on particular issues and some secularists and postmodernists are concerned whether the religious feminists, located as they are within patriarchal traditions, can be sufficiently feminist. But one could equally say the same for feminists who are located in Women's Studies Departments in universities within a dominantly patriarchal structure and engaged in a hierarchical enterprise, as I was. This is an example of feminists holding divided views as to what is in the interests of other women.

Intrinsically linked with academic feminism is the matter of who is able to possess the research and who is not. Liz Stanley describes the approach of academic feminists as a reformist one: 'For the last 20 years one of the aims of academic feminism has been to join [the official and unofficial gatekeepers of academic inputs and outputs]...but another [aim] has also been to dismantle at least some of the sources and uses of their power over "peers"' (Stanley 1990: 5). This is not dissimilar to the way in which many religious feminists work *within* religious traditions. Nevertheless, the idea that feminist research is by women for women suggests an altruism that structurally can be only partial. The idea that feminist research is for women also avoids the issue that there must be a sense in which the research is largely for the researcher.

Ethnography

Feminist methodology prioritizes the merits of qualitative over quantitative research (Oakley 1981; Stanley and Wise 1983; Finch 1991: 195). A great emphasis has been placed on the benefits of the 'small-scale, qualitative research methods which aim to make visible the experiences and needs of women' (Finch 1991: 195). This overlaps with the reality that feminist projects are frequently small-scale owing to financial constraints. Because qualitative methods are regarded as those which make gender issues most visible, many feminists see ethnographic methods as those best suited to feminist research. In the early 1980s much feminist writing was concerned with feminist research methods which drew on qualities that were viewed as being traditionally female (Oakley 1981; Duelli Klein 1983; Du Bois 1983; Graham 1983; Stanley and Wise 1983).

Judith Stacey takes a moral stance by questioning the justification for this belief in the ethnographic method as she is concerned about the possible exploitation of respondents. She suggests that the relationship between researcher and researched may appear as genuine friendship and egalitarianism, but mask the reality of a hierarchical relationship which is terminated on completion of the fieldwork. Stacey uses empathy, human concern and egalitarianism to describe the kind of ideal non-exploitative feminist relationship of which she approves and which has its basis in caring (Stacey 1988). But a great deal has been written by feminists about how women are the ones who constantly find themselves cast in the caring role: 'compulsory altruism' is the powerful phrase used to describe this (Land and Rose 1985).

At first it appeared that postmodernist or poststructuralist ethnography would solve the problem of 'masculinist' research methods. Using a 'critical and self-reflexive ethnography...like feminist scholars, critical ethnographers [tore] the veil from scientific pretensions of neutral observation and description...[they showed that] ethnographic writing is not cultural reportage, but cultural construction' (Stacey 1988: 24) and that ethnographic truths can be only partial.[4] Stacey envisages 'partially feminist' ethnographies which are 'accounts of culture enhanced by the application of feminist perspectives' as possible (ibid.: 26).

Stanley and Wise write how they looked for a methodology to be used in 'recovering the personal'. Working from an interactionist viewpoint (from which everything including structures and belief systems are in a constant state of negotiation) they were attracted to ethnography, with its 'egalitarian impetus' and its broad sense of data in terms of the everyday and personal as well as the relational. It appealed to them the more because it has been described as 'sociology without balls' (Stanley and Wise [1983], 1993: 138–42). Working, as I was, on a study of members of religious revivalist groups, ethnography, in terms of 'being there', proved to be a good way of meeting believers who had not been hand-picked to meet the researcher and to get an overall sense of group dynamics and gender relations. I here include participant observation in religious groups in cyberspace. This is because in order to understand it better, I wish to feel open to experience the attraction of the group. Further, an ethnographic dimension is important if one is to explore the interactional aspects of becoming and remaining a member of a revivalist group (Ayella 1993). Work with individuals alone will not reveal this interactional level.

As with any research method, there are contradictions in ethnography as a suitable tool for feminist research. A number of feminist scholars using a universalist standpoint seem to gloss over the issue of difference in claiming the ethnographic method. This is the other side of the egalitarian coin. Du Bois, for instance, in her statement 'The actual experience and language of women is the central agenda for feminist social science and scholarship' implied that women have one sort of everyday language, life and experience which they share (Du Bois 1983: 108). On the other hand, the more recent dismissal of the possibility of shared experience and therefore what might constitute feminist research has come about partly as the result of the development of feminist epistemology and partly because feminism has taken on postmodernism, deconstruction and difference. Stanley argues that ' "feminist standpoint" needs to incorporate a number of feminisms, including black and lesbian standpoints' (Stanley 1990: 33). At the same time, postmodernist anthropologists have pointed to the constructed nature of ethnographic accounts, that is, research as writing (Mascia-Lees, Sharpe and Ballerino-Cohen 1989: 9; Clifford and Marcus 1986: 15).

A debate between Judith Stacey (1988; 1994) and Elizabeth Wheatley (1994; 1994a) addresses some of these ethical and authorial problems in ethnographic research. Stacey (1988) is concerned how achievable the aims of empathy and egalitarianism are and thus implies that feminist research should be ethical. It is extraordinarily difficult, in a discussion of feminist methodology, to emerge from this bell jar of caring in which women have been placed.

Stacey sees two main areas of contradiction, the first being the fact in so far as ethnographic research depends upon the human relationship, that women can reveal things about themselves they might later regret or which could in some future time be used against them (Stacey 1988: 23). Stacey's second area of contradiction is that although the ethnographic method appears to lead to collaboration between the researcher and the researched, ultimately it is the researcher who authors the ethnography. Stacey is concerned that the ethnographic method, in being considered women-friendly, 'masks... a deeper form of exploitation' and opens up respondents to possible 'abandonment' and 'betrayal'. Further, that the presence of the researcher is 'an intrusion and intervention into a system of relationships... that the researcher is far freer than the researched to leave' (Stacey 1988: 24). I too would argue that the stance of phoney friend is exploitative, especially in relation to gaining information from disadvantaged groups.

Stacey sees a contradiction between feminist principles and ethnography in that the researcher ultimately owns the product even if it has been modified by informants, as has been the case with my interviews when I have sent transcripts for comment to informants. Stacey sees the ethnographic method as ultimately more exploitative than masculinist research methods (Stacey 1988: 24). I cannot help but see this as something of an overreaction. It is based on the idea that all feminists should be scrupulously 'moral'. Elizabeth Wheatley views the dilemma as 'not uniquely feminist in character' but as an ethical and epistemological problem all ethnographers face (Wheatley 1994: 406). I agree with her conclusion that the demand for a fully ethical ethnographic study as a feminist criterion makes 'insurmountable requisites for anyone' (ibid.: 407). She suggests 'rather than avoid any risk through abstaining from ethnographic endeavours, scholars might draw on diverse feminist insights in a sensitive manner when facing the dilemmas that are bound to emerge through the ethnographic process and product' (ibid.). But this brings us close to 'intentionality' as a criterion of feminist research (Poland 1990: 160–5). Intention, however, is flawed as a criterion by its dependence on the researcher being well informed by discourses, none of which, as poststructuralists have shown, are value-free.

I conclude that the only way to carry out a feminist ethnographic study without a complete sense of moral and ideological paralysis is to work empirically with the permission of informants and accept that one will end up being in a partially ethical position. For just as it is not possible to carry out research without a degree of objectification, so too in the case of a study undertaken in order to obtain a higher degree, it is not possible to be completely non-exploitative. Things are likely to be more equitable if the exploitation factor is recognized and which, being overt, can work both ways.

Method

Sources of respondents and interviewees

Data for this study were collected by means of a snowball questionnaire distributed amongst revivalists in Britain and information gained through semi-structured interviews with nine Muslim and nine Christian revivalist sisters of different kinds. Further material, drawn from participant observation both on news groups in cyberspace and in actuality, has been utilized as well as follow-up e-mail correspondence with Muslim and Christian participants in the United States.

Some 200 questionnaires were distributed over a two-year period. The 73 respondents ranged in age from 13 to 81. The age range of Christian respondents was between 15 and 81, the majority being between the ages of 20 and 40. The Muslims were younger: the entire group of 30 respondents were between the ages of 13 and 44, and of these, 23 were below the age of 30. Of the 43 Christians, the majority belong to house church or independent church groups, but four were conservative evangelicals. These four respondents belong to an organization called Men Women and God, a group of Biblical feminists who seek a gender 'equalitarian' interpretation of scripture and are drawn from different denominations but come under the umbrella of the Evangelical Alliance. Men Women and God has links with Christians for Biblical Equality, which is based in the United States. Christians for Biblical Equality describe themselves as 'an organization of Christians who believe that the Bible, properly interpreted, teaches the fundamental equality of men and women of all racial and ethnic groups, all economic classes, and all age groups, based on teachings of scriptures as reflected in Galatians 3: 28'.[5]

According to Valerie Griffiths, one of the founder members of the British association, the name of the group was intended to be Women, Men and God but it was registered wrongly here in Britain (though not in New Zealand), and the name stuck.[6] The views of Men Women and God are not typical yet they form part of conservative Protestant Christianity, which from the outside is portrayed as being unremittingly anti-feminist.

House churches are quintessentially postmodern church movements offering a 'pick-and-mix' menu of styles of worship and activities. These house churches range in style from Puritan culture to club ('rave') culture and some manage to include both. The various groups from which respondents in Britain come are: Christians in York, a fellowship which began as a plant from a Covenant Ministries church in the late 1980s, Covenant Ministries representing the most conservative network of the house church movement as described by Andrew Walker (1985); Jesus Fellowship, an independent church (described below); and Pioneer People in Cobham (Surrey) as well as other church groups who come under the Pioneer Network umbrella. Two of these Pioneer churches had women in leadership roles. Ten completed questionnaires were returned from Ichthus Fellowship whom I approached on the advice of a member of Men Women and

God on the grounds that it had a more enlightened view of gender equality. Both Ichthus and Pioneer were described by Ian Cotton (1995) in *The Hallelujah Revolution*. One respondent was from Vineyard, the church founded by John Wimber, ex-drummer of the 1960s band The Righteous Brothers. The three American evangelical feminists, all, in their late forties or early fifties, who participated in supplementary interviews, belong to Protestant denominations which are more mainstream: one was an Anabaptist and an ordained minister from the Brethren in Christ Church, one a Lutheran and the third a Baptist.

One conservative evangelical interviewee spoke of the house church movement as lacking in a knowledge of church history, but this bypassing of tradition is common to the majority of the UK groups in which I am interested. Pioneer People is, a good example. Not tied to any particular permanent building, they use a cinema in Leatherhead (Surrey) and leisure centres in the locality for their meetings. Their Sunday meetings attract up to 500 people in their congregation. They are flexible and focus on the individual. Like the other Christian respondents, the majority are white and middle-class.

This is not the case with Jesus Fellowship (also known as the Jesus Army), an Independent Baptist Church. Jesus Fellowship, which is a charismatically-based church which split from both the Evangelical Alliance and the Baptist Union in 1986, was founded by Noel Stanton in 1969. It appears to be successful in attracting young people who are experiencing difficulties, and appears to reach out especially to young men. Noel Stanton was a part-time minister at Bugbrooke Baptist Church in Northamptonshire, who, according to Fiona Macdonald, felt called 'in 1973, to establish a community along the lines of the early Christian Church'.[7] In the *UK Christian Handbook* (Brierley and Hiscock 1994/1995), I find that the Jesus Fellowship is an expanding church. This may be because of their use of all the modern methods of evangelizing, such as producing youth-centred printed material, utilizing the media, holding multi-media events, using the Internet and owning a conspicuous fleet of colourful buses which they use to meet the public.

Jesus Fellowship grew from 431 members in 1980 to 2,500 in 2001. During this period, Anglican, Catholic and other Baptist church attendance was decreasing. This is an interesting statistic as it helps to explain why I am not unwelcome when I ask questions. But there is also the possibility that Jesus Fellowship wishes to engage with enquirers whose aim is not to prove they are a 'cult'. Information on the Jesus Fellowship homepage on the World Wide Web sets out the Christian orthodoxy of their beliefs:

> The Fellowship is an evangelical Christian church with a charismatic emphasis and Baptist roots and is orthodox in doctrine, upholding the universally-accepted Christian creeds. It is linked with other churches and groups in the UK and overseas through the Multiply Christian Network.[8]

Jesus Fellowship has live-in and live-out members, and has a special ministry with young people for whom it holds rave-style worship sessions. But in Jesus Fellowship communities there is no television or rock music. This is an example of the combination of Puritan and club culture.

The three interviewees (as opposed to the ten respondents to the questionnaire) from Jesus Fellowship were middle- and upper-middle-class and highly articulate. They were hand-picked for me to interview and I do not think they reflected the class makeup of Jesus Fellowship as a whole. (See the issue of sensitivity to outsiders and impression management, discussed below.) Nevertheless, my impression was that they do reflect the beliefs of Jesus Fellowship and the questionnaires which were distributed for me by their communications officer do clearly reflect a wide range of backgrounds.

As mentioned above, the Muslim respondents were mainly from a younger age group than the Christians, their comparative youth perhaps being due to the route through which I accessed the Muslims. As with the Christian groups I started with the Internet.

The Muslim respondents came from a number of sources. The first source was Young Muslims UK (YMUK), which was founded in 1984. Most of its members were born in Britain, many into Muslim homes. The majority of members are of Pakistani origin, but there are also members from Somalia and the Yemen as well as white British converts. They are apologists in that they differentiate between culture and Islam. But in adapting their understanding of Islam to the conditions in which they find themselves, they are also reformists. For instance, as Zainab, a member of YMUK explained, YMUK is finding ways to be 'both Muslim and British'. A sister at a YMUK meeting which was held at the Islamic Foundation near Leicester, to which I was invited in March 1996, described how members born and educated in Britain know both the Western way and the Islamic way and have chosen Islam. Many of the YMUK sisters are reverts, who have tried the Western way and have become disillusioned.

The second source is an Islamic forum in cyberspace where I encountered members of a group who call themselves Submitters. The word Islam of course means submission, but their founder, Rashad Khalifa, an Arabic speaker and scientist, states in his intro-duction to his translation of the Qur'an that 'Submission' is the universal religion.[9] The Submitters are unusual in that they are mod-ern-day 'Qur'an alone' people or *Ahl al-Qur'an* (People of the Qur'an). They reject the *Hadith* (the sayings of the Prophet), the *Sunnah* (the example of the Prophet) and *Shariah* (Islamic law) as unsound and manufactured. They are mainly based in the United States and Canada, but there are also some Submitters in Britain.[10] Their 'Qur'an alone' strategy may well prove useful in societies that are intolerant of Islam. It lends them a degree of invisibility as Muslims, for instance, by rejecting the *hijab* (the headscarf) on the grounds that the Qur'an requires only that women should dress modestly, but does not suggest they should cover themselves from head to toe.[11] This private approach to Islam (in terms of both becoming less visible as well as in permitting personal interpretation of the Qur'an) is not new. A Qur'an alone strategy was used by the *Ahl al-Qur'an* formed in Delhi in the late nineteenth century as one response to the dreadful reprisals against Muslims by the British following the First War of Independence (the Indian Mutiny) of 1857–59. Submitters are also very unusual in following Khalifa's belief that the Qur'an is divinely constructed on the basis of multiples of 19.[12] Submitters clearly think that other Muslims are misreading the Qur'an and battles rage in cyberspace between them and more orthodox believers, who are appalled by their rejection of Islamic tradition and their belief that Rashad Khalifa, who was murdered in 1990, was 'God's messenger of the Covenant', based on Qur'an 3: 81, 33: 7 and 33: 40. When I inquired as to the history of the Submitters, Yasmin, a member based in the United States, replied that the movement goes back 'to the beginning of time'. She continued: 'According to the Qur'an, Abraham was the first to use the word "submitter" to describe one who worships and submits to God alone.'[13] So although they do not wear what I have come to regard as Islamic revivalist dress, these Submitters qualify as 'revivalist' in that they are seeking a 'pure Islam'. Yasmin expresses it in terms of their particular movement as being an expression of a pristine Islam which goes back to 'the beginning of time'. Only one respondent to the questionnaire, from Scotland, belonged to this group. Participant observation on an Islamic forum in cyberspace where this particular group has a powerful voice led me to encounter some opposing and more orthodox voices. One of these voices came from a member of Young Muslims UK who invited me to attend a weekend meeting of YMUK (see 'Access' below).

The third source of respondents and interviewees were Islamic societies at three universities in the North of England. Four interviewees from these sources are white British and Irish converts. All of them are married and have children, but none of them is a student. Linda explained that a lot of Muslims in Newcastle 'who do not feel they fit in at mosques which are specifically Pakistani or Iranian and which use languages other than English, meet up at the Newcastle University mosque'. They wear the headscarf in the same manner as the sisters from YMUK. That is, they show only their faces and hands in public. They, like the YMUK members, refer to the *Sunnah* and the *Hadith* as sources of legitimation. All four regard Islam as a total way of life.

The fourth source of Muslim respondents to the questionnaire was a mosque in the South of England where a group of young women are studying for their GCSE in Islam. (They are unable to take GCSE in Islam at school.) All of them have been born into Muslim homes; some are still at school and some at university. These young women have a high pass rate in the GCSE, some with as many as ten passes. One had four A levels. According to their teacher, many of them are the daughters of fathers who are taxi drivers and mothers who work at a mushroom farm. All these young women, including the youngest, who was 13, dress in what I would describe as the Islamic revivalist style.[14]

Some sisters whom I met through being referred on by other respondents or interviewees are members of the Islamic Society of Britain. Although only five of the Muslims described themselves as 'converts', many of the Muslims have tried living the Western consumerist lifestyle but have rejected it. Most of the Muslim respondents to the questionnaire are second-generation British Muslims, born to Muslim parents of Pakistani, Indian, Syrian or Moroccan descent. Among the interviewees the situation was reversed in that six of the nine were white European converts to Islam. The majority of the Muslim respondents and interviewees were highly articulate, often high academic achievers and some were professionally trained.

The majority of the Christians (29 of 43) described themselves as converts to Christianity even though many of them were born into Christian homes. This is because the majority are 'born-again' Christians with the exclusivity this implies. In contrast, of the Muslim respondents to the questionnaire, only five described themselves as converts or reverts to Islam. The rest were born into Muslim homes.

Access

It has been suggested that there are particular difficulties associated with studying proselytizing groups, not least the fact they may wish to convert the researcher or cease to cooperate when they realize that the researcher is not a candidate for membership (Gordon 1987). 'Conversion-oriented' groups may hold 'potential convert' as their only conceptualization of outsiders (Ayella 1993). I think the researcher may overestimate their personal appeal as a prize. Further, for reasons of public relations, it is not in the interests of a revivalist group to convert a potentially non-antagonistic researcher because, should the researcher join them, her findings would be devalued by the view that 'she would say that anyway'.

A more serious difficulty, in my view, is that of the sensitivity of the group to outsiders through fear of misrepresentation. This may be the result of adverse media coverage. For instance, a covert researcher (a journalist) posed as a homeless person in order to be taken to New Creation Community, Jesus Fellowship's Northampton Headquarters. She later describes them as a 'cult'.[15] Although it could be said that Christianity started out as a Judaic 'cult', 'cult' is a dangerous word as it alienates and isolates the group thus described. At the same time, a researcher who is anticipated to give a favourable report and thus improve public relations might be welcomed (Ayella 1993). This may take the form of 'trading' which enables access. In the later stages of my fieldwork I was able to send papers I had written to 'gatekeepers' who could then ascertain that I was not in the business of stoking the fires of Islamophobia or the vilification of Christian groups.

Muslims, in a post-communist, secularized society have been identified as the enemy of the West (Huntington 1993) and many Muslims live in Western countries as the 'Other' within (Turner 1994), and are pushed into a defensive position. Larry Poston, studying conversion to Islam in the United States, found that because Muslim groups were suspicious of his motives, it was impossible to get responses to his questionnaires. Poston had to resort to the published testimonies of converts (Poston 1992). Poston cites Yvonne Haddad and Adair Lummis as experiencing similar problems. More recently, Elizabeth Warnock Fernea (1998) has written about interviews she carried out with Muslims in the United States, who were mainly not converts and generally in positions of some influence.

This problem led me to expect that I, as a white, non-Muslim, might experience similar difficulties in Britain. I was surprised then, when, in the earliest stages of my study, I met a student member of Bradford University Islamic Association setting up his bookstall outside the university library and his immediate response was that I should meet some of the sisters. He was as good as his word and it was through this contact that I was led to my first informant. Further, when I approached an individual who declared himself, on an Islamic Forum in cyberspace, to be on the executive committee of Young Muslims UK, he not only agreed to distribute my questionnaire but also invited me to the YMUK meeting at the Islamic Foundation, even going to the trouble of meeting me at Leicester Station. Muslims who offered access were clear that they were interested in being better understood by non-Muslims.

When I approached Christian groups, I received a warm welcome from John Campbell, communications officer for Jesus Fellowship whom I first contacted by e-mail. Martin Scott of Pioneer People was also welcoming when I contacted him in response to reading his book *Women and Ministry*, a book which had been recommended to me by an informant. Both these contacts distributed questionnaires and helped to arrange interviews. E-mail has also been my first contact with some of the individual respondents to my questionnaires, and indeed, one of my questionnaires was completed by e-mail.

But it was not always easy. Some of the contacts I attempted to make by letter and e-mail and requests for distribution of my questionnaire were not successful. Letters to six Evangelical ministers and to two Muslim leaders in London, a number of e-mails to two Vineyard missionaries who were working in Berkshire (to whom I had an introduction from a Vineyard member from the United States) as well as an e-mail to a self-proclaimed member of Hizb-ut-tahrir, all met with a wall of silence. All these points meant I needed to be flexible in my approach to gaining information and at the same time attempt to make an analysis of the reasons why access is being granted or denied.

Ayella suggests that 'One should question the kind of access one is being given, ever conscious of the possibility of sanitization or impression management' (Ayella 1993: 111). On the whole this impression management is understandable by groups who feel they are considered 'fair game' by journalists and researchers. For instance, representation as a 'cult' has deeply practical outcomes. Not only are 'cults' 'considered by many to be deviant' (Ayella 1993: 108), but such labelling makes it more difficult for the group to mobilize resources (ibid.: 121). During a phone call in which I requested the opportunity to visit the Jesus Fellowship group in Sheffield (which was granted) the area leader suggested I would 'bowl googlies' at poor, unsuspecting young people. I was conscious of not wanting to 'catch people out'. But I could understand the pastor's concern and why it was that interviewees would be hand-picked. This is where participant observation helps as a means of getting a wider picture.

Participant observation

At the outset I felt that my most pressing need was to visit revivalist groups, not only to gain access to respondents but to get a feel of the social milieu in which they moved. The culture of a group can only be experienced by 'being there'. We learn about a culture by observing people and by participating (Spradley 1979: 8; Richardson 1991: 62). I therefore attended meetings, talks, worship, classes, lectures and exhibitions as well as visiting the homes and communal homes of believers to gain a more rounded view of the groups of which my informants are a part.

The most famous accounts of participant observation are generally of covert research where the researcher is cast in an heroic role. Examples of this genre are Lofland's (1966) *Doomsday Cult*, and Rosenhan's (1973) 'On Being Sane in Insane Places'. The reader is held in suspense at the possibility of the researcher being discovered in their duplicity, or worse, what if Rosenhan's researchers who got themselves admitted to psychiatric hospitals are not released? There are also strong ethical reasons against covert research. A study often cited to illustrate this is L. Humphries' (1975) *Tearoom Trade* in which the researcher acted as a 'look-out queen' for gay men having sex in public lavatories. Humphries then conducted a covert follow-up on his research subjects by obtaining their addresses via their car registration numbers. Yet Roger Homan points out that critics of covert methods tend not to be above criticism themselves in terms of their methods (Homan 1991: 119). He cites Dingwall (1977), who takes a high moral tone with regard to covert research but who was involved in drinking sessions with his subjects,[16] and Belson (1975),[17] who fed his subjects before interviewing them about their experiences of thieving (Homan 1991: 126).

This kind of participant observation is very much in the style of sociology as grand narrative. There is also overt participant observation where the researcher participates in order to observe, but there is a grey area here with regard to how overt can it be. This is especially the case in relation to proselytizing groups who might see the researcher as having been sent by God for some reason not yet revealed to the researcher (Richardson 1991: 67). Some feminist social scientists have wrestled with the issue of creating a more feminist kind of participatory observation which shares power between researchers and subjects (Gergen and Gergen 1991: 768). Gergen and Gergen call this 'dialogic participation'. I was participating in order to do experiential research and at the same time my aim was to encourage participation in my research project by the subjects of the research. This was not only for feminist ethical reasons but because the informants are the people who know how it is to live a life in conformity with revivalist religion. Although I was aware that ultimately I would have authorial control, I hoped my informants would participate in the process of interpretation. To this end I sent transcripts of interviews to all interviewees for their comments, and drafts of papers to some.

Participant observation is 'non-linear', being both verbal and nonverbal, and accesses data which would be outside the frame of a classic interview as a means of trying to ascertain the insiders' viewpoint. This is especially the case in terms of religious movements where the insider viewpoint is frequently obscure to the outsider (Jorgenson 1989: 9–12). Some researchers have even joined religious groups in order to engage in covert research. My whole instinct has been to do the reverse, that is, to be honest from the outset regarding my researcher role and to see how far this would allow me to collect data.

In November 1995 I attended my first Christian 'revivalist' meeting advertised thus by a Christian student group in York as: 'Toronto Blessing Come and See'. This was an invitation I could not refuse especially as it was a group to which one of my earliest informants belonged. I had decided from the outset that when I visited a group I should tell people that I was engaged in a research project, what that project was and what it was for. I also informed them that I was based at the University Centre for Women's Studies, not only so they could locate me if they wished, but also because of the, at times, strained relationship between feminisms and revivalist religions. I felt that the responses to that piece of information also constitute data. However, this may have prejudiced some groups against responding to my requests for access.

I soon discovered that the fact that members of a group knew I was a researcher did not preclude their welcoming me as a participant. This could, of course, be because I might be viewed as a potential convert (Richardson 1991). At the Christians York meeting, I decided to stand up when they did, sing when they did (fortunately the words of the hymns were projected onto the wall) and I think I smiled a lot. I came to this last conclusion as one of the participants asked me if I was there for 'business or pleasure'. Just 'being there' enabled me to absorb some of the atmosphere of a meeting and get a better picture of the group. I found out, for instance, that a number of the men were scientists and mathematicians – groups disproportionately represented amongst revivalist religionists (Barr 1977). Further, although I had read a great deal about the 'Toronto Blessing' and the poster for the meeting had mentioned it, I was disappointed to find that no one fell to the ground in the manner frequently described in the press at the time. I think the poster was an interesting example of a group turning media hype to its own purposes.

In March 1996 I attended a weekend workshop held by Young Muslims UK at the Islamic Foundation, where I was able to participate in a sisters' work group. The sisters all wore the *hijab* and were seated behind the brothers. Actually 'being there' gave me the feeling that they had not been 'relegated' to the back (as is so often imagined by non-Muslim observers) but that this was a choice, which allowed them, as young women, the freedom to operate away from the masculine gaze. I could see that the sisters were able to address the whole group from the stage and that they took a dynamic part in the overall organization of the event. For instance, one sister signalled from the back of the hall for a male speaker to hurry up because it was time to draw a particular item to a close.

I was able to visit the *masjid* (mosque) with the sisters, share their lunch (which appeared to be Kentucky Fried Chicken) and listen to a talk by a visiting speaker from Egypt. The talk was about marriage and I had expected the sort of Christian talk on the subject, about 'give and take', with which I was familiar. Instead it was a highly political talk about the importance of the family as the basic unit of Islamic society and the extended family as a support network which could liberate women to work for Islam. The visibly pregnant speaker pointed out that she would not be present if it were not for her extended family taking care of her children while she was in England. The act of being present at this meeting was informative in a way that talking with an individual alone can never be. It quickly abolished any stereotypical ideas I had about women who wear *hijab*. The speaker on the stage was certainly not without a voice. I was deeply impressed by the goodness, tolerance and kindness of the sisters, one of whom led me by hand from place to place if I was in doubt where to go. I could not help thinking that, because of their visibility, the sisters might be better Muslims than the brothers.

This contrasted with my attendance in November 1996 at a Leeds University Student Islamic Society 'Islamic Awareness Week' exhibition and talk where sisters had their own entrance and sat on one side of the auditorium and all three speakers were male. I found it interesting to observe the many degrees of veiling and numerous ways there appeared to be of wearing the *hijab*. My informant, who had arranged to meet me there, eventually came up to me fully veiled from head to toe in black, as I was leaving. She had been there all the time, but I had not been able to recognize her. But this 'being there' offered insight into some of the practicalities of the veil, for instance, the anonymity it can bestow[18] as well as a sense of what it feels like to sit on the women's side of a large auditorium. As a non-Muslim and being on my own it was pleasant to be seated amongst women. But I found myself concerned that all the speakers were male and that they were answering written questions from the floor on what seemed to me women's issues, for instance *hijab*.

I have also visited the Jesus Fellowship New Creation Farm and Headquarters in Northampton on two occasions. This gave me a completely different impression from the one I had obtained from visiting their website on the Internet and from reading their magazines. From Jesus Fellowship publicity I had gained an impression of brash exuberance, but my visit made me think them more like a monastic group who live a simple and wholesome lifestyle. These two impressions sit rather oddly together and called for further investigation. When I mentioned this to John Campbell, their media officer, he suggested that in today's world it was necessary to give such an effervescent impression in order to gain attention. My most lingering impression of New Creation Farm is the unforgettable scent of a profusion of mainly unobtainable, old-fashioned varieties of apples in the farm shop. Is this the perfume of a lost world or of late modern nostalgia? I fancy it is a little of both.

A visit to the Sheffield branch of Jesus Fellowship gave a different picture. In this respect I found it useful to attend a house warming party at a Jesus Fellowship Sheffield community house and a meeting for worship on the following day. There I was able to see that a cross-section of people in terms of gender and class attended. Nevertheless the vast majority of attendees were white. Many of the members at the house and at worship were utterly different from the hand-picked members I had met at the Northampton Headquarters. This was a ministry which incorporates marginalized people, ex-prisoners, young people in trouble, homeless people. When I visited, Jesus Army (Jesus Fellowship in action) were out on the streets at night, cooking baked potatoes to feed the homeless. Northampton Jesus Fellowship members do this in London too.

When I visited Martin Scott, one of the leaders of Pioneer People, at his office in in 1996 I had thought I should dress in a business-like manner to meet my stereotypical vision of an evangelical pastor. I was amazed to be greeted at the door by a woman who was dressed in leggings and to find Martin Scott wearing an earring through one ear and dressed in jeans. By 'being there' some of my prejudices and stereotypical images were melting away. In May 1997 I attended a

Pioneer People meeting at the Tolworth Leisure Centre, Surrey, where people were welcoming. The response to a request for prayer on an important issue for the group gave me an impression of a crowd of private individuals, each praying alone, a postmodern phenomenon of the 'lonely crowd',[19] a group of isolates, each with his or her own concerns. A cacophony of groans went up, as if a groping for some intangible reality was taking place. Individuals wandered around in prayer, some speaking in tongues, whilst one young man raised a staff over his head, Moses-like, his body quaking. Others went to the ground; a couple of men appeared to be prostrating themselves in prayer, like Muslims, whilst some women giggled on the floor. I wondered if the impression I had gained of the casualization of dress amongst these mainly white, middle-class suburban people was related to the fact they might find themselves on the floor.

Questionnaires

Early in my research process I sent out a pilot questionnaire to gain an indication of what kinds of questions I should be asking in interviews. It soon became evident that the completed questionnaires were a viable source of information in themselves.

Contacting the organizations from 'cold' and asking to have access to the sisters did not necessarily bring a positive response. But sending a sample questionnaire was a means of showing gatekeepers the kind of questions I wished to ask. So besides providing me with valuable information upon which I could draw for the interviews and proving to be a rich source of data in its own right, the questionnaire acted as an ice-breaker. Inquiring about the willingness of a religious organization to distribute questionnaires gave me something tangible to ask the men and women who were in leadership roles and therefore able to offer or deny access.

Another function of the survey was that it helped to establish a wider picture against which to measure the degree to which a particular respondent may be atypical when it comes to data acquired from in-depth interviews. But the quantitative part of the research is not a rigorous study. There are too many problems associated with trying to obtain a random sample from revivalist groups and the survey forms only part of a multi-method approach to gaining information.

Having accepted that questionnaires are not generally considered to be a feminist method I designed an open questionnaire which allowed respondents to answer questions in whatever way they pleased, writing as much or as little as they wanted in their own time and only if they wished to do so. I also worked at offering respondents space to suggest changes and to criticize the questions which are the content of the questionnaire. Suggestions for changes to the questions were forthcoming. A Christian respondent, for example, indicated that in her view a question concerned with rights was more appropriate to Muslims than to Christians. Other Christians, especially conservative evangelicals from Men Women and God, questioned the use of the term 'revivalist' as applied to themselves. Some Muslim respondents objected to the term 'obedience' in the question 'Does your religion require that a woman should be obedient to her husband?', preferring 'submission'. A Muslim researcher who completed a questionnaire suggested I remove the boxes which I had placed for the answers because 'respondents might write more'. I adapted the questionnaire as I progressed and therefore changes have been taken into account in interpretation of the data. At times I had to balance the fact that the feedback was data in itself with the desire to be open to make changes. For instance, the issue of the terms 'obedience' and 'submission' yields a rich vein for comparative study. Why did the majority of Christians *not* object to the term 'obedience'? To discover more I continued to use the term 'obedience'. This issue became the basis of chapter 3 of this book.

It was not possible, in the situation of finding respondents from revivalist groups where I was obliged to gain access through leaders, to ensure I was obtaining a random sample. This was difficult because of the pressure there is on leaders to engage in 'impression management' for fear that researchers might misrepresent their case in some way. It took Eileen Barker two years of negotiation with the Unification Church to reach a position where she could do research on her own terms, that is, to be given access to a list of all members, so that she might draw a random sample to interview. Further, Barker was allowed this freedom of access only because she was sought out by the Unification Church in order to carry out the research for them. This put her 'in a more powerful position to negotiate for a favourable research "bargain"' (Ayella 1993: 111). I had neither the time nor the power to attempt such a negotiation. Further, I was approaching a number of groups, some of whom would view me with suspicion. As a non-Muslim approaching Muslims and as someone with, at best, liberal Christian and at worst, post-Christian beliefs, I might be viewed as unsympathetic and something of a 'lost cause' by some evangelical and charismatic Christians. I knew that the groups would wish to show their 'better' side to the public.

Over a period of two years I distributed over 200 questionnaires. The highest return was from organisations from which I have had an overall 50 per cent return rate. The rest were completed by the snowball method, passed on by interviewees or respondents to the questionnaire. As the questionnaires were passed on by representatives I always enclosed stamped addressed envelopes with each questionnaire to avoid the need for their collection and perusal by the distributor. The latter did in fact happen in one case when a leader of one Christian group collected the questionnaires which I then never received.

Respondents to the questionnaire

The profile of the interviewees is not a pattern replicated by the 73 respondents to the questionnaire. Eleven of 30 Muslim respondents described themselves as Pakistani, four as Arab, one as Iranian, one as Asian and one as Anglo-Asian, five as white British and one as Irish. For the rest their ethnicity is unknown. Christian respondents were overwhelmingly white British with one white Canadian and a white South African, one black British and one Asian.

My interviewees were largely British-born, mainly middle-class and many had received higher education. This was no doubt influenced by the fact that in 50 per cent of cases I had to go through gatekeepers to obtain interviews. Gatekeepers selected articulate women to represent the movement to which they belonged. All the Christian interviewees are white and come from lower-middle to upper-middle class backgrounds. Four of nine Christian interviewees had attended university and one had professional training as a social worker. The Muslim interviewees came from more ethnically and culturally varied backgrounds than the Christians. Unlike the sample who completed the questionnaire, the majority of the interviewees (five of nine) were white converts to Islam. Three of these were converts from Catholicism, of whom two were Irish. The rest were born into Muslim families; one English Muslim was born in Egypt, another was Somalian and two were born to British, South Asian-Muslim parents. Four of the nine interviewees were attending, or had attended university, two at postgraduate level. The age range of the nine Christian interviewees was 21 to 73, six of whom were in their thirties and forties. The age of the nine Muslim interviewees was 23 to 46.

Interviews

The interviews took a degree of negotiation to set up and involved travel to the far North of England, the South of England (including London), the Midlands and South Wales. I also interviewed, or had ongoing dialogue with, eight interviewees (women and men) in both Britain and the United States, who were not involved as subjects but on whom I was able to call for information or advice. One of these discussions was carried out entirely by e-mail. At times there was some overlap here because some of my informants were also experts. For instance, among my Islamic informants there were two women who are researchers and another who has obtained an MPhil for an Islam-based study.

Because of the locations in which I have been obliged to meet informants and because of the need to build trust, I did not, in a number of cases, use a tape recorder. Anderson and Jack have written about the spontaneity of the exchange of a taped interview (Anderson and Jack 1991: 11), but how spontaneous can it be? I am aware that some people find the presence of a tape recorder daunting. James Spradley (1979) has written how recording is not always advisable as not only does it not substitute for rapport, but it 'may threaten and inhibit informants' (Spradley 1979: 74). In terms of its intrusiveness recording equipment has changed a great deal since Spradley was writing. But on my initial visit to the Jesus Fellowship in Northampton a group of sisters expressed relief that I had not brought a tape recorder. One of them remarked how when a visiting journalist had used one the group had remained silent. Immediately the journalist turned the tape recorder off the group had started to talk.

During interviews, I took notes, making an effort to get down key terms which would act as triggers (Spradley 1979: 74) to my memory once I started writing up the interview as soon as possible after the event. I also found it necessary to follow this procedure whilst using a tape recorder: once I lost the major part of an interview because my informant's telephone rang a few minutes into the interview and I switched the recorder off. When I switched it on again I omitted to depress both the 'play' and 'record' buttons. On other occasions, my interviewees have been so quietly spoken that I have had great difficulty in transcribing the tapes.[20] Not surprisingly, the best recording resulted from an interview with an interviewee who does some professional broadcasting.

Sometimes I found myself meeting respondents in places where, because the surrounding noise level would make recording impossible, it was not practical to use a tape recorder. For instance, I met Linda, a white British convert to Islam, at a large railway station. She had suggested, during a telephone call, that now her older children were at school we could meet away from her house. We spent the next few hours in a series of cafés where making a tape recording would have been impossible. I met another sister, whom I had previously met at the YMUK meeting, at London King' s Cross Station and, following her choice of venue (from what was available), I interviewed her in the burger bar there (where the interviewee drank only water, perhaps because, the food was not *halal*). I think that cafés do represent neutral spaces and this may lead to a relaxed conversation. There is plenty going on around and this helps to detract from what can at times be the intimidating process of an interview. Later, after I had gained some rapport with Linda, I was invited to her home to meet two other sisters and I was able to carry out a group interview and share lunch with them whilst their children ran around laughing and playing. The situation was relaxed and informal, but again not suitable for a tape recording.

Conducting the interview

Although the power relationship between interviewer and interviewee changes during and after the fieldwork process, there is an implicit power relation in the interviewer/interviewee relationship. For instance the interviewer knows the order of the questions whereas the interviewee does not. Further, the control that the interviewer holds over the interview process means that she can distort the flow of information. This can happen if the interviewer fails to listen carefully. Anderson and Jack suggest that the interviewer needs to learn to listen more to the narrator then to her own agenda (Anderson and Jack 1991: 12). Careful listening can help the researcher avoid the pitfall of scripting the narrator's account. This process takes place when the interviewer thinks she already knows what the narrator is saying (ibid.: 19).

There is also the issue of asking leading questions. If I ask a question such as 'what led up to your conversion to Islam?' I am perhaps suggesting a linear process where everything fell into place. It's a bit like the way that writing a CV invites you to represent all career choices as having been based upon deliberation as part of a rational career plan.

After carrying out my first two interviews, I realized that there is great value in having previously met my interviewees and having visited the organizations to which they belong. Apart from making for a relaxed feeling about the process and providing a sense of being open to ongoing dialogue, it made it possible to see the interviewee as *part* of something, as well as an individual. Initially, I had proposed carrying out 40 interviews, but in the event opted for a smaller number of mainly longer-term exchanges. These took various forms and included interviews, meeting for coffee or lunch, letter writing or e-mail, and telephone conversations. The interviews were loosely structured in that I had an overall plan of five areas I wished to address. These included: background and family; education; employment; circumstances surrounding conversion or reversion (if indeed either was the case) and the benefits of the religious system to the interviewee as a woman. I would then ask specific questions regarding issues that had been raised.

Life histories theory has influenced me to take the life-span into account. This proved useful, for instance, in my second interview with Laura, a white English, 24-year-old convert to Islam, when I asked her about her education, mainly as an indicator of class background. Laura informed me that she had been sent to a 'free school' where the child-centred education had left her with a sense of having missed out on real life. She said: 'There were no black people, no Asians. I felt I was not getting a broad experience. I knew others from normal schools and I wanted experience of normal life. Everyone was so privileged. I felt I was missing something so rich.' This did not fit the stereotypical view of a woman who wears *hijab*. Yet there are women from all manner of backgrounds who have come to wear *hijab*. For instance, the interviewee Maryam (see chapter 3) told me that she knew 'punks' who had converted to Islam. In the case of

Laura I found myself wondering whether this rejection of the model of child-centred education, which was fashionable in the 1970s, was perhaps a generational matter. The rigid structures of my own childhood had me longing for the kind of education where you can call teachers by their first names, but for Laura it had clearly seemed an inauthentic experience. Had its lack of structure made the ideological structures of Islam and the regularity of the practices in her daily adult life more appealing? Childhood experiences, as well as family background, must influence our later religious choices.

Power

Power is a theme which will resurface throughout this book. Although there is a sense in which I wish to challenge some outcomes of a blanket application of a Foucaldian analysis of power, I find Foucault's (1977) theorization of the situatedness of power irresistible. This is because it is a model that accommodates a recognition of the changing nature of power. In the case of feminist literature of the 1980s, the impression was given that interviewing is 'a cosy enterprise' (Phoenix 1994: 50), on the one hand, and that there was a moral imperative on the interviewer to recognise her power position, and, on the other, to compensate accordingly (Oakley 1981). The notion of power being on the interviewer's side can be overestimated. My experience, doing research for a doctoral thesis, was that I was dependent upon the goodwill of my informants. As an interviewer your future is in jeopardy if you do not get results. In this sense the interviewer is vulnerable, and I found that the absence of a discussion of this in the literature was disadvantageous. Ann Phoenix (1994) is a writer who does address the issue but in the main it remains unaddressed.

The power of the researcher is in the fact that she has a voice, and the literature regarding her power and the potential she has for exploiting the interviewee is plentiful (Oakley 1981; Stacey 1988; Finch 1991). However, considerably less has been written on the reverse position. Phoenix (1994) has pointed out that the balance shifts throughout the research process. At first, during the fieldwork stage, the power is with the individuals who may admit or deny the researcher access to informants; then it shifts to the informant in that the researcher is dependent upon her provision of information. There have been times when I have gained no response to my requests for interviews, admission or distribution of questionnaires and this has left me wondering whether the problem was lack of interest or outright rejection of my project. A researcher at the fieldwork stage is not necessarily in a powerful position at all. Phoenix writes about her negative experiences as a black fieldworker. She writes of the neglected theme of how 'most published material has discussed projects over which the researcher had some control rather than the more common experience where the feminist researcher has no control over the research process' (Phoenix 1994: 49). Donna Luff (1999), imagining the impact of the interview would be one-way, found discomforture not in rejection but in moments of rapport with her interviewees, women in the 'British moral lobby'. She reports that she was 'usefully confounded' by having her stereotypes unsettled by her 'anti-feminist' interviewees and points to the contradictions and fracturedness of power relations in the interview process (Luff 1999: 694). Nevertheless, once she has possession of the data, the balance of power rests with the researcher. This is because she has now become the author. But even this is not as unproblematic as it may appear. There are many considerations in the presentation of material which must be reflected upon. There are issues involved not only of understanding the views of those interviewed, and (if one wishes to keep the door open to the possibility of further research) maintaining their goodwill, but also the consideration of the ways in which the material will be received by others.

Phoenix gives an example of the difficulties at the fieldwork stage from her study of mothers under 20. An interviewee who lived at home with her parents was forthcoming. They sat in the kitchen while the parents, who were unemployed, sat in the sitting room, separated by a partition wall and serving hatch. She writes: 'I had not got very far into the interview when her father came in, told me to turn off the tape recorder and enquired why I was asking questions about him and his wife. My explanations about getting background information fell on deaf ears' (Phoenix 1994: 51).

Phoenix writes that 'the dynamics of race, social class, the issue being researched, and the intersection of the agendas of interviewers and interviewees all have as much impact as gender on the interview situation' (ibid.: 55). Sometimes it was obvious to Phoenix that after appointments made by telephone, 'a minority of white interviewees

[were] visibly shocked to see me when I turned up on the doorstep' (ibid.). I felt a little like that about my age. If my first contact was by telephone I let people know that I was not a young researcher in order to avoid the mutual embarrassment of their visible surprise.

There are also issues of power associated with interviewing members of proselytizing groups. Gordon (1987) writes how such groups may not understand how the researcher can appear to understand but at the same time not be persuaded by that understanding to believe. Three months into his study Gordon was asked if he 'knew the Lord yet?' When he replied in the negative he was warned that he had had plenty of time and that the Lord would deal particularly harshly with him. Gordon writes: 'These are the kinds of pressures that lead field researchers to experience fear of expulsion, anxiety and guilt' (Gordon 1987: 272). This is an example of where honesty is used by the researcher in the face of proselytization. I too was told at a group interview that God deals particularly harshly with those who hear the word of Islam and do not follow. The pre-Vatican II Catholic child in me is not impervious to the threat of hell.

Oakley (1981; 1993) has demonstrated the importance of allowing the researched to question the researcher as a means of redressing the balance power. Interviewees who are believers may well ask the researcher questions about their own beliefs. For instance, during my second interview with Laura, she asked my view on polygamy. Although I recognize that there are a number of perspectives from which polygamy may be viewed, I felt I had to say that I was not in favour of it. I felt I could not lie in order to ingratiate myself with her and yet I think my response led to a degree of mistrust and possible misreading of my intentions.

In attempting to create a dialogic process I decided that, after each interview, I should send informants a written transcript either of the tape (if a tape recorder had been used) or of the notes of what I understood them to have said. In the latter case, this was a means of double checking my information as well as an opportunity to ask subsidiary questions which may occur to me after the event. Further, it gave an opportunity to the interviewee to comment and correct me if they thought I had misunderstood them. Chilla Bulbeck (1997), who used this method in her interviews with three generations of Australian feminists, writes that this method allows 'a space for reflection and editing' and 'encouraged frankness at the point of narration'. I found this generally to be the case as the interviewees know that they can edit at a later date. For this reason, and after the episode with Laura (described below) I shifted to a pattern where I requested permission to use the content of the interview *after* the transcript had been edited and commented upon by the interviewee.

But this method is not without its problems. Bulbeck found that a number of respondents, by editing, made themselves appear less racist, less critical or less confused than their transcript might have suggested. I think this was a problem to a degree with interviewees who see themselves as ambassadors for their religious position. There is an example of this in the conversations I had with one interviewee who throughout stood by the Islamic requirement for a wife to submit to her husband. Only later, when we were parting company at the railway station after a shared lunch and a two-hour interview spread over an afternoon, did I get the impression that she might have a different personal feeling on the issue but that she believed that, because of her loyalty to Islam, her personal feelings did not come into it.

Although the sending of transcripts and interview notes for comment worked very well in general and proved to be a way of continuing an interview in writing, it did backfire in its initial stages. My first Muslim interviewee had kindly invited me to her house. This had been my second visit to Laura's home and I felt that we had built up a rapport. She had been very open on the first occasion but she said she wished her husband to be present for the second interview, 'in case she got something wrong'. I explained that I wished for her view on things and that I was interested in her life and how she had come to Islam as a convert some three years earlier. In retrospect I realize that Laura saw herself as a representative for Islam. After the interview I sent her my typed-up notes of the conversation which I left unembellished on purpose. In each case of Laura's words which I had noted down I was careful to write: 'Laura said'. This is because I wanted to make clear which were her quoted words and which were my impressions or compressed notes as I did not wish to put words into her mouth. This may have read rather strangely because I was devastated to receive a letter which told me that in my 'first draft' I had a 'mocking tone throughout' and that I was clearly biased on 'the women's issue' and that what I was doing was a 'complete waste of three years'. Laura put no address on her letter and said she had moved. As far as I understood it, I was feeding back what she had said. But I must have gone through a selective process in choosing what to write down and also, as shown by Linda's (another interviewee's) comments, there were times when I misheard things. However when this did happen, according to Linda's response, it was usually a matter of a single word. I found it hard to believe that what I wrote down could be *so* extremely different from what Laura had said.[21]

So what went wrong? Katherine Borland (1991) has written about interpretative conflict, for instance, in her feminist reading of her grandmother's narrative – an idea with which her grandmother strongly disagreed. But the notes I sent to Laura hadn't even reached the interpretation stage. I think the problem was that I imagined my informant would understand that my write-up of the interview was in note form and that it was not a 'first draft' of my thesis at all. Further, not all my interviewees had had the opportunity of a university education. I needed to be aware of this and now realize that some may not be able to accept that in the research process it is necessary to ask the difficult questions as well as the easy ones. As can be seen elsewhere in this book (chapter 3), I pressed and pressed Maryam, an interviewee with a research degree, on the issue of 'obedience' to the stage where she was annoyed, but we retained an understanding and I was able to send Maryam a paper on the issue of submission, which I subsequently wrote, for her comments. The incident with Laura may have resulted from lack of forethought on my part and was deeply unnerving in the initial stages, when I knew I had so many interviews to go. I was left with an awareness that, with all my subsequent interviews, welcome could change to outright rejection at any moment. It showed me that there is a high level of emotional work involved in the research process, especially at the fieldwork stage.

A year after the second interview, Laura returned my notes with her amendments. She wrote:

> The relationship between men and women in Islam is just and gentle in all situations, and the women are to be respected and treated honourably in all circumstances. It seems strange to me, that people are constantly picking holes in Islam which is fundamentally a just and gentle way of life, when the society they love

and defend so much is full of adulterers, paedophiles, murderers, rapists, thieves, etc.

So when I look back on the interview, I realize that I was assumed to be on the attack, and in defence of secular society.

Difficult issues – caught in the crossfire: reframing[21]

The first angry letter from Laura had come just over a year into my research process, not long after a confrontation with colleagues who could not believe that I was not in some way coming from the same political standpoint they perceived my interviewees as having, that is, a religious 'fundamentalist' point of view, right-wing and anti-feminist. As one colleague put it, I was interviewing people she 'would not even speak to'. It is actually far from the case that the politics of either Christian of Islamic revivalists are universally of this kind, but one only finds this out by talking with people and not just assuming it is the way they are. As well as meeting one or two who might indeed fit the bill of the stereotype, I have also met feminists who work from within the religious traditions and who take a reviv-alist stance. Could it be that there are women who are anathema to feminist research at the close of the 1990s and the beginning of the new millennium? The implication of heresy brings me back to the religious theme. I was already aware that there is a whole spectrum of social/political views amongst revivalists just as there is amongst feminists. But I found the experience of having my morality and my politics questioned in this way disturbing. I would be the first to agree that religion *can* be problematic in women's lives. That is the very reason why I was researching the issue. Coupled with the mis-understanding with Laura I felt like giving up, but at the same time I was aware that this must surely be *data*, even if it was of an unanti-cipated and unwanted kind. Nevertheless, it was the very stuff of ethnographic fieldwork. I was greatly relieved when through the recommendation of two people who believed in my efforts, I came upon accounts by two writers who had similar experiences.

First, Nilufer Göle, a sociologist writing about veiling in Turkey, has written how, in attempting to remain exempt from aligning herself with either group, 'engaging nonengagement', she became caught in the crossfire between Islamists and secularists, each group not liking what she had to say and how she was dislocated (Göle 1996: 23). This helped to explain how, engaging in such a piece of research, one runs the risk of becoming caught in the crossfire between secularists and revivalists. In this case, neither group will be happy with what the researcher has to say. It was probably this kind of experience which led Göle to state in a television interview in 1994[22] that there is such a thing as 'secular fundamentalism'. Religious revival is an issue which inflames not only believers but secularists as well. Both groups can be equally sure that the view of the other is untenable and when this view takes over all possibility of dialogue ceases.

Second, Faye Ginsburg (1997) wrote about how, as a pro-choice researcher who was carrying out research amongst 'pro-life' activists, she found herself being identified by colleagues with the beliefs of the subjects of her research – a case of 'mistaken identity'. In her anthropological research with right-to-life grassroots activists in the United States, she found that, when she presented her work and tried to 'explain the way the world looked from the point of view of these "natives", [she] was frequently asked if [she] had, indeed, become one of "them" '. Ginsburg continues:

> Unlike the Nuer, Australian Aborigines, or a variety of American subcultures, the people I studied are considered by most of my colleagues to be their enemies. When I offered representations that rendered the right-to-life position sensible or even as powerful as it is to those who adhere to it (as any good ethnographer must), often my 'objectivity' or results were called into question, framed by queries of whether I had 'gone native'.
>
> (Ginsburg 1997: 285)

Ginsburg points out how in socio-cultural anthropology 'Malinowski's axiom – that the ethnographer's task is to represent the native's point of view – is still widely accepted' (ibid.: 283). She suggests that rarely do audiences confuse the anthropologist with the natives and that 'Malinowski's talent for grasping the native's point of view... has not been mistaken for his becoming a Trobriand Islander' (ibid.: 284). Ginsburg writes how she 'shifted from a strategy of bridge building' which sets up the researcher as 'spokesperson' for 'the native' and began to use her interviewees' own words rather than her own voice and devices. This 'helped to recreate the

counter-intuitive encounter' that she experienced with the informant, 'drew attention to the interpretations offered by informants'
and 'resituated the ethnographic case in the context of historical
material, thus drawing away from the immediacy of politics and
toward broader cultural patterns that are often "too close" to see in
one's own society' (ibid.: 285). I felt there were similarities here with
my own difficulties and as a result I decided to write up and report on
my research, as far as possible, using my respondents, own words.

A great deal has been written about ethnographic writing and how
representation may be a distortion because of the power relation
between the authorial voice and the less powerful 'natives', yet Ginsburg suggests that little has been written about the reception of
ethnographic texts. The issue becomes all the more complicated
when one knows that the text will be read by some respondents,
one or two of whom are researchers themselves, as well as other
researchers coming from different perspectives.

Ginsburg's paper is helpful in that it gives the problem of 'mistaken
identity' a theoretical base and considers ways of approaching communication with a hostile audience. I felt that her article gave me
hope of finding ways of 'reframing' my research process and product.

More recently my attention has been drawn to a paper by Donna
Luff (1999) who carried out research among those she describes a
'anti-feminist'. Luff describes how she felt ill at ease during moments
of rapport that she achieved with some of the women during the
interview process. The contradiction of enjoying talking to a woman
a feminist 'shouldn't even talk to' is experienced as uncomfortable
and challenging. In articulating and making an analysis of this internalized crossfire, Luff draws the readers' attention to the issue that
feminism *can* be 'recruitist' making the evangelical assumption that
feminism is the solution to all women's problems (Luff 1999: 694).
Luff's analysis points to a situation where there can be shared interests between feminist and 'anti-feminist' women. These interests are
issue-based, for instance concern over pornography, and will not be
shared across the board, even amongst feminists at any given time.

Mixed methods

The largely unexplored problems of interviewer powerlessness at
the fieldwork stage and of representation of material have not been

the least of the difficulties involved in this study. In any feminist research project there is an underlying, unresolvable epistemological conflict regarding the existence and non-existence of a feminist knowledge. In terms of praxis there is the dichotomy between the view that a feminist researcher should not objectify women and the view that a complete lack of objectification is impossible in the research process. The feminist research project therefore is not without its conflictual moments. I came to the view that in all these issues it is necessary to accept the impossibility of pleasing all feminists. In order to address the issue of objectivity I decided to be eclectic in my use of methods, employing them reflexively in relation to the particular interviewee, informants or religious group and came to the conclusion that 'best practice' will at best be only partial. By 'reflexive' I mean having the capacity to monitor and modify methods as the situation develops as well as observing and exposing my own impact on the research process. Qualitative methods lend themselves to reflexivity and, for this reason, my study is largely qualitative, not because I imagine them to be less 'objectifying' than quantitative methods.

I am left with the sense that feminist research can indeed be only partially feminist (Stacey 1988) and that, in order to attempt to build as rounded a picture a possible, the use of eclectic methods is justifiable. I am not trying to produce a scientific study. It was not possible to find symmetrical samples from the different groups. For instance, the membership of Pioneer People tend to be white, approaching middle age and middle-class. Jesus Fellowship, it was explained to me by their communications officer, have an age gap between a core who are at the centre of things, many of whom are around the age of 40, and youth who are on the periphery. When, in a telephone conversation, I asked Jihan, who I understood to be a 'core worker' from Young Muslims UK, if it was possible for me to meet women who were core workers and women who were more peripheral in order to get some kind of balance between the Christian and Muslim groups she said, 'Oh, you mean women who don't give a damn.' It turned out that anyone who is committed in Young Muslims UK is understood to be a core worker because together they form a vanguard of youth in the cause of Islam.

The painter Henri Matisse is reported to have said that 'exactitude is not truth'. I believe this to be the case. The overall picture can get lost in the disproportionate concentration on one aspect of detail. I believe I create an overall picture by using multiple methods which give a sense of different angles from which the issues may be viewed. I am producing a 'collage' rather than a realist portrait. For instance, some people may be able to say things in response to a questionnaire that would not be possible in a face-to-face interview, especially because of the anonymity a questionnaire affords. On the other hand, an in-depth interview will bring out the nuances of meaning. But some of the women I have interviewed twice, over the space of a year or more, have (as I have) visibly shifted in their beliefs and practices, which are constantly being negotiated. To have both accounts as well as a background of visits adds to the texture of the account of religious affiliation. To visit someone in her home gives a sense of the person's immediate environment and relationships. To visit the group with whom she associates gives insight into her culture and the gender relations, dynamics and behaviour of the group of which she is a part. The reception of the presentation of data is another part of the whole, part of a picture where groups alienated from each other develop their discourses at first through polemic and then even through *perceived* polemic where each 'side' understands itself to know the nature of the other without listening to what individuals have to say.

3
Marriage, Obedience and Feminine Submission

The fact that some women choose to join religious movements which emphasize the importance of binary gender roles suggests that they find some positive advantages in adopting this position. They cannot all be victims, especially when the choice is apparently freely made in a liberal democratic environment. A number of writers have explored ways in which women empower themselves through religion and especially through fundamentalist-like movements (Afshar 1991; 1995a; Ozorak 1995; Gerami 1996; North 1996; Brasher 1998; Karam 1998). Shahin Gerami counters the blanket anti-women stereotype of fundamentalism by not only listing the negative effects of fundamentalism but by producing a list of positive impacts which fundamentalism has had for some women, especially in the case of Islam in the Muslim Middle East (Gerami 1996: 156). Among the positive effects of fundamentalist discourse in the United States, Gerami, rightly suggests 'the reaffirmation of motherhood as a legitimate feminist agenda' (ibid.). Brenda Brasher (1998) takes a similar position with regard to 'fundamentalist' women in the United States. She refers to the power women can wield within the confines of their religious community, a community that also regulates the behaviour of men.

Feminine submission

In order to explore the degree to which women's submission in marriage may be consensual in the present day, how women understand the notion submission and in what ways they might find it to be a positive experience, I asked respondents and interviewees to give their reactions to the concept of obedience in marriage. In the case of some Christian interviewees I inquired about their attitude to the extension of their submission to include masculine authority within the church. Although I discovered that some of my respondents prefer the word 'submission', I am here using the expression 'obedience' because it is the term to which respondents have responded in both questionnaire and interviews. Although the surveillance of women and the regulation of sexuality and gender are characteristic of many traditional forms of religion, what Christian and Islamic revivalisms have in common is a reputation, among many secularists and liberals, for the policing of gender boundaries and roles and the blanket subjugation of women.

Although the stereotype of women who choose a revivalist way is one of mute submission to male regulation I quickly discovered that, on the issue of female submission in marriage, my informants held a range of positions on the continuum of submission to masculine authority. Some do submit to male leadership while others engage in forms of feminist struggle within their religious traditions against patriarchal interpretations of their holy books. What they all hold in common is a sense that revelation is paramount (the Qur'an in the case of Muslims, the Bible for conservative evangelicals, and the Bible and the ongoing revelation of the Holy Spirit for charismatics) and whatever their position might be regarding submission to masculine authority they take it in respect to their interpretation of that revelation.

Amongst those who embrace submission I found a complexity of interpretations of what submission or obedience might mean. Among my respondents and interviewees there were a number of ways in which women shaped their understanding of what they do and how they negotiate power relations within marriage. The range of understanding is wide and includes notions of absolute obedience, though in my sample this was the exception rather than the rule, to ideas of pleasing God and maintaining spiritual harmony by accepting the judgement of men. At times this cleaving to the decision-making of men was more tokenistic than actual. But submission to masculine authority for some, within marriage, in terms of the husband, or outside marriage, in the case of divorced, widowed or never-married women, to the direction of the masculine church leadership, conveyed a sense of spiritual freedom. Others saw self-denial or self-emptying, expressed through submission, as a means of paving the way to a blessed hereafter. This was particularly the case for some Pentecostal/charismatic Christians, who emphasize submission as a means of self-emptying (*kenosis*) which is perceived to be a route to empowerment through becoming a vehicle of the Holy Spirit. Although one Muslim interviewee appeared to follow a path of self-denial as a spiritual discipline, the phenomenon of Christian self-emptying as a road to enrichment is a spiritual strategy for which I found no direct parallel among my Muslim revivalist respondents and interviewees. This leads, in the context of this chapter, to an emphasis on the Christian case of self-emptying as a route to fulfil-ment. It will be counterbalanced in the next chapter where there is an emphasis among the Muslims upon empowerment which they seek through claiming their Islamic rights, a strategy for which I found no parallel among my Christian informants.

The concept of submission

The words 'submission' or 'obedience' may be found in various Eng-lish translations of the Bible and the Qur'an, and both holy texts lead some interpreters to believe that it is the duty of a wife to 'submit to' or 'obey' her husband. St Paul's Letter to the Ephesians 5: 22–24 reads:

> Wives, be subject to your husbands as you are to the Lord. For the husband is the head of the wife just as Christ is the head of the church, the body of which he is the Saviour. Just as the church is subject to Christ, so also wives ought to be, in everything, to their husbands.[1]

And Surah 4:34 of the Qur'an (the Marmaduke Pickthall translation) reads:

> Men are in charge of women, because Allah hath made the one of them to excel the other, and because they spend of their property (for the support of women). So good women are the obedient, guarding in secret that which Allah hath guarded.

Yet some modern writers have argued that the idea of feminine obedience in marriage has neither a Qur'anic nor a Biblical basis.[2] As mentioned below, some writers suggest that the requirement for feminine submission has been selectively drawn from the Bible. For instance, Randall Balmer compares the present-day high profile given to feminine submission by some evangelicals with the fact that St Paul's insistence that women should keep their heads covered has not generally been taken up (Balmer 1994: 47–62). The focus of this chapter is on the current use of the concept of feminine submission. I am not concerned here with what might be the 'true' interpretation, only that there are Muslim and Christian women who believe in the necessity for submission in marriage and who act accordingly.

'Obedience' is a word which may still be used in the Church of England marriage service (by the bride only) if the bride and groom elect that she should do so. It is also a word connected with monasticism, associated with the vows of poverty and chastity. Perhaps the Christian connotations are one of the reasons why some of the Muslims were unhappy with the term. 'Islam' of course means 'submission' in the sense of submission to God. A number of Muslims called my attention to the Islamic principle of *shura* or mutual consultation. They claimed it was not so much a situation of 'obedience' but, because the husband has the casting vote, it was more a position of the woman stepping aside, should mutual consultation fail to bring about agreement. This 'tie-breaker' view is shared by a number of Christian respondents and interviewees. There may have been another reason for the general dislike of the term 'obedience' amongst the Muslim respondents and this connects with the deep suspicion with which Muslims regard anything which for them borders on idolatry (*shirk*). This concern, which also has its basis in the Qur'an, is mentioned repeatedly. Surah 3: 64, for instance, reads:

> Say: O People of the Scripture! Come to an agreement between us and you: that we shall worship none but Allah, and that we shall ascribe no partner unto Him, and that none of us shall take others for lords beside Allah.[3]

One part of the Qur'an may be used to provide insight into the interpretation of another. If the Qur'an tells women they should be obedient to their husbands, the fact that the command that none should stand between a believer and God is paramount may be taken into account in understanding the power relations within marriage: all submission is to Allah alone. Thus, marriage and obedience are contextualized within this primary relationship with Allah and the desire to submit to Allah's wishes and commandments as expressed in the Qur'anic teaching.

My aim is to consider reasons why some women believers might accept submission in marriage to be a requirement and the strategies they use in order to negotiate their freedom without causing religious offence. To this end, in the questionnaire, I posed the question: 'Does your religious belief require that a woman should be obedient to her husband?' Below I shall discuss the responses, comments and conversations which resulted from this question, in the questionnaire and in relation to the interviews.

The question

Asking a question is not always as straightforward as it might seem. In attempting to understand the reasons why some women would accept so apparently retrograde a position in terms of gender power relations I shall first examine what I meant by the question and how it may have been understood by respondents. Some respondents may have taken the question under discussion to mean, 'Does Christianity/Islam require that a woman should be obedient to her husband?' rather than ' Do *you personally* believe that a woman should be obedient to her husband?' From the completed questionnaires I have found evidence in replies to questions other than this that sometimes an inquiry is not read as I intended it. For instance, in responses to the question 'Have you had to give anything up in order to practise your faith?', two replies suggested that the question was read with the emphasis on 'had', that is they understood it to mean 'Have you been compelled ... ?' I did not mean it in so forceful a way. This may be an interesting reflection of 'mistaken identity', as discussed in Chapter 2. Working from a different perspective, the respondents assumed I was viewing them as a stereotype. In this case, the answer was shaped, to some degree, by reaction against an imagined stereotype which the respondent believed the questioner to be perceiving in the respondent.

The majority of both groups (27 of the 30 Muslim respondents and 30 of 43 Christian respondents) answered the question: 'Does your religious belief require that a woman should be obedient to her husband?' in the affirmative. I shall deal with the Muslim responses first.

Muslim responses

With regard to the degree of obedience a woman should offer her husband the respondent was asked to choose from three qualifying statements ranging from unconditional obedience to a flexibility in approach.[4] Fifteen of the 27 Muslims who replied to the obedience question in the affirmative chose the second qualifying statement: 'A woman should only be obedient to her husband when he is right in his judgement' (two of these also ticked statement three), some adding comments such as, 'If it is according to Islam and in the Qur'an. If not she can disobey him' or 'Only if he doesn't go against the Prophet's teaching'. Four Muslims who answered the obedience question with 'yes' chose the third statement: 'A woman should use some degree of flexibility in deciding when to be obedient.' Seven chose statement four, 'other' and made similar comments about how a husband need only be obeyed in righteousness. Two of the 27 answered with 'yes and no'. One of these explained:

> The Qur'an tells us that the male and female were created, amongst other reasons, to find peace and tranquillity with each other. The wife should 'obey' her husband in all matters of righteousness. However, if the husband is encouraging the wife to be unrighteous, then he should not be obeyed.

Three other Muslims, all of whom were married converts to Islam, made a similar point and indicated *Shura* (mutual consultation) as the Islamic way. A theme of 'mutual submission' is also one which was picked up by biblical feminists (participants who were members of Men Women and God). Significantly, unlike a number of Christian respondents, none of the Muslim respondents chose the first statement which was unconditional: 'A woman should be obedient to her husband in all things.'

I interpret this result to mean that the respondents hold the Qur'an to be the highest authority. This helps to keep the husband in order in that the wife will obey him only if he is being Islamic according to her understanding of the faith. It also makes the wife's obedience in any particular matter dependent upon *tafsir* (interpretation of the Qur'an). This means that each issue must be approached in the light of the Qur'an.

Some respondents and interviewees took exception to the word 'obedience'. One respondent, a convert to Islam, was forthright. She wrote, 'I don't like the word "obedient". Women and men are a mercy and blessing for each other and are advised to consult *each other* about everything and consult the children when they can understand. So "obedience" smacks of subservience to me – not acceptable.' A Muslim interviewee who is not a convert also made her dislike of the word evident. I found myself brought to task by Maryam, a woman in her early forties with a research degree and a longstanding marriage to a GP. I felt she was avoiding the issue of obedience when I tried to question her about it. So I kept bringing up the subject and eventually Maryam became quite annoyed:

MF: So maybe the problem is that there's a secular idea of obedience that I'm bringing in.

Maryam: I think so. There's a very negative connotation which I picked up as well from what you say. I don't like the word 'obedience'. It really bugs me.

MF: I asked that question because I mean I'm interested in finding out how the stereotypes are in reality. And I think the obedience thing is part of the stereotype. For instance, like you were saying how the stereotype is of Muslim women being non-assertive.

Maryam: I don't think a really good Muslim woman is [non-assertive]. I think the non-assertive woman is somebody who has taken on the role of obedience and feels she has to wear certain clothes to please a man and to do certain things. She is not her own person.

This problem of particular words being understood differently in secular and religious contexts has been addressed by Mary Anne Wichroski (1996), who speaks of 'meaning inversions' in her research fieldwork amongst members of a cloistered order of nuns. The mismatch in meaning between herself and her informants was caused not only by 'unshared cultural assumptions, but... [by] the actual use of common words themselves'. It was pointed out by the Mother Superior that Wichroski's interpretation of the interviewees' words 'were culturally biased' (Wichroski 1996: 273–4). I think this kind of differing interpretation of a common language took place in my interview with Maryam.

Wichroski writes:

> I also came to realize that their vows of poverty, chastity, and obedience are not self-explanatory terms; that is, poverty means 'having just enough' and chastity may not be so much a separate vow but another form of poverty... that is, separation from friends, family and social relations on the outside create an inner void to make room for spiritual fulfilment. Similarly, the vow of obedience conjures up visions of blind adherence to formal rules. Yet their definitions of hierarchy and authority were not consistent with this: for the cloistered nuns, hierarchy means in order of closeness to God, what comes first – not deference to the power of a punitive authority; nor did it mean that those who were more highly educated and could hold office were held in higher esteem than those performing physical or domestic labour. All forms of labour were considered done in the service of God.
>
> (Wichroski 1996: 274)

Although it is dangerous to make cross-faith assumptions regarding meaning I think the term 'obedience' is problematic because, viewed from a secular frame, it has implications of an unthinking, 'knee-jerk' or robotic following of authority. Submission is perhaps a gentler word, which implies that one is giving up one's authority and submitting to another for a reason. It may also be regarded as a voluntary act.

Christian responses

Thirty-one of the 43 Christian respondents to the questionnaire answered the obedience question in the affirmative. These responses came from members from across all Christian groups except, predictably, Men Women and God, the biblical feminists with an 'equalitarian' agenda. One respondent answered 'yes and no', and the 81-

year-old respondent, an Ichthus member, gave her position on submission in marriage to be 'under discussion!'[5] Although I felt the
respondent probably wrote this comment with a twinkle in her eye,
I nevertheless felt this reply demonstrated how, in a living faith
community, people of all ages can be challenged to change. Of the
31 who answered in the affirmative, ten (from different Christian
groups), chose the first statement: 'A woman should be obedient to
her husband in all things' – the statement with which *none* of the
Muslims agreed. Six of the ten contextualized the obedience in terms
of Ephesians 5: 21–33: the husband must love and respect his wife, 'as
Christ loved His Church'. One of these respondents represented wifely
obedience as being the easier option in this context. Six chose the
second statement: 'A woman should only be obedient to her husband
when he is right in his judgement.' Two chose the third statement: 'A
woman should use some degree of flexibility in deciding when to be
obedient'. Thirteen chose the fourth option: 'other'. Of these, six
mentioned the necessary context as one where the husband loves
and cherishes the wife, three represented it as a 'tie-breaker' if the
couple are unable to reach agreement, and two, although they had
answered 'yes' to the obedience question, represented it as mutual
consultation. One of these declared the husband the head of the
house and another said that she thought that a woman would not
have to obey if the husband's request was 'unbiblical'. The Muslims
tended to recommend an evaluation of the degree of the husband's
conformity to Islam through *tafsir* (interpretation of the Qur'an) and
some of the Christians recommended a similar approach with regard
to the New Testament, while some others unconditionally accepted
the headship of the husband.

Submission in evangelical Christian marriage

Feminine submission in marriage is not limited to fringe elements of
the evangelical church. In May 1998, the Southern Baptist Convention in the United States proposed an addition to the 1963 Baptist
Faith and Mission Statement which was accepted in the following
month. The amendment read: 'A wife is to submit graciously to the
servant leadership of her husband even as the church willingly submits to the headship of Christ.'[6] There is a drive amongst some
American evangelicals to get women back in the kitchen. A website

devoted to 'biblical manhood and womanhood',[7] which also offers a discussion list and a feature entitled 'A woman's place', informs us that each time we visit the site we can read about a different woman who accepts the complementarian position. Even today, in evangelical Protestantism and the new churches, unmarried, widowed and divorced women are (generally speaking) dislocated. As in Islam, marriage to a believing man is regarded as a holy state (Brasher 1998: 131). Protestantism, in following Luther, has largely enforced this view.

Yet in Peter 1: 3. 7 we find: 'Wives, in the same way, accept the authority of your husbands, so that, even if some of them do not obey the Word, they may be won over without a word by their wives' conduct, when they see the purity and reverence of your lives.' This New Testament directive goes a long way to explaining why some evangelical women might consider unconditional submission to be a means of winning a husband over and points to hidden leadership through example. But this kind of unconditional submission can have frightening repercussions. The biblical feminist and writer Catherine Kroeger, in a meeting in London,[8] told me that on this account some women from fundamentalist churches in the United States are told by their pastors they should not cover their faces if they are beaten by their husbands.

Mary Stewart Van Leeuwen (1990) quotes Genesis 3: 16, which reads:

> I will greatly increase your pains in childbearing
> with pain you will give birth to children
> Your desire will be for your husband
> and he will rule over you.

Van Leeuwen sees the possibilities of abuse amongst those who take the Old Testament as a literal guideline as coming from two directions:

> There are two opposite ways we can abuse our God-given exercise of accountable dominion. The first (the man's sin) is to try to exercise dominion without regard for God's original plan for male/female relationships. But the second, the peculiarly female sin, is to use the preservation of those relationships as an excuse

not to exercise accountable dominion in the first place.

(Van Leeuwen 1990: 46)

In other words, this verse from Genesis is used to justify the oppression of women, and some Christian women, according to the writer,
hide behind the words in order to avoid decision-making and leadership. Do women who agree to obey their husbands in all things, as
Van Leeuwen suggests, merely wish to get 'off the hook' in terms of
decision-making? Certainly there is a period in the lives of many
women when they need support and assistance in the tasks of
child-rearing, and it may be that in finding themselves with a lack
of alternatives they give up their independence as part of a trade-off.
Karen, in a supplementary interview, illustrated such a response. She
and her husband joined a Baptist fundamentalist church when their
two sons attended the Baptist school. She suggested that people who
believe in gender equality within the church change when they have
school-age children. She wondered whether this is related to the
enormous expenditure of energy parenting requires: 'They have no
time to think for themselves. One thing that can be said about
fundamentalism is that there are answers for everything.'

Although a number of Christian respondents to the questionnaire
wrote how they believed in total submission to their husbands, these,
as Brasher suggests, were mainly unmarried or newly married
women. Brasher cites Lynn Davidman's (1991) research amongst
unmarried women converting to Orthodox Judaism as articulating a
stronger pro-male line than married women (Brasher 1998: 156).
Brasher finds this situation echoed among the women of the two
evangelical congregations in her research and points out how single
women tend to support the rhetoric regarding feminine submission
in marriage. She sees this as a form of expression used in courtship
language which softens after the reality of the lived experience of
marriage. Among my Christian interviewees (as opposed to respondents to the questionnaire), although some women appeared happy to
embrace submission to male leadership in the church, they did not
suggest that unconditional obedience to a husband was a necessary
concomitant. Two of my nine British Christian interviewees, Jill of
Jesus Fellowship and Libby of Pioneer, had chosen to remain single.
Jill, who accepted the 'necessity' of masculine leadership by the elder
of the church, celebrated her commitment to celibacy, which was

'like a wedding', and Libby (see below), who takes a biblical feminist position, said she would not marry unless she could find an egalitarian relationship.

I wanted to find an interviewee who was in church leadership in one of the new churches but who accepted the idea of feminine submission in marriage, to see how this worked out in 'real life'. How could anyone live out the apparent contradiction between being a woman in church leadership who submits to masculine authority in marriage? I was fortunate to be introduced to Sally, the leader of a thriving fellowship in South Wales. I specifically wanted to ask her how she, as church leader, dealt with the apparently conflicting issues of leadership and submission. Sally said there were problems: [My husband] still has to cope with people's reaction. Because I'm in church leadership they think he must be a wimp. But because he's secure he copes very well.'

Whilst talking with Sally I realized she was describing a different concept of leadership from the usual top-down model, associated with church structures. She described it as 'very much a giving away of power'. Sally even described her work as fitting in with her role as a mother – an unexpected description of church leadership:

> As a mother with four children leadership suits me because I can work my hours so that I can pick the children up from school and not go out until they are in bed in the evenings. There are also occasions when I can do certain things with them there. I think it is also healthy for the church for there isn't the expectation, as a senior leader, that I should do everything. Rather that I should release others.

I asked Sally how she handled the situation in the home regarding submission in marriage. Sally wrote in a follow-up letter:

> In the home Mike [her husband] has the casting vote in our relationship although, because of the element of mutual submission, it rarely comes to that. In fact the only major decision in which he has had to take that role was about which house we should buy seven years ago. We couldn't agree so he took the decision and in fact circumstances have proved him right.

This is the 'tie-breaker' idea of submission. From this point of view, God simply chose the male to take this role, which simplifies things considerably. The bad news for wives is that the husband has the final say, but the good news for wives is that their husbands bear the ultimate responsibility to God for their decision. A Christian respondent who states that she had promised in her wedding vows 'to love, honour and obey' explains that, in her view, her husband's role is the more 'difficult' because he has to 'love, honour and worship'. The respondent sees his role as demanding because, like the women among the congregations studied by Brasher, she believes that if the man makes a selfish decision and causes his wife unhappiness, he will be answerable to God for his wife's response (Brasher 1998: 148). Interestingly, I found this also to be a Muslim qualification of the power invested in the husband. Regarding the 'tie-breaker' where the husband has the final decision, the same Christian respondent wrote: 'If you are stuck on a decision, the husband makes the final choice. But this is not easy for him; it carries a lot of responsibility. For example, if it turns out to be the wrong decision, he would be to blame.' She explained the 'tie-breaker' in terms of, 'God says you can't have a democracy of two'. I was intrigued because these words could not possibly be in the Bible in this form. The respondent had given me her name and address in case I wanted to follow up. I wrote and asked her where in the Bible it says this. I received no reply and I can only think that my question was taken to be oppositional. But I found it interesting that she appeared to be putting words into the mouth of God. It may be that in some of the more conservative restorationist churches women are not encouraged to read the Bible themselves but take their knowledge second-hand from the male leadership (Malet 1998). If this is the case it represents an interesting reversal to pre-Reformation conditions.

These different kinds of responses represent two ends of the spectrum of opinion of women who choose to submit. The almost token, in the home only and only when there is a deadlock kind of submission of Sally is far from the kind of submission which always bends to male leadership. Yet the interviewees who accept this kind of full-blown submission clearly are not without a dynamism of their own.

Leadership and submission

As mentioned above, for some Christians the requirement to submit to the authority of the husband is extended to church elders who, in the house church movement, are almost invariably male (Percy 1996). This requirement centres on the issue of headship and authority, for instance in Paul: I Cor 11, and is a selective interpretation which has been hotly contested by biblical feminists, who claim that 'head' does not mean 'boss' but 'source' (Kroeger, in Hull 1989: 267; Kroeger, Evans and Storkey 1995: 343) and relates to the view of reproduction held at the time, that a woman was a kind of incubator who did not contribute genetically to the makeup of the offspring (Gundry 1980). Translations of the passage differ. The St James translation of I Cor 11: 3–4 makes it plain that the requirement for feminine submission is general: 'But I would have you know that the head of every man is Christ; and the head of the woman is the man; and the head of Christ is God.' The later New Revised Standard Version (NRSV) differentiates between 'woman' and 'wife': 'But I want you to understand that Christ is the head of every man, and the husband is the head of his wife and God is the head of Christ.' In interviews both Ann from Christians in York and Freda from Jesus Fellowship mentioned and accepted the requirement for submission to the authority of the church elder. In some cases the requirement to submit to masculine authority seems to be even more general. Karen, now an evangelical feminist, in a recent communication suggested that when she was a member of a fundamentalist Baptist church in the United States, 'wearing pants with a zipper like a fly... [was seen as] usurping man's authority'.[9]

A way in which the agreement to be obedient 'in all things' as well as submission to masculine authority in the church fellowship may be perceived is as a strategy to attract men to the group. As mentioned in chapter 1 this has an historical basis. Put in an historical perspective, female submission was used by Protestant fundamentalists in the United States in the early twentieth century as a means of shoring up masculinity. They attempted to enforce a selective interpretation of past conditions in order to reinstate the rights of men. Preachers such as Donald Grey Barnhouse and Billy Sunday, in a reaction against the 'feminization' of religion (that is, the majority of church attenders were women), took a theological approach and emphasized the masculinity of God. This was known as 'muscular Christianity'. Islam does not seem to have the 'problem' that Christianity has of a 'feminized' image. If anything, in this respect, the stereotype of Islam is the opposite.

This kind of 'reclaiming' of Christianity for men (as if they ever lost control of it) continues in terms of the Promise Keepers in the United States and more recently in Britain, and in literature which echoes the ideas of muscular Christianity, for example in *Recovering Biblical Manhood* (now on line)[10] and David Pawson's *Leadership is Male* (1988).[11]

I have noted that Jesus Fellowship, which has a ministry with disadvantaged young people, appears to reach out in particular to young men. In order to do so they hold men's events. For instance, a meeting entitled 'Men Alive for God' was held in October 1997. This was advertised in *Jesus Life*, the Jesus Army's quarterly magazine, in a leaflet which proposed: 'Join over 600 "uncaged lions" for a "wild" day of friendship, "roar" power and vision.'[12] This boosting of masculine self-confidence is a means of building up young men into leadership positions.

Claire North suggests that women who join such male-oriented groups often have a history of sexual abuse (North 1996: 12). None of my interviewees said anything that would support this, although two of the respondents to the questionnaire did. In the questionnaire I asked: 'Did stressful experience play any part in making your religious choice?' Ten Christians (but none of the Muslims) answered 'yes'. Of the Christians, six related the stress to the breakdown of relationships and separation, whilst two mentioned an abusive relationship. Two others described how they were fearful of rejection or failure. North suggests that the attraction of male-dominated Christian groups which offer 'cleansing, healing and escape from the shame and hurt of the old life' whilst still dovetailing with the 'wider patriarchal culture' are attractive to 'vulnerable' people (North 1996: 19–20). I can see that the safety of a predictable and more benign hierarchical relationship to men in power might represent a refuge after the unpredictability of an abuser. Further, the presence of masculine authority, regulated by Scripture and by a fellowship, might feel like a protection from the threat of the return of the abuser. North, in her critique of such groups, accedes that, 'The other draw was the huge amount of love and commitment to others in the fellowship. There was a sense of real community and the knowledge that you could drop in on someone at any time' (ibid.: 19). The Jesus Army literature can give the impression that a number of their converts have been abused, but I think this may be because they have a particular ministry with marginalized young people, some of whom will have been abused. I do not think this pattern is transferable across all house church or independent church fellowships, or even across a particular fellowship. My interviewees from Jesus Fellowship (Jesus Army), three in all, were middle-class women, all apparently untraumatized.

As Freda, a Jesus Fellowship member, has described, some of the men who come to Jesus Fellowship with severe difficulties are built up into leaders. I interviewed Freda, who is in her seventies and lives in a Jesus Fellowship community house in October 1996. Freda spoke of how she saw the advantages of male leadership in the community in which she lives. She is awaiting surgery for an arthritic condition and has a problem with mobility. I was struck how by living in community Freda gets all the help she needs. Other members assured me it is help that is freely given, a return for help given to them by Freda in the past. I asked Freda to describe her attitude to the male leadership. She replied:

> Being in submission to the male set-up gives a sense of security. It is very biblical. It is important because the whole present trend is for women to have a more authoritative status. I don't agree with it at all. I wouldn't like it if 'Paul' wasn't head of this house and a woman was, it's a security. The leaders have a meeting. To see young men coming up to a leadership position, to see them growing into maturity.... If you met some of our elders, they have been drug addicts. You know it's only God who has been doing the work.

Freda's reference to submission to masculine authority being 'very biblical', as well as a respondent's comment that a woman might not have to submit if her husband's request was 'unbiblical', caused me to ponder what 'biblical' means in this context. Historically, marriage has been understood to mean very different forms of relationship, as the biblical feminist Patricia Gundry (1980) has shown. In the Old Testament there are marriages which are polygamous and/or temporary, as well as slavery. So Gundry traces the perceived Christian 'divine order' for marriage in the present day to the influence of the medieval order of things (Gundry 1980: 49). This exposes a different kind of 'biblical' marriage from the one that has generally been considered as fitting the Western Christian paradigm of respectability. Further, considering some of the practices to be found in the Bible, the idea that a woman should submit only to a 'biblical' demand leaves the man a great deal of scope for abuse.

Jill, a team leader social worker and a celibate sister in her early thirties, from another Jesus Fellowship community house, described the male and female roles within their church and how she did not perceive it as oppressive:

> Celibate brothers have certain roles. We need each other for the body [of the Church community] to be united. The world puts value on what we *do*, but Jesus was prepared to give his life. He didn't want to be a big shot. I prefer to take my example from Jesus and the women who inspire me. But the public image of sisters is that our brains rot to vegetable.

So Jill draws a line between the way 'the world' perceives women and women's role, and the way her church does. Within the church she has status but she knows that this is not understood by 'the world'.

Freda, like Jill, was no mouse. Freda had been born into a well-to-do family and had been married to a diplomat. Now divorced, she showed no trace of bitterness over her husband leaving her for another woman. Both interviewees were strong, intelligent and accomplished women. I cannot help thinking these sisters are engaged in a kind of hidden leadership.

There is a way in which submission and self-abnegation may be seen as a means through which Pentecostal and charismatic women are able to claim authority in this respect. Mary McClintock Fulkerson (1996) has written about the pioneer Pentecostal women preachers of the Church of God, Cleveland, Tennessee, who, were 'experts in the rhetoric of self-denigration and submission to men [where] "I am nothing, nothing, nothing..." is a favourite refrain' (McClintock Fulkerson 1996: 131–41). The writer is trying to find ways to extend the boundaries of feminist theology 'to interpret the working of Christian traditions in the lives of non-feminist women' (ibid.: 131). In selecting these Pentecostal preachers, who are white, working-class women, she uses a poststructuralist frame to show that there are subversive elements to their self-abnegation. This is a very interesting view, one applicable to some of my interviewees and respondents. McClintock Fulkerson suggests that, through an attitude of 'I'm so nothing it's pitiful', the Pentecostal preacher women become vessels to be filled with the spirit and to speak for God (ibid.: 140–1). It is only by being empty that they can become a channel for God: by becoming the least they become the most. Further, it is a kind of protection against accusations of witchcraft and spiritualism because the very 'nothingness' of the woman proves it *must* be God working in her. Rather like the contrast in 'before and after' advertisements, the *less* a person is perceived to be before their upliftment, the *more* they are perceived to be used by God afterwards and the more they glorify God. This is very like Freda's emphasis on young men, who were formerly 'drug addicts' coming to a leadership position. This is intended to communicate the fact that the previous degradation of the men in question is testimony that their elevation to leadership can only be the work of God. So the worse the condition of the potential leader before God took charge, the better the actual leader subsequently displays the 'wonderful works of God'. There is an interesting parallel here: the fact that Muhammad is reputed to have been unable to read is seen by Muslims as a proof that the Qur'an is the direct revelation of God. His illiteracy means that he could not have produced such a work of poetry and wisdom himself.

When it comes to submission/passivity, because of our acculturation, many Western women will win hands down in a competition between women and men on who can be the most self-emptying (Miller 1976; Lorber and Farrell 1991). Here is a way in which this psychological hobbling, which has been inflicted upon women, may be used to advantage because it is the criterion of receiving the Holy Spirit, a power with which no believer can argue. In this respect and context self-abnegation, self-denial, submission and self-emptying (*kenosis*) can be seen as a means of empowerment (Coakley 1996).

Responses that disrupt the stereotypical image

Muslims

Maryam, the Muslim interviewee quoted above, said later in our interview that the man 'had the last say'. In order to get her to discuss the issue further I showed her a table I had made of the comments of respondents to the questionnaire on the issue of obedience and I pointed to one in particular which read:

> The Qur'an and the example of the Prophet (peace be upon him) refer to 'mutual consultation', kindness, wisdom and consideration. In other words, teamwork. If ultimately when a proper, genuine compromise cannot be reached and if the man involved is a good, practising, thoughtful man, ultimately he has the final say. But if, for example, he is demanding three cooked meals a day, and using this as an excuse for his wife not to go out to see her friends, this is an unIslamic demand, not kind, not reasonable and not backed by Qur'an or *Hadith*. In a situation like this, the woman has the right to refuse but must, of course, balance other aspects of their relationship in her decision.

Maryam's response was as follows:

Maryam: Well, she says ultimately if he is a good thoughtful practising man he has the final say. Well that's not right, really. Because even if he's not a good, practising, thoughtful man he still has the final say.

MF: He still does?

Maryam: Oh yes. (laughs)

MF: So that is obedience, isn't it? What is it if it isn't obedience? What would you call it?

Maryam: Well, I'll just say that if a woman is putting as her higher aim her rights and is not putting as a higher aim to keep away divorce from her household . . . because the devil said there is nothing he celebrates better than splitting a man and wife . . . because it is such a basic foundation of society. It may not be perfect but it's what we've got and to stick with it if you can, unless it's an absolutely abusive relationship, is very important to

Islam and I don't think any Muslim would argue with
that.

Maryam defies the stereotype with her humour and with her quiet
dedication. Being with Maryam was to be in the company of someone who puts herself under a spiritual discipline. She gives the
impression of being someone set upon a way from which she will
not be diverted. There is no sense of an easy option here, no opting
out of responsibility. At the time for prayer the interview stopped and
Maryam allowed me to stay in the room and read. I felt honoured.

Linda, another interviewee, is a convert to Islam and the mother of
three children. She teaches a group of teenage girls at a weekend
Islamic school. Linda put the Muslim refusal of unconditional submission in context when she spoke of 'a problem for young English
girls of a lack of self-esteem'. She said that when they get married
they think they should give themselves wholly to a man: 'This is
giving men (other human beings) power they don't deserve.'

Zainab, a single postgraduate student of law in her early twenties
and born into a Muslim home to Indian parents, was clearly not keen
to give herself wholly to a man either. I asked Zainab if she intends to
marry. She said that if she is to marry she wants 'someone who knows
that Islamic marriage doesn't imply rigid role play'. 'I couldn't marry
someone who wants me to stay at home and produce babies.' She
spoke of the 'psychological benefits' of work and felt that confined to
the home she would 'go crazy'. I asked how would she meet such a
man. She said it could happen through university. Zainab told me she
had a friend who had an offer of marriage from someone who would
be away for half the week and she saw the non-suffocating possibilities of this as ideal. She said she may never have children but she
couldn't talk to her parents about this. It struck me that young
Muslims in Britain who know the Western way, the ways of their
parents and the Islamic way are able to make positive choices regarding the best these systems have to offer.

I was left with the impression that the obedience question was
more complicated than it had at first seemed. Certainly, Zainab,
although an Islamic revivalist who, quite possibly, would answer
the obedience question on the questionnaire (on paper) in the affirmative (as most of the Muslim respondents did), was not interested
in being submissive to a man in the way her parents might interpret

the idea or in terms of the stereotypical view – in fact, Zainab described the relationships of her parents' community as 'based on inequality of the sexes'; Linda clearly saw the idea of giving herself to a man as unIslamic; whilst Maryam appeared to accept submission on the grounds (of her understanding) that it was a requirement of the faith which was the means by which she traversed the difficulties which life threw up at her and which led ultimately to Paradise. I believe this spiritual goal was more important to Maryam than any merely human relationship. Even if the majority of the Muslim respondents to the questionnaire answered 'yes' to the obedience question not all the Muslims agree on how that should be worked out in everyday life. Further, there is something deeply pragmatic about Maryam's statement. I do not know whether she was saying that she agrees with the dynamic within marriage, of which she speaks, or whether she was simply stating that it exists. I believe it is the case that many secular marriages and partnerships will also take this form. Maryam's is the voice of long suffering which puts the spiritual goal before all else. This is surely the submission of which the Muslims and Christians speak when they say that submission is to God and not to man. Obedience to God helps to make sense of suffering, and suffering that is unavoidable is accommodated as a spiritual exercise. Theodicy, the means of making sense of the phenomenon of suffering, is perhaps the whole purpose of religion (Berger 1967: 53–80). But do submission and self-emptying of personal desire not come so much more easily to women who have been trained to put others first?

Christians

Claire North writes as a former member of a house church which she describes as having been comprised of three-quarters women and a quarter men. She suggests that the only qualification for being an elder was being male even though there were so few men to choose from (North 1996: 19–20). What North does not mention is the fact that there are women who are active members of the house church movement today who would agree with her statement and that some of them are trying to change things from within. Libby, a single woman in her thirties and a well-known speaker and musician on the international evangelical/charismatic circuit, is an example of someone working within the house church movement alongside others who want change. She is no 'victim'. I asked her if she wanted to get married. Her response was not unlike Zainab's:

> It would take a really 'magical' man, if I can use that word, for me to marry. I'm not interested. I think, as you get older, what you feel about marriage changes. I could only cope with being married with a man who together we'd look at the house, who'd look at the radical family, who'd actually say jobs aren't gender-based. If we had children (I would like to be able to say) 'Will you stay home John or Eric and look after the children? Don't just expect looking after the children to be the woman's role.' So I think we would need to be two people in a very similar belief system or even just prepared to talk about it. But there aren't many men like that ... yet. So I'm very happy being single. I find it more positive than negative. . . .
>
> As I travel, which I do quite a lot, within denominations, I think at Pioneer we have looked at a lot of issues of women, of singleness, of family and we are changing mindsets. Because it has to happen in the mind first before it can change in practice and we are asking a lot of difficult questions. Maybe that's why it's called 'Pioneer'. How it actually gets worked out in practice, as you know, takes a lot longer. For example, the women: I cry when I look at a whole platform of men. I think 'Where are the women? Where are they?' And so therefore we do need to look at fast-tracking women, taking affirmative action, not just to recruit tokenistic women . . . but I know they're out there.

The night before I interviewed Libby I had attended a Pioneer meeting where the speakers were mainly male. Further, the wife of a writer on women's issues in the ministry stood up and said how she saw her role as looking after the children to release her husband for ministry.

My other interviewees from Pioneer held a variety of views on the position of women within the church and Libby was the most radical. But it was interesting to meet Carol, also a member of Pioneer Fellowship, who had for some years taken a secondary role to her husband but was now feeling challenged by the church to review her role. She said:

> There's no church policy on women. You're free to be who you are and what you feel is right for you and your family. So there's no

kind of... In fact, if anything, it is a challenging thing, you know 'Come on women... take your place'. I think I'm prone probably to passivity and find it easier to hide behind the front door and let my husband get on with it. I feel very challenged by this at the minute. Especially with the new phase the church is going through. I'll have to stop just being this woman at home. No one has made me do that. I think I have become that through all sorts of things. Lack of confidence maybe. I find the church very encouraging, very challenging. I think again... it probably hasn't always been that way. I think when we first joined the church it was more male-oriented. I think it's been a developing thing.

It is plainly wrong to assume that all the house church movement or all members of any given church hold the same position on the continuum of the submission of women to masculine authority. It is clear from the questionnaires that there are differences within and between house churches and to claim that they are all inevitably 'fundamentalist' in their attitudes to women is to accept a caricature of them. The interviews throw light on the ways in which women involved in revivalisms see their role in relation to men in connection with the reality of their lived relationships.

Submission is a complex issue

The interviews and completed questionnaires demonstrate that the cultural and practical meanings of submission and obedience within marriage are complex and differ not only inter-faith but also intra-faith. They also differ across age, socio-economic standing, geographical location and marital status. It is a subject which does not lend itself to simple generalizations. Not all Muslims or Christians concur on the meaning of these terms, nor on how they should be understood in terms of their practical lived experiences. There are, in fact, considerable similarities between the views of educated, articulate Muslim and Christian single women who are wary of marriage and what it means to them in terms of personal relationships.

What was unexpected was that although the majority of the Muslim and Christian respondents to the questionnaire thought a woman should submit to her husband in marriage, none of the Muslims and only ten of the Christians thought that this submission should be unconditional. Six of these ten put the unconditionality within the context of the husband loving and cherishing his wife. Linda put this Muslim refusal of unconditional submission in context when she spoke of what she described as 'English girls' lack of self-esteem, in that they think they should give themselves wholly to a man. When no man deserves or warrants that.' For Linda the implication of giving oneself wholly to another human being is nothing short of idolatry; that is, putting a human being before God. Thus, my respondents and interviewees who choose submission in marriage are not necessarily abasing themselves before the altar of men. In this case the caricature of women who submit out of victimhood is mistaken.

There are some interesting parallels in the responses to the obedience question between the manner in which a variety of Christians and Muslims deal with the issues. Maryam, the Muslim interviewee, like a number of respondents, drew my attention to the fact that I had chosen the word 'obedience' even though this is frequently not used within the religious contexts. Both groups seem happier with the word 'submission' and would readily agree that their first concern is submission to God. Amongst both the Muslims and the Christians there are those who accept and those who reject submission. Many comments by those who accept pointed to the view that submission should be located in a religious rather than a secular context, as a means to a reward or end which is regarded as ultimately better, either for the self or society in general.

A number of respondents, both Christian and Islamic, made comments which indicated that a wife should obey only if her husband was in accordance with their holy texts. This gives plenty of room for negotiation. But proportionately more Muslims than Christian took this position.

The Epistle of St Paul, to which the Christian respondents refer, does, at least superficially, appear to demand submission in all things. This understanding of the text, selected for compliance as it may be, is currently being re-emphasized. Nevertheless, this interpretation is also being questioned by some members of the Christian groups, a re-evaluation which is taking place from within. This means that present activity in some of the house church fellowships is far more dynamic in terms of gender relations than the stereotypical view of them would allow. Yet, as Libby pointed out, even where there is a will for change, the greater proportion of men in leadership roles remains in evidence.

Both Muslim and Christian responses show that there is no one particular way of being a Muslim or Christian revivalist and that disagreement and struggle take place within the movements. At times it is hard to untangle leadership and submission. At times there appears to be a hidden leadership role which takes the form of submission. For me, submission and leadership are inextricably linked. The one who directs or has authority in this context depends upon the submitters for his own leadership position, be it in marriage or as church leader. In this way the submitters are the leaders through their voluntary submission.

4
Rights and Responsibilities

In this chapter I consider the kinds of entitlements participants feel they gain from their religious affiliations, especially in terms of the rights and responsibilities conferred by the holy texts. This is followed by a discussion of the extent to which (if at all) feminist discourse enters into revivalist discourse, and its application in everyday life. To facilitate this process an initial examination of the question of rights and responsibilities conferred (or denied) by holy texts in Islam and Christianity and how these have been interpreted by my interviewees and respondents is appropriate. Although the term 'rights' is frequently used in relation to the duties and privileges conferred upon women by Islam, its origin is in Enlightenment discourse. Nevertheless the idea that there should be regulation of the responsibilities, entitlements and protections of women in terms of marriage, inheritance and the tasks of motherhood is as old as Islam.

The notion that this might be an encouragement for affiliation with a faith community which offers such entitlements is in keeping with the concept of rational choice theory: the proposition that people base their religious choices upon a process whereby they weigh the benefits against the disadvantages of a religious system. Muslim interviewees and respondents were asked if they felt their rights as Western women were enhanced by Islam. Given that a number clearly did, I wondered if there was a similar incentive within the new Christian (house and independent) churches and if there was some way in which Christian respondents felt their entitlements as women were enhanced through their religious affiliation. To this end all respondents to the snowball questionnaire were asked first, whether they felt women's rights were adequately protected by Brit-ish law and, second, if they thought their rights had been improved by their religious choices and if so in what way.

I use the term 'rights' loosely as in Britain, unlike the United States, there is no Bill of Rights which stipulates the freedom, justice and equality guaranteed to citizens by the state. Nevertheless, in Britain there are many 'rights' in terms of privileges and protections which are underpinned by English (and Welsh) and Scottish law and also by EU law in provisions such as the Social Chapter of the Maastricht Treaty. Freedoms in Britain largely depend upon these protections. I also used the term 'British law', in the case of the questionnaire, loosely, to mean the law of the land in which a British person lives. At least one respondent lives in Scotland and so the term 'the law of England and Wales' would not be appropriate.

I have also utilized data collected from e-mail interviews with some members of the International Community of Submitters[1] – the North American-based organisation described in chapter 2. These are mod-ern-day 'Qur'an only' people or *Ahl al-Qur'an* (People of the Qur'an). This kind of Islam is sometimes described as Protestant Islam because of its emphasis on the personal and private in the practice of religious duties. Submitters reject the *Hadith* (the sayings of the Prophet), the *Sunnah* (the example of the Prophet) and *Shariah* (Islamic law) as unsound and manufactured. Even though they do not wear the *hijab* (veil), Submitters take an Islamic revivalist stance as they regard their kind of faith commitment as 'pure' Islam. I have also included data collected from participant observation at a Young Muslims UK weekend at the Islamic Foundation near Leicester (see chapter 2) and on an Islamic forum in cyberspace. In this section I discuss the answers given by respondents to the snowball questionnaire and interviewees with regard to their perception of their rights in law as well as the privileges which they feel accrue from their religious affiliation.

Rights

In Islam there are particular unequivocal rights set out for women in the Qur'an. These rights include: a woman's entitlement to be housed, clothed and fed by her husband and to retain her own money without contributing towards the upkeep of the family

(Qur'an 4.34). A woman has the right to payment for suckling a child, particularly in the case of divorce (2: 233 and 65: 6) and the right to be paid upon the consummation of marriage (*mahr*) (4: 4 and 4: 24). Marriage not necessarily being a permanent state means there is the possibility of guilt-free divorce. Further, the woman has a right to inherit half the amount of a man, but as some of my interviewees have pointed out, they cannot be disinherited and they may leave their own money to whomever they please. Women also have the right to education.

When it comes to the issue of 'rights' there is a major difference between the two groups of respondents. Where the Muslim respondents generally answered that they had gained rights through their affiliation to Islam and while there is a place for rights and responsibilities within Islam, evangelical and charismatic Christians do not generally use the language of rights within the religious context. This may be because Christianity, historically, reacted against the prescriptions and proscriptions of Judaic law embodied for Jesus in the Scribes and Pharisees who lived according to the letter of the law and whom he branded as hypocrites: clean on the outside and unclean within.[2] St Paul, addressing Judaizers among the early Christians, wrote how the law equates with the 'flesh' and faith with the spirit (Galatians 3). He suggested that the law was a curse in that no one, however much they tried, could keep it. He claimed that through the death of Jesus, Christians were now justified by faith.[3] Consequently, in early Christianity, there is a sense of being 'above the law'. This emphasis may be one of the reasons why some Christian respondents consider the idea of 'rights' to be alien or irrelevant to their belief. But the root of this lack of a language of rights may also be in Christian self-emptying, the origin of which may be in the dying/rising God of Christianity whose death leads to renewal, and where the symbolic death of baptism leads the believer to a fuller life. The figurative death of the self is productive of regeneration and life eternal. This difference is also reflected in the previous chapter regarding submission to masculine authority in marriage, conditional amongst Muslims and unconditional for some Christians, which results from an emphasis on self-abnegation (*kenosis*), in order to become an empty vessel for God's work. This giving over of the self and the negation of autonomy is the 'fishbone' which Daphne Hampson (1996), as a feminist, finds hard to swallow and which leads her into a post-Christian feminist position. Although there is an implicit reward for Christians – eternal life, sainthood, heaven, God's Kingdom on Earth and even the suggestion that prosperity follows a right orientation of faith in some house church fellowships – there was no overt mention of reward among my Christian respondents and interviewees. Reward might come for the Christians but they should not set out with the explicit intention of gain. Yet I found some of my Muslim interviewees were quite happy to talk of reward as a motivation for their action.

Even though Christianity does not use the language of rights, 17 of 43 Christian respondents to the questionnaire wrote in response to my questions that their rights had been enhanced through their religious affiliation. Although the language of self-abnegation is frequently used amongst evangelicals, Pentecostalists and charismatics, there is a stream of evangelical feminist thinking which discerns the promise of equality within the gospels. This is a concept which is more on a par with rights. These biblical (evangelical) feminists constitute a minority and their message, coming as it does from *within* conservative Protestant evangelical circles, is all the more powerful. As mentioned above, biblical feminists believe this promise of equality is given in the letter of St Paul to the Galatians 3: 28. As mentioned above, this idea is presented by evangelical feminists not so much as an equality in terms of rights but in terms of 'equality to serve' (Hull 1989). Nevertheless, it presents a picture of gender equality which is based on an egalitarian rather than a complementarian model.

The egalitarian view of cross-gender equality contrasts starkly with the selective way in which the requirement for feminine submission is frequently understood in evangelical circles. As discussed in the previous chapter, St Paul's injunction for women to submit to their husbands has been selectively enforced.[4] It may be argued that the language of self-abnegation doubly oppresses women because they are already expected to live out a role of self-giving as mothers, carers and nurturers and that this may be a treble oppression in the case of black women. The womanist theologian Jacquelyn Grant has described her discomfort as a black American woman, with 'the ease with which Christians speak of such notions of service and servant' (Grant 1995: 204). Referring to inequalities in society based on racial discrimination and oppression as well as slavery, Grant points out that 'some people are more servant than others'. So Grant finds herself asking questions about the source of feminist theology being 'women's experiences' and asks: 'Which women's experience is the source of [feminist] theology?' (ibid.: 208). The language of servant-hood can be construed to be a language of whiteness (ibid.: 200). Interestingly, it is the language used in the white Southern Baptists' addition to their statement of Baptist Faith and Message which requires that 'A wife is to submit herself graciously to the servant leadership of her husband'.[5] The Pentecostalist preachers, who self-abnegate as a means of empowerment, of whom McClintock Fulk-erson (1996) writes (chapter 3), are white and working-class. Grant's association of servanthood with the language of whiteness has rele-vance to the discussions of biblical feminists who tend to be white and middle-class and who claim the right to be 'equal to serve'. Yet there is also a way in which this validates the biblical feminist approach, which starts from the text of the Bible rather than from a spurious notion of a global kind of 'women's experience' or an idea of a universal kind of woman's life. Grant's essay is entitled 'The Sin of Servanthood' and the sin is that of a white-dominated society that turned black people into a servant class. Grant resolves the issue by suggesting that 'The church does not need servants, as oppressively conceived of and experienced by many; the church needs followers of Christ – disciples' (Grant 1995: 216).

For many modern Christians, especially those associated with char-ismatic renewal, the emphasis is on individual salvation and a personal Saviour. This contrasts with Islam where the emphasis is on a godly society and the Islamic state. For some Christians, God's Kingdom may be considered as something to be established in the here and now, but for many it is projected into the hereafter. For the latter who may hold the millennialist view, history is projected as an inevitable downward spiral and the worse conditions become, the more they may be perceived to be the fulfilment of prophecy that heralds the Second Coming. This kind of worldview does not necessarily encourage an interest in human or civil rights. Yet some house church and independent church groups *do* feed the hungry and house the homeless, and it is difficult to determine whether they are motivated by the need to evangelize or by the desire to build a just society. There are, of course, many within the mainstream and other churches who fight for social justice and some respondents have voiced such views.

The approach believers take to the redistribution of power and wealth, which is suggested in the Magnificat (Luke 1), depends upon whether they believe God will take care of that redistribution or that we humans are supposed to help the redistribution along. Dualists who shun the world may assume that redistribution takes place in the spiritual realm only and that the issue is of no earthly concern. Those Christian respondents who showed a lack of interest in 'rights' seemed convinced that if they have Jesus in their lives, everything else will be taken care of.

Because Christianity does not make a comparable provision, within Christianity, rights are granted by the constitution of the individual nation or group of nations as in US or EU law. Often, as in Britain, these rights have, in their formation, been subject to Christian influences. Muslims in a Western democracy are subject to the law of the land but they may also draw upon the laws of Islam in order to clarify their religious, civil and familial duties and rights within a Muslim community.

Pre-Islamic and pre-Christian conditions

The concept of 'pre-Islamic' and 'pre-Christian' traditions may seem to imply antiquity but from the point of view of the religious traditions there are pre-Islamic and pre-Christian conditions in our present society. This is especially the case from the viewpoint of the apologist who stresses the division between religion and culture. For the Islamic revivalist, *jahiliyya* (pagan, ignorant society) and likewise, for the Christian revivalist, 'the world' (the domain of the enemy), are ever present. Although it is not possible to define the authentic state of early Christian or Islamic communities, nor the exact condition of the first-century and seventh-century CE worlds respectively into which they came, there is a strong indication that both Christianity and Islam improved the conditions of women over the previous customs. This is not to imply that Judaism does not make provision for women. I speak only of the specific historical and cultural context. Here are some examples: In the Muslim case, with regard to inheritance among the pre-Islamic Arabs it seems that 'Under the laws of inheritance, succession was confined only to able-bodied male relations who could take up arms to defend the tribe against foreign aggression. Wives, mothers, sisters, daughters, minors, incapable, and infirm male heirs had no right in the estate of the deceased' (Chaudhry 1991: 193). In the event that there are no sons of the deceased Surah 4: 11–12 of the Qur'an gives a variety of proportional distribution between other female and male relatives. Amina Wadud-Muhsin sees this as an improvement on pre-Islamic conditions because females, as well as distant relatives, are not to be disinherited. She comments that this is true of the pre-Islamic customs still prevailing today where the inheritance of female offspring may be given to a male relative, however distant (Wadud-Muhsin 1992: 87). Some of my informants see Islamic inheritance rights as an improvement over the customs of the communities in which they have grown up. An Irish convert to Islam, for instance, wrote that 'being Irish and Catholic everything went to the boys, or at least, the eldest boy' and she therefore saw her right to inherit under Islam as an improvement.

Historically, Christianity can be viewed as improving conditions for women over pre-Christian conditions if one considers, for instance, the account of John 8: 3–11, when Jesus condemns the practice of stoning. A woman, accused of adultery, is brought to Jesus by the Scribes and Pharisees who ask: 'Moses has ordered us in the law to condemn women like this to death by stoning. What have you to say?' The Scribes and Pharisees are portrayed as looking for a way to catch Jesus out, hoping he will transgress the law. After some time Jesus responds: 'Let anyone among you who is without sin be the first to throw a stone at her.'[6]

Even when not written as a commandment within the New Testament, biblical feminists are able to read metaphorical meanings within the New Testament which affirm the full personhood of women and improve the status of women over the pre-Christian conditions. Patricia Gundry uses this method when she points out that women were not permitted to act as witnesses in the culture in which Jesus was born and yet 'Jesus chose women as the first witnesses to His resurrection' (Gundry 1980: 46). This drawing on the example of the life of Christ is not unlike the manner in which Muslims draw upon the example of the Prophet (*Sunnah*). Zainab exemplifies this method when, in order to demonstrate that, in her view, Islam was not originally a patriarchal religion, she describes the Prophet as mending his own sandals and his clothes. In the Qur'an there is provision made concerning women acting as witnesses. The most conservative view, based upon 2: 282–3, is that a woman *alone* should never act as a witness[7] yet even if this *were* the Qur'anic intention (which I do not believe it is) it would still be an improvement over not being able to be a witness at all. A more progressive reading is that the Qur'an actually makes an improvement in women's status in requiring that they do not act *alone* as a witness in the case of financial transactions only,[8] either because it may have been that women (at the time) were not sufficiently versed in financial matters (Rahman 1979) or because they might be coerced (Wadud-Muhsin 1992). Thus the second woman in the requirement for two women witnesses acts as a support. This is not unlike present-day notions of empowerment which employ citizen and peer advocacy. Wadud-Muhsin writes:

> ... considering that women could be coerced in that society, if one witness was female, she would be easy prey for some male who wanted to force her to disclaim her testimony. When there are two women, they can support each other – especially in view of the term chosen: if she *(tudilla)* 'goes astray', the other can *(tudhakkira)* 'remind' her, or 'recall her attention' to the terms of agreement. The single unit which comprises two women with distinct functions not only gives each woman significant individual worth, but also forms a united front against the other witness.
>
> (Wadud-Muhsin 1992: 86)

Nevertheless, the more liberal reading is not generally accepted by the wider faith community which applies the Qur'anic provision by analogy to marriage witnesses and elsewhere. Perhaps this is an example of one of the reasons why many revivalist women have chosen a path with more consistent and predictable outcomes by taking a more literal view of Qur'anic legislation which they use to claim their *stated rights*. This is because if it can be shown to be a declared right in the Qur'an, the believer who wishes to please Allah cannot refrain from granting it. Pre-Islamic and pre-Christian conditions can also be perceived by apologists to be *within* Muslim or Christian cultural interpretations of specific groups within the present day. For instance, in a more extreme example of this position, Yasmin, a Submitter and therefore (as explained above) a believer in Qur'an alone, scornfully refers to Muslims who follow the *Sunnah* and the *Hadith* as members of 'the sect of Mohammedans'[9] regarding them as followers of Muhammad rather than of Allah. She sees them following the word of Muhammad rather than the word of God in the Qur'an. In this way also, a Protestant evangelical contributor to the same Islamic forum as Yasmin[10] constantly referred to Roman Catholicism as 'apostate Christianity', believing his own brand of Protestantism to be representative of a return to an authentic New Testament Christianity which pre-dates Catholicism. Both Islamic and Christian revivalists are looking to an 'ideal' and 'pristine' form of their respective faiths which they believe can be stripped of all cultural baggage. It is, of course, highly debatable whether this is possible as revivalisms carry the cultural associations of their time and place.

In a poignant example which affects the everyday lives of Muslim women, Maryam related how a lot of (Muslim) men choose to ignore the precepts of Islam and follow their own cultures. She gave the example of a Sheikh, a holy man and teacher of Islam who does not play by the rules and whom she thought should have known better. She related how he was talking to a group about Muslim inheritance laws. He told them how a woman's money, according to Islam, is her own and how she does not have to pay for maintenance of the home. Someone asked 'Does your wife know this?' The Sheikh answered, 'No, No way!'

Improvement may be made where pre-Islamic and Islamic conditions coexist in modern societies. An example of *Shariah* offering superior justice over custom is given in the case of 'Aziza bint Hassan b. Fadl, a Bedouin woman, who, in 1906, took her husband to court, demanding an annulment of their marriage on the grounds that it was against *Shariah* law. She had been given in marriage without her consent by her brother, according to Bedouin custom. A Bedouin woman, according to custom, had no legal standing yet she presented her own case in court without representation by an agnatic relative (Shaham 1993: 193). 'Aziza's husband told the *Shariah* court that he had married her according to the custom of Allah. Shaham points out that at this time, although Bedouins identified with Islam, their knowledge of its teachings was frequently limited. 'Aziza, who was taken by force and the marriage 'consummated', had escaped the next morning. 'Aziza's representation of herself in court was valid according to *Shariah* but was not in accordance with Bedouin custom.

By turning to the *Shariah* court, this woman was able to claim her Islamic right which offered her superior status to customary law. In this case the *qadi* (or judge) did not dissolve the marriage on the grounds of the woman's complaint that she had not consented, because that would be hard to prove, but he tackled the issue by relying on the husband's evidence that the marriage offer had not used the expressions considered valid for this purpose by the *Shariah*. The expressions 'marriage' and 'giving in marriage' were not used. 'Aziza gained her annulment. This is a clear example of the enhancement of women's' rights through Qur'anic legislation in the twentieth century.

The right to marry freely (that is, not to be forced into marriage) as exemplified in the account of 'Aziza is an important right conferred by Islam. But 'Dr Hadi', an Egyptian speaker who addressed the Young Muslims UK meeting on the subject of marriage,[11]suggested the importance of not upsetting the extended families (which freed women to work for Islam) which already exist in the British South Asian communities and that it was necessary to bring them round, and to wait to marry if necessary. But she spoke strongly against the practice of enforced marriages, describing them as 'a waste of many good sisters'. She asked if there was no authority people could turn to in such a situation. The answer from the floor was that there was no one because the families of South Asian origin had become selfish living in Britain and that they think it is no one else's business. Dr Hadi suggested that YMUK should work on the problem. She said they should work out amongst themselves how to deal with the issue and that they should visit families where enforced marriage is practised.

Whether or not a provision in a holy book is seen to be an improvement depends largely upon hermeneutics, who has control of interpretation and whose view is recognized as legitimate. In the case of both Islam and Christianity the orthodoxy historically has been defined by men.

Respondents to the snowball questionnaire and rights under British law today

The majority of respondents to the snowball questionnaire answered the question 'Do you think that women are adequately protected under British law with regard to: a) marriage; b) divorce; c) mother-hood; d) employment; and e) control of personal finance?' Four of 30 Muslims abstained from answering, another said she didn't know enough about the law to answer and one was unable to affirm that women were adequately covered in any of these respects. She wrote: 'I'm sorry – I'm not just being stubborn but I would find difficulty with all these in terms of adequate protection.' In all, 23 of 30 affirmed that there was at least one of these areas in which they felt women were adequately protected by the law. Of the 43 Christian respondents, seven made no entry and four said they did not know. Three respondents, all from Jesus Fellowship, wrote that they were not interested, one writing: 'I'm not interested in feminism so I cannot comment.' I found it interesting that the everyday legal protection enjoyed by women in a liberal democracy was regarded by this respondent as 'feminism'. It was no doubt feminism that obtained such rights in the first place. Jesus Fellowship literature tends to equate feminism with extremism: for instance an account of a testimony by Jay Mansfield in *Jesus Life* recounts how, prior to her conversion, 'Jay had developed a hatred of men and this led her into feminism'.[12] Why does man-hatred have to be a prerequisite of feminism? What about respect for humanity as a prerequisite? In response to the question, a member of Men Women and God wrote: 'I'm not sure what you mean', but then went on to write that her own experience in each of these areas had not been difficult in terms of 'protection under the law'. She added: 'The law is not particularly just in many ways, because it is more concerned with property than with people, but this affects men too.'

Over half the Muslim respondents thought marriage law ade-quately protected women and this compared with a third of the Christians. Half the Muslims thought women had sufficient protec-tion in terms of divorce, as did a third of the Christian respondents. A third of the Muslim respondents and a quarter of the Christians thought that women were adequately protected in motherhood. A Muslim and two Christian respondents stated that they felt that the importance of motherhood was not recognized, whilst another Mus-lim wrote about the need for flexible working hours and the problem of women who work outside the home effectively doing two jobs. In terms of responsibilities, one Christian respondent thought that 'we need to encourage women's *responsibility*[13] to children in education especially' and a Muslim respondent thought that women in divorce tend to get custody of children 'to the detriment of men'. This questions the assumed 'right' women have to custody of their children in British society. This could, however, change as it has in the United States where poor women are penalized in this respect and often lose custody to the richer father (Chesler 1990). But there is also an assumption that the woman invariably *wants* custody of the child. This of course may not always be the case.

In terms of employment protection less than a third of the Muslims and a third of the Christians thought that women were adequately protected under the law. This shows a fairly low level of satisfaction with the degree of statutory employment protection generally. A Muslim respondent pointed out that 'those married and available for work but unable to find work are discriminated against by social security' as they are unable to claim unemployment benefit. Two Christian respondents actively criticized employment protection in terms of the fact that many women, because of family commitments, are part-time, sessional or temporary workers ineligible for sick pay, holidays and pension rights. With regard to control of personal finance a third of Muslims and Christians thought women were adequately protected. A member of Men Women and God added the proviso: . . . '*if* a married woman has personal finance'. A Muslim respondent who is a Submitter wrote: 'Surely this depends upon personal circumstances and not the law.' This latter remark illustrates the individualistic leaning of the Submitters and their emphasis on liberal interpretations.

Issues which emerged showed some dissatisfaction with the law as it stands in relation to marriage and divorce, motherhood, employment rights and protections and financial matters. In other words, there was less than 50 per cent satisfaction across the board. The answers which I found the most unnerving were those of a minority who seemed oblivious to any need for legislation in order to protect women's rights.

Rights and religious affiliation

Christian responses

As mentioned above, some Christian respondents did not see the relevance of the question about rights. This is perhaps the case if

Christianity is viewed as a personal religion which is also about self-emptying. Yet there are many ways in which Christianity can be interpreted and one of these is as a faith which stands for social justice. There was a range of views in this case. Jesus Fellowship, which feeds and ministers to the homeless and whose leader recently stated that the Jesus Fellowship was interested in 'economic equality',[14] registered a low level of interest among sisters regarding 'rights'. Some Ichthus members and members of Men Women and God were at the other end of the spectrum with a knowledge of the law as it stands and a concern for the welfare of women. Apart from the core differences described above, one of the reasons for the lack of interest on the part of Jesus Fellowship members may well be the fact that whilst not all members live in community, the majority of my particular respondents do. This is an enclosed situation which means that a person may be out of touch with issues such as employment conditions, personal finance, and so on. This is especially the case if they work from a common purse. Also, from the questionnaire, I gauge that the situation of a number of respondents from the Jesus Fellowship has been drastically improved by living in community and their present sense of increased well-being may mean they are currently not concerned about 'rights' issues.

Overall, the impression of the Christians was that they did not gain in rights through their religious affiliation, with more than half answering that they did not gain or that the question was not applicable in the Christian case. Nevertheless, 17 respondents answered 'yes' and one answered 'yes and no', but in doing so expressed the kind of feeling voiced by the other 17 who answered in the affirmative. She wrote: 'Christianity does not confer rights on people in this sense ... I know who I am and am confident to live that out.' A sense of enhanced status and opportunity was reported by a number of the Christian respondents who answered in the affirmative. Two wrote of 'knowing what to expect' in Christian marriage as a gain, but these were young unmarried or shortly to be married women. Five respondents mentioned equality with men before God or in the church, whilst another six wrote of the importance to them of being valued as a woman or having their role as mother and homemaker respected and supported. One of the latter was also working as a GP.

A respondent who was a church leader wrote how historically the answer to the question regarding the enhancement of rights was 'no' but now it is 'yes'. She said she was given 'positive affirmation in the church leadership role, acceptance as a person in my own right, increased self-awareness and security [and] given the right to express my views and influence systems where appropriate'. This sense of personhood was also shared by others, for example in the statement: 'I feel I am valued as a *person*' and was perhaps even echoed in the sentiment: 'If I am a child of God I don't have to worry about rights'. This latter was from a member of Men Women and God. Yet I was surprised that a biblical feminist should be unaware of the interplay of legal rights and protections and life within the church. For instance, if 'rights' are unimportant why should women have the vote, indeed why not go back to a system of slavery? But another respondent, the oldest, pointed out the contingency of it all: 'Christianity teaches a high standard of love/care/consideration [in and out of marriage] and *in as far as this is practiced*[15] women's "rights" are more readily recognised.'

Like one Muslim, a Christian respondent pointed out that the fact that abortion was regarded as a sin might appear to be a loss of women's rights. Both thought that it was rightly regarded as anathema. The 20-year-old Christian wrote: 'You could say because I now don't believe in abortion, my rights as a woman have been decreased, but as that is a heartfelt belief, not a religious rule, I don't see that it diminishes my rights as a woman.'

Muslim responses

Unlike the Christians, the Muslim respondents were almost unanimous in their agreement that their rights had been increased by Islam. Twenty-eight of 30 Muslim respondents to the questionnaire answered the question in the affirmative. One who did not wrote 'not so much increased as clarified', and the other, the youngest Muslim respondent, made no entry. Sixteen respondents gave issues connected to finance and work and finance in marriage as the ways in which they saw their rights enhanced, including three who stated categorically that they found the right *not* to work an enhancement to their rights within marriage.

Four respondents suggested the superiority of rights which are God-given, according to their belief, over any merely human law. This unreliability of mere human laws was also mentioned by a Christian respondent. Qur'anic inheritance rights were considered to be an improvement over British secular ones by five Muslim respondents who answered in the affirmative, divorce rights by seven. Three of the Muslims mentioned the right to keep their own family name in marriage. The right to education was named by four respondents but above all the affirmative answer was given by Muslim respondents in relation to marriage, motherhood and divorce and financial interests within these contexts as well as security. Marriage, motherhood and divorce are discussed next.

Marriage, motherhood and divorce

Walker mentions that unlike many evangelical circles, in some house church fellowships, divorcees are welcomed and able to remarry (Walker 1987: 207). This point was echoed by Linda, a Muslim interviewee who related how she was able to get a guilt-free divorce and subsequently marry a 'good husband'. A Jesus Fellowship respondent, a single parent of two sons, wrote how she had found protection for her family. Walker suggested that such a communal structure will appeal only to a limited number in the Western culture of autonomy. However, since he wrote this, the movements have grown and seem to have an appeal to many, maybe *because* of the pressure for competitive independence which forces women with child care needs into an intolerable situation of being breadwinner, carer and supporter without any kind of support themselves. The importance of this should not be underestimated. Rights within marriage and divorce conferred by Islam figured large in terms of Muslim responses.

A number of Christian and Muslim respondents mentioned their right to be treated well in marriage. The Christians expressed it as 'knowing what to expect in marriage', whilst the Muslims stated that they had the right to be treated kindly in marriage. This puts boundaries and an element of surveillance into marriage as an institution, a sense of a silent witness within marriage to whom the partners are both accountable.

Two Muslim respondents mentioned their freedom to marry whom they wished regardless of nationality as an important improvement over custom. One respondent mentioned respect for motherhood as important. The right as a mother not to work, mentioned above, is an important factor at a time when the feminization of the workforce has taken place and there is pressure on mothers to work outside the home. This has led to the double and treble burden of which Islamists complain (Afshar 1991: 316). Further, 14 Muslim respondents alluded to their financial rights within marriage, that is the right to be provided for by the husband, to keep their own finances separate and not to have to contribute towards household bills. Three Muslims referred to their financial rights in divorce, that is, the right to maintenance, and a further five respondents referred to their right to divorce itself if the husband does not fulfil his responsibility and, as mentioned above, another wrote positively of the possibility of 'guilt-free divorce'. This right to divorce and remarriage within a religious framework is indeed liberating when seen from, say, a Roman Catholic viewpoint where divorce and remarriage are not permitted. This can mean being forced to choose between one's religion and one's emotional, physical and financial well-being. This has produced, for instance, a diaspora of women who are scarred by domestic violence and rendered homeless in terms of their religion.[16]

Islamic feminist approaches to claiming Islamic rights

As has been discussed, Islamic feminists differ from biblical feminists in terms of taking a gendered and complementarian, rather than an androgynous and egalitarian approach. The similarity between the two groups is that their forms of feminism are derived from holy texts rather than from secular discourse, although it is arguable that there is necessarily some dialogue with and input from secular ideas.

Riffat Hassan, a Muslim feminist, who, like the Submitters, leans to the position of 'Qur'an alone', has concluded that despite patriarchal attitudes, which she sees as evident in Muslim culture, the Qur'an, 'which to Muslims in general is the most authoritative source of Islam, does not discriminate against women' (Hassan 1991: 59). From my point of view, Submitters are most notable for the implications of their rejection of *Hadith* in terms of their interpretation of the Qur'an regarding women. The Submitters, in accepting *only* the word of the Qur'an, are able to bypass the religious establishment and make their own interpretations of the rulings concerning women. My initial impression was that Submitter women are very liberated in the 'all American' way. Yasmin wrote: 'Islam is the only religion that propagates equality between men and women. ... Unlike any other religion Islam has specific laws benefiting the women. *Islam therefore appears to be fitting into the emancipated status of today's women.* To understand this one needs to understand the Qur'anic view of women.'[17] This portrayal of Islam as a modern religion which has been waiting for the rest of the world to catch up is an apologetic stance which can be traced to the nineteenth century,[18] and is in keeping with the suggestion that feminism derives from Islam (see below).

One of my interviewees, Zainab from the more orthodox Young Muslims UK, shared this view of an Islam which was at the outset a progressive religion for women. She explained: 'Islam as a religion for them [women], before God, is the same as for men.... I don't think Islam embodies a concept of patriarchy.' She gave historical reasons, as those described above, but backed this up by turning to the *Sunnah*. 'Tradition has it that Muhammad used to mend his own sandals and wash his own clothes. It is a tradition in the *Sunnah*. This is an example of how Islam is not patriarchal.' Zainab also suggested that an examination of the lives of 'early Muslim women' who were 'very bold women' can only lead to the same conclusion. Zainab attributed the frequent distortion of the teachings of Islam regarding women not only to 'elements of patriarchy from the previous culture' but also to the fact that 'the vast majority of illiterates are women, and the learned men, the *mawlanas*, often make reactionary interpretations and this is taught to women'. One of the great achievements of sisters who are Islamic activists is the success they have had in claiming their right to an Islamic education and the means to interpret the Qur'an for themselves. My interview with Zainab helped me to understand how one of the sisters I had met at the Islamic Foundation (in March 1996) was able to live in what she described as a 'role exchange' with her husband who looks after the children while she goes out to work.

The fact that over the centuries the interpretation of the primary sources of Islam has been under masculine control is countered by women who are Submitters who turn to the Qur'an alone and thereby secure for themselves the possibility of a great deal of freedom in the interpretation of Qur'anic ruling on women's dress. Yet, within Islam in present-day Britain there are intimations of a changed view of a feminism, based upon women's rights – at least from some Muslims. For instance, there have been assertions that the revelation of the Qur'an in the seventh century is the source of feminism. The Muslim Parliament, drawing on a North American Muslim source, has made one such claim on the world wide web.[19] There may be some justification for this. I have already mentioned how Rana Kabbani has pointed out that Muhammad's teaching gave women economic independence in the seventh century whereas in Britain it was not until the passing of the Married Woman's Property Act (1870) that married women were able to control their money (Kabbani 1993: 36). Today, there are women who, through their own religious scholarship, are reclaiming Islam. They do this by taking the Islamic sources, especially the Qur'an, and making their own interpretations. When women have an Islamic education they are able to claim the rights for women which are enshrined in their holy book.

Muslim women, like many feminists, are divided on how to combine liberty and domesticity. As mentioned above, two of the ways in which Ghazal Anwar suggests the sources of Islam may be read in order to make progressive readings for women (and which I find to be the most appropriate to my interviewees and respondents) are the apologetic and the reformist ways (Anwar 1996: 57). Apologists for Islam take the route of complementarity, as do Islamic activists for women's rights. They claim that the needs of women and men are basically different, but they maintain that the Qur'an has given women specific rights. This makes for a problematic relationship between feminists who follow a Western egalitarian model and Islamic feminists whom they regard as 'essentialist'.

Apologists explain the reason why these Qur'anic rights need to be fought for by making the distinction between Islam and culture, for instance between Pakistani culture and Islam, so they might say that it is Pakistani culture which oppresses them, not Islam (Lyon 1995: 51–2). Reformists claim that the sources of Islam have previously been misread and that the distinction between the revealed text and its interpretation is of primary importance (Anwar 1996: 57). Yasmin, the Submitter, wrote: 'We must be careful not to confuse the words and deeds of Muslims with Islam. Islam is not determined by what Muslims may think, say, do or believe. Islam is defined for Muslims, by God, in the Qur'an.'[20] The reformist approach is to suggest that the Qur'an offers liberation to women, but that its liberating message has been distorted by male domination of the interpretative process. Members of all the Muslim groups involved in this study use both these reformist and apologetic strategies.

In this regard women's rights activists in the context of Islam draw on both modernist and Islamist schools. In applying Islam to the problems in Western societies women find that they are turning colonialism on its head. They are using modern Islamic discourse to address very modern problems in the West, as in the pressure to be liberated and autonomous at the same time as being a provider and a nurturer in the case of child care. These solutions are illustrated by some of the responses to the questionnaire regarding the right not to work and the financial arrangements within marriage where it is the husband's duty to support the family. It seems to me that while the Christians who submit in marriage get all the Christian responsibilities they get no such benefits as these. Islamic revivalist discourse allows a woman to concentrate on child-rearing without feeling obliged to go out and earn. If she does earn money she is allowed to keep it as her own. To some Western feminists this may seem like a retrograde step, but five of my interviewees, all of whom were mothers, also described it as a relief.

In terms of revivalist groups, apologists and reformists alike, as complementarians, tend to hold the view that to deem the needs of women and men to be the same is oppressive to women, placing them under a double and treble burden of nurturing inside the home, working outside the home, at the same time as consumerist society requires them to stay glamorous and young. Andrea Dworkin has suggested that as an alternative the 'equal but different' scenario is problematic because it has been cynically used in the United States in terms of race (Dworkin 1988: 191–2) to oppress groups. I would argue that, although an overemphasis on difference leads to a loss of political cohesion among feminists, a recognition of difference *per se* does not necessarily militate against equality. The recognition of differences in order to compensate for or disregard them in relation to specific situations is important to the political notion of equality. The needs of women are different at different times. In Britain today women are expected to be equal in the workplace at the same time as the welfare state is shrinking. This means that there is more pressure on women to be carers and nurturers. Women who choose 'complementarity' represent one solution to this dilemma.

Women's *tafsir*

Both apologists and reformers turn to the Qur'an as a means of establishing and claiming their Islamic rights, and *tafsir* (interpretation of the Qur'an) by women is the most powerful strategy for making headway in this respect. This is because 'unlike many Christians in relation to the Bible, Muslims (not just revivalists) generally believe that the Qur'an is the "direct verbatim word of God"' (Shepard 1987: 359). As Khadija C, a Submitter, put it: 'Islam is defined for Muslims, by God, in the Qur'an.'[21] So if a woman can prove the authenticity of her claim for her Islamic rights it would be a foolhardy believer who, wishing to please Allah, would prevent her from obtaining them. Obtaining these Qur'anic rights relies not only on proving their legitimacy, but also on being part of a community of believers who are campaigners and who, in the spirit of *da'wa* (mission), want to show that Islam is the better way.

In an interview in *Q News* in 1994, Anisa Abd El Fatah, Chairwoman of the National Association of Muslim Women in North America at that time, described a programme which enables women to utilize this strategy, a programme 'designed specifically for women coming from a woman's perspective and encouraging women towards Islamic scholarship'.[22] It takes the form of a newsletter which 'goes to women in the privacy of their own homes' and includes '*Hadith* methodology and literature' and an Arabic tutorial. Conservative Muslims, like the Sheikh mentioned by Maryam, are unlikely to object to this, yet it provides women with a means of obtaining their Islamic rights.

Linda, who converted to Islam more than ten years ago, used both *tafsir* and the division between culture and Islam in the following example. She has three children and became a Muslim during a previous unhappy marriage to a husband who was a non- practising Muslim. Linda's present husband is from Lebanon. She explained that when a couple get married in Lebanese culture, the woman pools her income with her husband's. But in Islam, 'A woman's money is totally her own and she doesn't have to disclose her income. It is the husband's job to support the family.' Interestingly, this requirement on the husband to provide protection and sustenance for his wife in the tasks of reproduction and child care depends, at least in part, upon Qur'an 4: 34, which is the verse which arguably gives permission to a man to beat his wife. No wonder it is necessary to value the verse and to find ways in which to dilute the husband's apparent right to chastise his wife physically, either by questioning the translation of the verb *daraba* as 'to beat' as do the Submitters and as suggested in the Introduction, or by the more orthodox revivalists by selectively using *Hadith* to neutralize or modify the meaning.

At a Young Muslims UK meeting, a *Hadith* was used to modify the impression that it is permissible for a man to beat his wife. A sister explained how the verse was meant ironically, that there was a *Hadith* which relates how Muhammad picked up a twig (*miswak* – wood used as toothpicks in Arab countries and North Africa) and indicated that it was only with such a stick that a man should beat his wife. In other words, he should not physically chastise her at all.

Linda said she was firm on the requirement that she should be allowed to keep her own money, when she and her present husband married. She said this was because her first husband took her Child Benefit. Her current husband was prepared to listen and looked at the references in the Qur'an. Linda described him as 'A man who gave me my rights...he doesn't infringe my rights.' She commented: 'For a good marriage you have to find someone who wants to please Allah.' Clearly such a husband is pivotal to gaining Islamic rights within marriage.

Feminist and non-feminist strategies

In order to ascertain how feminist these strategies might be it is necessary to attempt to find how the term 'feminist' is regarded by my interviewees. As indicated in the literature (Karam 1998), the Muslim interviewees were generally reluctant to have the term 'feminist' applied to themselves. This did not surprise me when I considered the historically difficult relationship between feminism and Islam. Rana Kabbani has suggested the alternative term 'gender *jihad*' as one that has its roots in Islam (Kabbani 1992: 36). Zainab from YMUK said she preferred to be described as a 'woman's rights activist within Islam' as 'feminist' has connotations she does not want. Khadija C responded to my inquiry that she was happy to be called an Islamic feminist 'if you define it [feminism] as being connected with the rights and status of women'.

Some of my interviewees are mothers who are taking advantage of their Islamic rights to raise their children without feeling obliged to work in paid employment outside the home. Their rights may seem a little inverted to an older generation of women who fought for the right to get out of the house. Yet for feminists there has been a conflict between freedom and domesticity. These women have found one particular way of solving the dilemma during their child-raising years.

Although some Western feminists have assumed that Islam can only be oppressive to women and that Islamic feminism can only be in the service of patriarchy, by utilizing Parvin Paidar's minimalist definition of feminism as 'aiming to increase women's rights, opportunities and choices within any ideology or context' (Paidar 1995: xi) it may be possible to work toward a cross-cultural and more inclusive understanding of feminism which respects differences, many of which may prove to be irreconcilable but which resists the situation of a multiplicity of postmodern Western secular feminisms united only in their refusal to acknowledge the legitimacy of women's struggle for rights *within* Islam, evangelical Christianity and other religious traditions.

Although the responses of the Christians were varied, some regarding 'rights' as being of no interest to them, others acknowledging the impact of legislation upon women, the majority of the Muslims did not take issue with the idea that 'rights' might be of some significance to themselves. Even though there are Christian influences behind many of the entitlements we have in Western democratic societies' systems of law, there are no 'rights' for women set out in Christianity in the same way as there are in Islam. The Qur'an gives guidance in terms of duties and entitlements and it may be that the concept of 'rights', in relation to the Qur'an, is an imposition of Enlightenment discourse. Nevertheless specific and overt verifiable claims may be made by women in Islam in contrast to a Christian culture where enrichment is often thought to come through self-denial and self-emptying. The apparent Christian disinterest in rights may also be explained in terms of the snowball questionnaire having been distributed in a modern Western state based upon Christian influences. For the Christians the need to establish particular kinds of rights may not feel so pressing. Islamic respondents coming from a different tradition have examples of struggles to establish an Islamic state elsewhere.

These Western women, who are not interested in rights, and who seem willing to give up their new rights only a few generations on from winning the vote, the right to their own property, money and custody of their children, do not perhaps consider how their lives would be affected if these rights, which are underpinned by law, were removed. Ruth Page (1990) begins her account of the work of Elizabeth Cady Stanton's impact on women's lives with an incident which illustrates the position of Western women in the nineteenth century:

> In 1869, Hester Vaughan was a 20-year-old woman, deserted by her husband, who had become a servant in a Philadelphia household. She had been seduced, became pregnant, and was dismissed. Destitute, she delivered the baby alone in an unheated garret and collapsed. Twenty-four hours later mother and child were discovered. The baby was dead and Vaughan was charged with infanticide. Tried without counsel, forbidden to testify, she was found guilty and sentenced to hang.
>
> (Page 1990: 17)[24]

Here is an account of a woman with no right to make testimony in court, no right to life or liberty. There are signs of a backlash in the United States against the new rights of women. For instance, as mentioned earlier, in June 1998 the Southern Baptist Convention voted an addition to their 1963 Baptist Faith and Message statement that: 'A wife is to submit graciously to the servant leadership of her husband.'[25]

Some of the Christians who are millennialists see the present day as 'end times' and therefore 'rights' are of little consequence in the face of the predictions of the Book of Revelation. Yet some of the house church and independent fellowships have a programme of social responsibility, as do the mainstream churches. In Islam, society is important. Submitters, like some of the Christians, make a private and American-influenced interpretation of their faith. It therefore comes as no surprise that an informant who is a Submitter suggests that personal finances are surely a matter for the individual and nothing to do with the law.

At times there is an anti-feminist agenda among the Christian hierarchicalists but this is not general. Some Christian respondents and interviewees actively call themselves feminists. There were areas of overlap between Muslims and Christians, one such being concern about marriage and the sense of 'knowing what to expect in marriage' which results in a kind of regulation of the married state. The holy text enters the marriage as a third party which facilitates scrutiny of the behaviour of the partners and recourse to the religious teaching. This is especially a safeguard in terms of the behaviour of the husband. In a secular situation there is no regulation except through private agreement. There was also overlap in terms of the desire for respect for motherhood, particularly in terms of financial provision which allows women to concentrate on the tasks of mothering free from financial insecurity and anxiety. The areas of difference here were being allowed to marry whom one wants (this is important against custom), the right to divorce and financial rights within that situation, and inheritance. None of the Christians mentioned divorce or inheritance as having been a particular issue for them.

5
Modesty Codes and the Veil

Even though there are moments of overlap, modesty practices and the issue of head covering, which have significance in both traditions, are treated differently in Christianity and Islam. They also have different forms of expression in the diverse faith communities which make up these two major religions. This chapter is in two sections: the first concentrates on Islamic revivalist practices in relation to segregation and veiling, and the second on Christian revivalist practices in relation to dress and decorum.

Modesty and head covering in Islam and Islamic revival

The discourse of the *hijab* (the veil or covering, or veiling) is situated within the location, community, ethnicity, socio-economic group and so on, in which it is worn. There is no monolithic meaning of the *hijab* in respect of gender relations. A stream of writing over the last two decades has aimed to examine the various meanings of *hijab*, especially in the Middle East (Makhlouf 1979; Mernissi 1991; 1991a; Ahmed 1992; Odeh 1993; Göle 1996; Karam 1998; Yegenoglu 1998; El Guindi 1999; Moghissi 1999). Some writers are reframing the *hijab* as a sign of resistance (Karam 1998; El Guindi 1999).

Veiling has been interpreted not only in terms of attire but also as practices of architectural separation (Mernissi 1994). There are ways in which this segregation from men can be construed as liberating (Oakley 1982), but it may also be problematic when women are excluded from decision-making processes. Like the nature/nurture debate which defies an ultimate solution, the definition of what it is that constitutes resistance is equally difficult to define for all time. This is because resistance is contextual and what comprises resistance in one situation is collaboration in another. The significance of the power of the veil, where it is not mandatory, is frequently missed: in the United Kingdom, for instance, far from being a sign of conformity and fulfilling the function of making the wearer invisible, the converse may be the case. In the non-Muslim Western context, the more a woman covers herself the greater is the degree to which she becomes a spectacle. In eluding the masculine gaze she becomes the focus of non-Muslim scrutiny (Franks 2000). Not only does this reverse the intention behind adopting Islamic dress but it also draws our attention to Western societal values and the requirement for the exposure of women's bodies as a matter of conformity. Instead of living out the stereotypical Western view that *hijab* represents passive obedience to Muslim men, Muslim women who adopt Islamic dress in the revivalist cause in Britain and the United States today need to be articulate and assertive.

Hajib and *hijab*

Separation *hajib* and covering *hijab* are not synonymous in Islam (Mernissi 1991). The Qur'an requires both male and female modesty in terms of women and men lowering their gaze (Qur'an 24: 30–32) but, according to Fatima Mernissi (1994), there are two kinds of separation through veiling which take place in Islam. The first relates to an architectural division of spaces which came about in the Qur'an when a curtain descended between the public and private domain (Mernissi 1991), between the Prophet together with his wives and the companions in the Qur'an 33: 53:

> O ye who believe! Enter not the dwellings of the Prophet for a meal without waiting for a proper time, unless permission be granted you. But if ye are invited, enter, and, when your meal is ended, then disperse. Linger not for conversation. Lo! That would cause annoyance to the Prophet, and he would be shy of [asking] you [to go]; but Allah is not shy of the truth. And when ye ask of them [the wives of the Prophet] anything, ask it of them from behind a curtain. That is purer for your hearts and for their hearts.[1]

The second kind of covering, *hijab*, is referred to in Qur'an 24: 31 and relates to dress and decorum:

> And tell the believing women to lower their gaze and be modest, and to display of their adornments only that which is apparent, and to draw their veils over their bosoms.[2]

Interestingly, this command follows verse 30 which reads: 'Tell believing men to lower their gaze and be modest.' Although both women and men are required to be modest, the emphasis in practice tends to be on the modesty of women. An amusing photograph in *Q-News* illustrates this: two veiled women, only their faces and hands showing, sit on a beach accompanied by two men in swimming trunks. The caption reads: 'What about the men's *hijab*?'[3] Nevertheless, there is overlap between the two kinds of veiling because the *hijab* in terms of dress, whilst marking her out as separate in the context of the Middle East, allows a woman to move between traditionally female and male spheres. For women it is 'a holy, sanctioned and acceptable means by which to broaden and further their political, social and cultural space' (Karam 1998: 12). This reading of the veil as a means of entering the public domain rather than as an exclusion from it is unpopular in some secular and Western feminist circles.

Hijab: criticisms and counter-arguments

Many secular feminists, Muslim feminists and feminists from within other religious traditions make a critical reading of veiling. According to some Muslim and interested Western feminists veiling has no justification in the Qur'an (Wadud-Muhsin 1992: 10; Karam 1998: 134). Basing their view on Surah 33: 28–32 some suggest that the *hijab* applied historically to the Prophet's wives, the 'Mothers of the Believers', and not to other women (Stowasser 1984: 32; Afkhami 1995: 13). Another suggestion is that it was associated with aristocratic practice among ancient Persians, Romans and Jews (Afkhami 1995: 13). Fatima Mernissi suggests that it was a mode of dress adopted by privileged women in order to signal that they were neither prostitutes nor slaves who had been forced into prostitution and whose heads were habitually uncovered (Mernissi 1991a: 182–8).

Amina Wadud-Muhsin (1992) describes how at the time of the revelation of the Qur'an, women who belonged to wealthy and powerful
tribes were veiled and secluded as a sign of protection. Wadud-Muhsin
makes a cultural interpretation of veiling as affording women
who are not economically advantaged the right to modesty also,
'however it is observed in various societies' (Wadud-Muhsin 1992:
10). To back up this position she quotes the Yusuf Ali translation of
Surah 24: 31 concerning the parts of the body which may be exposed
as 'what [must ordinarily] appear'. This allows for a more flexible
interpretation from culture to culture. The Qur'an acknowledges
the virtue of modesty and demonstrates it through the prevailing
practices. In Wadud-Muhsin's view, the principle of modesty is
important – not the veiling and seclusion which were manifestations
particular to that context. According to all these writers veiling is
based either on cultural practices which they see as separate from
Islam or upon historic detail relating to the Prophet's wives.

Stowasser (1984) and Mernissi (1995) both write about the spatial
meaning of the *hijab* as 'the sum total of practices connected with the
seclusion of women' (Stowasser 1984: 32) which 'identifies the
woman trespassing beyond her assigned private space as someone
who does not belong' (Mernissi 1995: 42). According to Mernissi,
veiling women is 'veiling resistance' (Mernissi 1994: 85). Denise
Kandiyoti (1997) expresses a similar view by suggesting that in Iran
the veil and segregation are a means of social control. All these
writers see veiling as retrogressive and a means through which men
oppress women.

Yet even if the *hijab* was and is a masculine imposition it may not
be necessary to decide for all time that veiling is either ultimately
liberating or oppressive, justified or not justified by the Qur'an, but to
recognize that women can and do make subversive and feminist
readings of patriarchal discourses. Oppressive readings can be turned
on their heads. What is collusion in one context may be viewed as
resistance in another. Karam quotes Michel Foucault: 'I'm not posit-
ing a substance of power. I'm simply saying: as soon as there's a
relation of power there's a possibility of resistance. We're never
trapped by power: it's always possible to modify its hold, in determined conditions and following a precise strategy.'[4] Karam sees Egyptian Islamists' defiance to state laws not only as resistance but as a
form of power. Karam is not alone in this view of women and

Islamism in the Middle East as a form of resistance (Afshar 1998; Ask and Tjomsland 1998). Karam writes how Foucault has provided a means of seeing the female body 'as a site of disciplinary power. ... To ground this in Egyptian praxis, Islamists both male and female, are also using the body as a site of power; whence their views on the necessity of veiling' (Karam 1998: 29). So rather than being read as a sign of oppression, the *hijab* is also a symbol of defiance and of rejection of the Westernized way. A poststructuralist analysis has been used, not only to define the *hijab* as 'an inscription of power relations on women's bodies' (Brenner 1996: 670) but equally the same theoretical base may be used to suggest that the veil is a sign of resistance which has potential for 'destabilizing and refiguring those relations of power' (ibid.). Some feminists see veiling in this light. Islamist women as well as Islamist activists for Women's Rights see it in a positive light.

The interpretation of veiling as exclusionary is a view currently held by some writers (Moghissi 1999) and there is no doubt that the practices of covering and separation can be oppressive. Yet this architectural separation of women from men can be restated from the feminine point of view as the exclusion of men from the world of women (Oakley 1982: 332). Oakley quotes an account of this separation from Makhlouf (1979) as an illustration. She describes the exclusion ritual of *tafrita*, a social gathering in the Yemen for women where no men are allowed. Makhlouf describes how the women arrive veiled in black and remove their cloaks at the door:

> The women wear their best clothes and display their jewellery. ... Upon entering a women's *majlis* [sitting room] one is taken by the glimmer of all the colours and brocades, by the chatter and music, the pungent smell of tobacco, the heady smell of incense, the sweet fragrance of perfume. ... Women enjoy smoking the *mada* [water pipe] and about one third chew *qat* [a stimulant shrub] which, they say, cools the body and relaxes it after the fatigues of the day. There may be some riddle guessing, story-telling and joking at a *tafrita*. Always there is music ...
>
> (Makhlouf 1979: 22–3, in Oakley 1982: 332)

Oakley writes how an 'early warning' system operates with regard to the intrusion of men into the gathering. Any man entering a house where a *tafrita* is in progress 'is required to say "Allah! Allah!" loudly a number of times while climbing the stairs of his house, so that the women hearing him, are able to change their comportment and cover their faces before he sees them' (Makhlouf 1979: 28–9 in Oakley 1982: 333). Oakley writes: 'This exclusion ritual contrasts with the simpler and more common entry of a veiled female into an all-male social group. While serving meals, for instance, women are able to learn a great deal about male society, whereas men are not allowed silently to witness female society in the same way' (ibid.). This surely is the whole point of interest here. The feminist enterprise is not to establish for all time whether the *hijab* is or is not oppressive, but to look at ways in which Muslim women may and do use it to their own advantage.

Why is the *hijab* such a potent symbol of Islam?

The discourse which relates to the position of women in Islam is a minefield, loaded with political, economic and religious agendas, both inside and outside Islam. This state of affairs has its roots largely in colonial history and Christian expansionism. Leila Ahmed (1992) has described how feminism was historically appropriated by colonialists in Egypt in an attempt to disrupt Islam. Repeated attempts by colonialists, postcolonialists, modernizers and secularists in, for instance, Algeria, Egypt, Iran and Turkey to remove the *hijab* by legislation or by force have served only to reinforce the potency of the veil as a symbol of Islamic revival. Further, the outcome of colonial interest in liberating oppressed Muslim women produced in the minds of many Muslims a close association between feminism and cultural imperialism and neo-imperialism (Kandiyoti 1991: 7).

Lama Abu Odeh (1993) has written how young women in Jordan, Algeria and Egypt who adopt Islamic dress signify their affiliation to revivalist movements by wearing the veil in a way that is different from the more liberal style of their mothers (or even their grandmothers). Many women of the previous generation showed some of their hair. The 'scarf' of what Odeh describes as 'fundamentalist' dress typically shows no hair at all (Odeh 1993: 27). As identifying a Muslim man by his dress is frequently impossible, women through their visibility act as the emblems of Islamic revival; by their attire and decorum they confirm the degree of Islamification of the group (ibid.: 26). This visibility means that, especially in a non-Muslim society, the conspicuously Muslim woman becomes an ambassador for Islam.[5] The veil has become a signifier of so much more than modesty; for whatever reasons women wear the veil, it is seen as a political statement. This in turn means that the 'scarf' becomes a target of those who would wish to disrupt Islam, even in the present day and ultimately serves to reinforce only further the power of veiling.

In the twentieth century, secularizers such Ataturk in Turkey and Reza Shah in Iran introduced dress reform as part of their programmes for modernization. The greater the attempts to remove the *hijab*, the more women adopted Islamic dress, and the *hijab* became even more inextricably linked with an anti-secularist agenda and more deeply embedded as a symbol of Islam.

The *hijab*, in the Muslim world, although not exclusive to revivalist movements, has become a signifier of initiation for young women into Islamist movements. It also fends off male intrusions and gives a sense of 'untouchability'. Odeh points out how, in the Middle East, public sympathy is often with the veiled woman and this can mean that the non-veiled woman feel powerless in the face of sexual harassment. This increases the pressure on non-revivalist women to conform. Feminists in the Arab world are usually middle-class and able to avoid such harassment as they have their own cars (Odeh 1993: 29). The veil gives an immediate solution for women who have to travel by public transport or walk in the streets (ibid.: 32). In Egypt, some poor students have not only adopted the veil as a means of avoiding sexual harassment but also because they cannot afford the expensive Western clothes worn by the upper classes (Turner 1994: 92). Bryan Turner writes that an upper middle-class form of the veil has even become fashionable in some parts of Cairo (ibid.). The gain is an instant solution for women seeking work or education, but the loss is the implication that women should minimize their contact with men, which, professionally, puts women in a liminal position.

Symbolic meanings are, however, complex and subject to change. Turner gives the example of the veil during the Iranian revolution, the wearing of which was a sign of opposition to the Shah's regime, and commitment to Islam and to Shi'ism. The veil also offered women anonymity so that they could not be identified by the secret police. Later, on a global scale, the veil became a symbol of a general commitment to Islamic revival.

Odeh has written how in Jordan, Algeria and Egypt in the 1970s, Western women's clothes carried a ' "capitalist" construction of the female body: one that is sexualized, objectified, thingified', by being identified with consumerism. Because capitalism coexisted with pre-capitalist social formations in postcolonial societies 'women's bodies were simultaneously constructed "traditionally": "chattelized"... terrorized as trustees of family [sexual] honour' (Odeh 1993: 27). This led to a conflictual situation between 'seductive' and 'asexual' formulations of the body which resulted in the impossible balancing act of being the 'attractive prude' (ibid.: 28)

The emblematic status of the *hijab* cannot be avoided. Karam writes with regard to Egypt today, 'There are no unveiled Islamist women' and goes on to describe the various degrees of veiling. These range from *hijab* where the scarf covers the head and neck and any 'body wear' covers the arms and legs, to *khimar*, a wider round scarf of various length with the front of the scarf pulled down to conceal the forehead, the 'rest of the clothing for the *khimar* centres on a shapeless one-piece, one-colour garment, usually a dull grey, blue, brown or black' (sometimes gloves are worn) through to *niqab* 'which consists mainly of a complete face cover with a narrow opening (the opening may be simply two slits for the eyes)' (Karam 1998: 135). There is an equation between the degree and kind of veiling and the woman's commitment to revivalist Islam and how far she is prepared to go in terms of her commitment. Brenner writes that Islamic activists in Java can read the beliefs of a woman who wears *jilbab* (Women's Islamic covering) by the way she wears it. For instance, they can tell what activist group she belongs to (Brenner 1996: 691).

In 'First Sex' (1994), a documentary on Channel 4,[6] women in Turkey who wear the *hijab* were interviewed. Wearing the veil in a situation where it was banned for public sector employees was not a means of furthering one's career. An unemployed teacher was interviewed. She was not allowed to wear the scarf to work in school and the *hijab* was banned in universities. Yet Nilufer Göle (1996), who must have been researching her book at the same time as this documentary was made, writes how wearing the *hijab* in Turkey helped students gain status 'as new female actors of Islamism, acquire and aspire for "symbolic capital"[7] of two different sources: religious and secular.' This demonstrates how women who wear Islamic dress bear different meanings for different groups, even in the same place at the same time.

Yesim Arat has suggested that the promotion of the 'individual right' of a woman to wear the *hijab* in a society which discriminates against it might be a kind of Trojan horse which imports a strand of liberalism into Islamic discourse in Turkey (Arat 1990: 21). She sees this agenda implied in *Kadin ve Aile* (Woman and Family) which 'might well be initiating its clientele into ideologies which in the long run can be used to challenge the confines of Islam' (ibid.: 15). Here is an example of the influence of liberal and feminist discourses which render the call for a return to 'tradition' a changed, and ever-changing, discourse. The *hijab* has a chequered career and is a focus of political forces. At times it bestows status in relation to the conventions of the society in which it is worn and at times it puts women in a peripheral position. Symbolic meaning varies with the specificities of location and socio-economic status and in relation to the constructions placed upon it by the observer. It may do both simultaneously within the same society but in different contexts. Further, Islamic dress has for many become the badge of resistance against Western consumerist culture. The fact that it is read as a sign of politico-religious allegiance in the revivalist context is unavoidable.

Hijab in Britain

In present-day Britain, there are many different ways of wearing the headscarf; some are traditional and associated with the diverse Muslim cultures from which women come. Islamic revivalist dress tends to take the form of wearing the *hijab* so that it covers the forehead and is pinned beneath the chin, below which loose body covering leaves only the hands exposed. But there are other ways or degrees of wearing *hijab* and some women cover themselves completely. There is a difference in, say, adopting the *hijab* in a present-day liberal democracy and an Islamic state where it is mandatory or in a situation where wearing the *hijab* officially prevents employment in state institutions, as has been the case in Turkey. In Britain, the wearing of Islamic dress is a sign of difference and, contrary to the stereotypical view that Islamic revivalist women who wear the *hijab* are passive victims, in order to wear Islamic dress in many parts of Britain today they have to be courageous.

The diversity of ways of wearing the *hijab* in Britain was evident at an Islamic Awareness Exhibition talk given at the University of Leeds on 14 November 1996. The women had their own entrance and sat on one side of the auditorium according to the requirement for spatial separation and they wore the *hijab* in a diversity of ways. Some were wearing the scarf in what I have come to see as the 'revivalist' manner, that is, fastened under the chin and covering the chest so that the whole face is visible but no hair and no neck can be seen. Then there were women who fastened the scarf turban like, so it covers all the hair but exposes the neck. A few women were completely covered in black veiling, from top to toe, with no opening for their eyes. I discovered later that one of my interviewees who had suggested she would meet me at the talk was dressed in this way. I was unable to recognise her until she approached me with her baby on her arm. I had previously met her at her house where she had been wearing the scarf. Interestingly, she said rather indignantly 'I waved to you' as though I should have responded, but the fact was I neither recognized her nor had I seen her waving, would I have been aware that she was waving to me. This made me realize that a woman who wears such a veil is able to claim the gaze, to see out and identify people. Perhaps there is a feeling that the recognition should be mutual. Like Brenner, who writes about Islamic activists who adopt Islamic dress in Java, I have found my Muslim interviewees to be strong and assertive women. In Java, as in Britain, Islamic dress is neither legitimated by the state, nor is it 'traditional' (Brenner 1996: 690).

Experiences of women who wear the *hijab* in Britain today

While a woman who wears Western dress in an Islamic country may be criticized for wearing too little, Muslim women in West find themselves criticized for wearing too much. In order to try to understand further what it is like to wear the *hijab* in a Western liberal democracy today, the particular questions in the snowball questionnaire which are the focus on issues of modesty were: 'Have you had any problems, in secularized society, following the modesty codes of your religion? If "yes" specify difficulties'; 'How does following the modesty codes of your religion help in your everyday life?' and a further question which asked: 'Have you experienced any problems in relation to your religious choice and your ethnicity?'

Of the 30 Muslim respondents who completed the questionnaire, 13 answered the first question in the affirmative but a further six respondents mentioned Islamic dress in answers to the third question. In all there were 16 answers regarding the difficulties encountered through choosing to wear Islamic dress and 13 of these specifically mentioned the *hijab*.

The issues were as follows: five wrote that wearing the *hijab* was a problem but didn't specify in what way, two said they met with hostility through their dress, two had encountered discrimination in school and employment: one respondent said she had experienced difficulty in getting a job because of it, but added: 'Once I found a job, they [colleagues] had no problems. In fact [they] realized I was human like them'. Four wrote that they had met with overt racial harassment and/or abuse. This included two white (one English and one Irish) converts to Islam. One of these mentioned abuse where she lives, but wrote that in more middle-class areas 'I get seriously avoided as if I might do something terribly embarrassing'.

Another respondent, the daughter of an Indian father and an English mother, wrote how the inability to 'locate' an English Muslim worked in two ways, some members of the white community hurled racial abuse whilst 'Many Muslims, more influenced by their cultures than faith find it hard to comprehend an "English Muslim" '. An Irish Muslim who described racial abuse wrote: 'Since I became a Muslim and adopted Islamic dress including the scarf (I hate the term veil) I have been called many things some of which I don't care to mention here . . . "white Paki" being the cleanest so far. I have been spoken to as though I neither speak nor understand English.' The experience of this respondent is not unlike that of Naima Radouane, a 41-year-old woman who felt convinced that she should wear the *chador* and to whom *Q-News* devoted an article. Naima reports how she has been called names, lunged at with a knife, thrown off a bus and old acquaintances have turned their backs on her.[8] In the next issue of *Q-News* a contributor wrote:

> Naima Radouane 'turns heads wherever she goes'. Where is the modesty in that? Although due to her choice of clothes no one would be 'lusting after her body', it is quite clear she is facing hostility because of what she wears. However if she was interested

in being modest she could wear normal loose fitting western clothes. If she did this she would not be bullied.[9]

Indeed, the way to become less visible (if that is the aim) is probably to wear something beige from a high street department store. But there is an interesting issue here: that a Muslim woman can be confronted on the streets of Britain for not revealing enough of her body. This is modesty in reverse.

I imagine there are not many women who dress like Naima Radouane in the locality. To local people who are used to communicating with a face that bears many of the signs of communication and many clues to the nuances of what is being said, including cues for speech and on how one's own words are being accepted, the blank wall of the *chador* might be unnerving. No doubt the responses to the *chador* are fuelled by media reports which represent it as being inevitably forced upon women and as part of a scheme to control women as is reported in the case of the Taliban in Afghanistan (Gohari 1999). But Radouane herself is quoted as saying: 'The years of my life I spent not dressed like this I used to walk in the street like anyone else without any problems whatsoever. People would stop to have a chat and would often compliment my baby daughter.'[10] The reader is not informed how she used to dress, but presumably she was still a Muslim at the time when she was not ostracized. This kind of statement was also made by my interviewees, especially two Irish and one English converts to Islam, in a group interview at the home of Linda. They spoke of situations ranging from the abusive to the comical relating to their experiences of how they are perceived. Like two respondents to the questionnaire, Elaine said she hated the stereotype of 'headscarfed, subdued and repressed'. Elaine, a woman in her mid-thirties, previously a practising Catholic and a former 'trainee blue button' at the Stock Exchange, said that at that point in her life she had been 'able to drink anyone under the table'. She is a strong and expressive woman and it would be difficult to imagine how anyone who had the opportunity to talk with her could imagine her to be 'subdued and repressed'. Julie, an Irish convert to Islam, suggested that people in Ireland think that women who wear headscarves are nuns. She recounted how a sister who is Irish is mistaken for a nun when she goes back to Ireland and often gets offered a seat on the train. Maryam also commented on similar kinds of confusion. She said:

Some people cross the road. They don't all know I'm Muslim. Some people come up to me and say 'Oh I thought you were Mormon'. And other people think I'm a nun and wonder why I have a child... when my little boy says 'Mummy'...

Linda said that when she makes a telephone appointment to see someone who does not know her, 'you try to find language to warn people that you are a Muslim'. She said: 'You turn up at the office and their mouth drops. A respondent wrote how she thought that due to her dress and her ethnicity, 'I am stereotyped and therefore am having to constantly justify and explain my actions/beliefs'. Another described how, as a student, she was cut off from interaction with other students: 'The main problems are not due to my interaction with society, but rather the way society sees me. I want to be able to feel safe, without verbal/physical abuse from people. Also a lot of people don't seem to understand how Muslim women may interact with other people and student life revolves around the bar.'

Although British society defines itself as liberal it clearly expects women to have particular experiences and to define themselves in specific ways. Traditionally in Western culture women are the object not the subject, of the gaze a view that has been reflected and transmitted through a long history of Western art where women are displayed in the nude, reclining position. This pattern of 'male looking/ female "being looked-at-ness"' has been reinforced by cinematic imagery (Mulvey 1975). The disruption of this pattern of the masculine gaze is not taken lightly by many women or men. This is because 'the panoptical male connoisseur' has been internalized by most women who 'stand perpetually before his gaze and under his judgement. Woman lives in her body as seen by... an anonymous patriarchal other' (Bartky 1988: 72). This disruption of the established hierarchy of the gaze happens especially when a woman is entirely covered because, unsurveilled, she is able to claim the right of scrutiny. Afshar has pointed out the 'gaze reversal' implied in the practice of veiling: the woman, in covering herself, avoids being the 'object of the gaze' and instead looks out, becoming the spectator with free access to gaze upon men.[11] This is only the case if the veiling is complete. One Muslim in a supplementary interview gleefully described how she experienced the claiming of the gaze represented by wearing the *chador*, on a visit to Saudi Arabia, as 'going out there like Candid Camera'. But in the Western context, if she frees herself from the masculine gaze the Muslim sister becomes the object of the non-Muslim gaze instead. The *hijab*, as generally worn by my respondents and interviewees, still arouses a degree of antipathy from the 'host' community.

The problem, however, is not in the non-Muslim community alone. A teacher of a GCSE in Islam group suggested that the girls who were from Pakistani and Moroccan families who wear the *hijab* to school are treated with hostility by some of the Pakistani boys. For this reason she thought that the Islamophobia Report[12] did not go far enough in that it treated aggression as coming only from the non-Muslim community.

Ameena Mohammed appeared on the front page of *Q-News*, high-kicking and wearing a tracksuit and *hijab*. She is Britain's first female Muslim Thai boxer.[13] In the same issue, Dr Zaki Badawi, described as a 'liberal' of the Muslim College London, advised that Ameena 'will make the *hijab* look ridiculous'. Ameena comments: 'Personally, I think a large extent of the objection to my doing Thai boxing has its roots in the restrictive attitude of many cultured Muslims who have a more narrow and restricted stereotype of a Muslim woman than even many non-Muslims. If mixed training sessions were not a problem they still would come up with something else.'[14]

Perhaps Dr Badawi's response was fuelled by concern about a different kind of reaction to *hijab* from non-Muslims. This different response was voiced by Zainab who was born into a Muslim home to British parents of South Asian origin. She suggested that wearing the scarf is seen by non-Muslims as 'very unBritish' and women who wear it are even seen as 'fanatics' or 'terrorists'. This perception is also expressed in a contribution to the University of Essex Islamic Society website, which quotes Naheed Mustafa, a Canadian-born Muslim woman, who explains: 'In the Western world, the *hijab* has come to symbolize either forced silence or radical, unconscionable militancy. Actually, it's neither. It is simply a woman's assertion that judgement of her physical person is to play no role whatever in social interaction.'[15] The idea that women in Islamic dress may be viewed as terrorists was echoed by two respondents who completed the questionnaire. This perception, which is the opposite extreme to the 'subdued and repressed' model, no doubt owes something to the linking of Islam, fundamentalism and fanaticism and 'un-reason' by the media (Esposito 1991: 156). Perhaps if a woman does not fit into the 'subdued' stereotype she can be construed as exemplifying the aggressive opposite. There may also be a kind of racism here, because white Muslim respondents and interviewees did not suggest that they were regarded in this way. Many non-Muslims appear to believe that a white Muslim woman cannot have made a dynamic choice for Islam and that they therefore clearly match the 'subdued and oppressed' model. The veil hides their femininity and they are regarded as traitors to the race because it is deemed that they have denied their 'superiority'. Mary Maynard has pointed out that 'It should not be forgotten, for instance, that it is not necessary to be black to experience racism, as the experiences of the Jews and the Irish and current events in Europe testify' (Maynard 1994a: 21).

The comments of the respondents and interviewees show some of the difficulties of interaction within a society which is largely nervous of Islam. Given that there are problems associated with wearing the scarf, why do some women choose to wear it? Answers to the questionnaire revealed that 11 of 30 Muslim respondents believed that following the modesty codes of their religion meant that they generally gained respect. Three said they gained respect for wearing the *hijab*. Obviously this respect must come from a different sector than the hurlers of abuse. The younger women and those who were at school also said they gained in respect. Eight said that they were protected from sexual harassment or from being seen as a sexual object, one of them also commented that it helped her not to act in a flirtatious manner and that men 'either ignore me completely or if they have to engage, they can only do so with my face/brain'. Four other respondents wrote how because of Islamic dress they were not judged by how they looked. As one respondent put it: '[It] liberates me from the bondage of being a commodity.' Another commented how at work it stopped men from regarding her 'as a busty brunette in a tight top'. Two respondents wrote how wearing Islamic dress reminded them of their religious duties. Three interviewees described a pleasure in gaining their own space and not receiving unwanted touching by men.

Maryam, who is the daughter of an Egyptian father and an English mother, has been a Muslim all her life. She explained in an interview why she had chosen to wear the scarf. Maryam had commented that she wore it to avoid *fitna* (strife) and on the surface this sounds like an unassertive kind of position to take. She suggested that the identifiableness of Muslim women meant that 'You have to behave' and that by being immediately recognizable women have to be more courageous. Maryam had not always worn the *hijab*. She used to find it difficult and showed me photographs of herself wearing hats and polo neck sweaters. Maryam, who in an earlier chapter is quoted as describing submission to her husband in marriage as an Islamic requirement, went on to describe how she had chosen to wear the *hijab* against the wishes of her husband:

> My husband was a bit, to be honest...was a bit worried and nervous when four years ago I said that I would like to wear it properly. And he said: 'You are going to attract attention to yourself and it is unfair if you attract attention to yourself because I, being a foreigner, get a lot of attention anyway and if we sit in a hotel, people will stare at us doubly.' And I said, 'Well, I'm sorry about that', but I felt I had to be true to myself.

So Maryam confounds the stereotype by wearing the scarf against her husband's wishes. When I asked Maryam what made her start wearing the scarf four years ago she replied:

> It was mainly the Bosnian War. It was also, I had met Muslims at the University Mosque, who were determined that there was a correct way to wear the scarf and what I was wearing was a stage towards it but it wasn't really correct. That was one factor. But what gave me the courage to do it was when I realised that just around the corner from us in Europe there were these people being killed because they were Muslims. I met Bosnian Muslims here in England, most of them were not aware of much of their religion, they used to go round to the pub with the Croats. They didn't wear scarves, they didn't identify themselves much, the majority [as Muslims], and they were being killed for it. And I thought, my gosh, if this sort of thing can happen then it doesn't matter really to blend in...there's no point. I would like to stand up and be counted. Here I am, there's no sort of beating around the bush and hiding it and in that case I think I will wear the scarf because if you're going to die for it you're going to die. I mean, I'm not suggesting that the British, hopefully, would ever turn like that.

It just seemed such an incredible thing so close to home and it changed my psychology and it gave me that extra courage to stand up for my convictions.

Maryam counters a number of Western stereotypes in relation to Muslim women. First, she is a white, English Muslim (there have in fact been white Muslims in Britain since the nineteenth century[16]), she is not a member of the British South Asian communities, and she is not a convert. Second, her husband did not force her to wear the *hijab*, it was not the result of docile comformity with the wishes of her husband; in fact he was reluctant for her to do so. Maryam, an educated woman with an MPhil in Religious Studies, decided to wear the *hijab* as a response to the plight of other Muslims during the Bosnian War, who were being persecuted for their Muslim identity even though they had not adopted what she would regard as an Islamic way of life, and she had to assert herself against her husband in order to 'stand up and be counted'. The treatment she receives, as a middle-class, white English Muslim is thought-provoking from the observer's viewpoint. Maryam's comments are in keeping with those of the respondent who wrote how some middle-class people tend to ignore her as if she is going to do something 'terribly embarrassing'.

Maryam pointed out in the interview that she knew punks who used to shave their heads. After they had converted to Islam, and used to high visibility, they were able to adopt the headscarf with ease. This is because, in the context of British society, rather than hiding a woman the *hijab* works in reverse and turns her into a spectacle. This is where the veil 'destabilizes and refigures power relations' (Brenner 1996). It does so not only by producing anxiety in some non-Muslims who cannot comprehend how a white woman could choose to wear the *hijab*, but also in disrupting power relations within Islam through this assertive act. Maryam shows herself to be either more courageous or more 'Islamic' than her husband, or both.

For me, the comments of converts to Islam are revealing in that they know what it is like to be on both sides of the fence. One respondent experienced discrimination by non-Muslims because of her ethnicity, on the grounds that she is a white Muslim. Some non-Muslims found themselves unable to accept the idea of a white woman wearing the *hijab*. The white Muslims find themselves crossing a boundary and thrust into situations which, to some degree, parallel the realities which British Muslims, whose parents originated from South Asia, Africa or the Middle East, may have experienced all their lives. As the youngest respondent, a 13-year-old Moroccan school girl from Surrey, put it, 'I experience racism everyday, especially at school because some people think that because of my religion I am very different'. Yet at the same time she writes how her religion helps her in everyday life and the problems that she might face during the day. Wearing the scarf clearly takes courage yet the benefits outlined by respondents and interviewees outweigh the drawbacks.

The issue of the division of space was apparent at the talk of the Islamic Society of the University of Leeds mentioned above. I have to say it felt comfortable to sit amongst women and the system worked whereby everyone could ask questions of the speakers because questions in writing were collected and taken to the panel. But there are positive and negative things to be said about women's space. There is a problem if it puts women in a liminal position and excludes them from policy-making. However, Linda thought that non-Muslim perceptions of the division of space were laughable. She related how she and her husband had gone to speak to some social workers as consultants on Arab culture. A member of the audience asked a question about women not being allowed to sit with men. Linda explained that if the plumber was coming to her house, she would arrange for her husband to be there. The social worker asked: 'Don't you feel you've lost your autonomy as a woman?' Linda laughed at this idea which she found absurd and pointed out that she would stay at home if a female visitor were coming to see her husband.

Some writers as well as my informants see the concept of 'veiling' as providing protected space and contest the notion of an architecture of oppression. Oakley (1982), following Makhlouf (1979), makes a good and unusual case in this respect, for a Western feminist of that time. In the context of the United Kingdom the woman who wears the *hijab*, in averting the masculine gaze, becomes the focus of non-Muslim scrutiny and speculation. Yet although on the one hand the veil makes the wearer stand out as different, at the same time she avoids the scrutiny given to a sexual object and the issue of being judged by her appearance. My interviewees and respondents to the questionnaire indicated that there are many ways in which they gain benefits through wearing the *hijab*, even though they also have to deal with antipathy from non-Muslims and some Muslims.

Modesty and head covering in Christianity and the new Christian churches

Modesty codes are not the same thing in Christianity as they are in Islam and, further, there are differences in their interpretation *within* the religions. In Christianity there is a teaching on head covering in the Epistle of St Paul I Cor 11: 4–11:

> Any man who prays or prophesies with something on his head disgraces his head, but any woman who prays or prophesies with her head unveiled disgraces her head – it is one and the same thing as having her head shaved. For if a woman will not veil herself, then she should cut off her hair; but if it is disgraceful for a woman to have her hair cut off or to be shaved, she should wear a veil. For a man ought not to have his head veiled, since he is the image and reflection of God; but woman is the reflection of man. Indeed man was not made for the sake of woman but woman for the sake of man. For this reason a woman ought to have a symbol of authority on her head, because of the angels. (NRSV)

Although currently some restorationist churches take this directive as universal and therefore as applicable to themselves, in general in the Christian churches this is not the case. It is interesting to speculate why this might be. It is, after all, a recent change in interpretation. Pre-Vatican II Catholic women could not enter a church if their heads were uncovered and, spending some of my time in Wales as I currently do, I still see women going to Welsh chapel on Sundays wearing their hats.

On the face of it it is difficult to see how anyone could make a feminist reading of such a text, yet biblical feminists and others attempt to do so by a number of means. The first is to regard the directive as contingent to that particular time and situation in Corinth which Paul was addressing, that is, the particular problems associated with the new church community, many of whom would have been pagan converts from a multiplicity of religions. Other means include contesting the translation of particular words or by making a subversive reading – in this case, choosing to read the passage as giving women a voice.

A New Testament text which deals not so much with head covering as with feminine submission, hairdressing and modesty is 1 Peter 3: 7:

> Wives, in the same way, accept the authority of your husbands, so that, even if some of them do not obey the word, they may be won over without a word by their wives' conduct, when they see the purity and reverence of your lives. Do not adorn yourselves outwardly by braiding your hair, and by wearing gold ornaments or fine clothing, rather, let your adornment be the inner self with the lasting beauty of a gentle and quiet spirit, which is very precious in God's sight. It was in this way long ago that the holy women who hoped in God used to adorn themselves by accepting the authority of their husbands. Thus Sarah obeyed Abraham and called him lord. You have become her daughters as long as you do what is good and never let fears alarm you.

The first part of this passage has been discussed in the chapter on feminine submission. The biblical feminist Catherine Kroeger has drawn attention to the fact that this proscription on braiding may be connected to the practice of braided hair being seductive in the cult of Isis, and she cites Apuleius' *Golden Ass* 111.8–9; Xenophon, Anthia and Habrocomes 1.11.5–6 as evidence.[17] The references to Sarah in 1 Peter might be differently read by Womanist theologians. What Sarah did in forcing her slave Hagar to have a child by Abraham (Genesis 16: 1–6) seems to the modern mind repugnant. The Womanist theologian Delores. S. Williams (1993) has linked this example of the oppression of a black woman with the possibility that black women in the United States might be forced to be surrogate mothers of white babies. So how can Sarah be seen as admirable or as a role model for modern women? But Kroeger (forthcoming) makes a biblical feminist reading of the passage. She writes: 'Even the best of biblical ancestors had their flaws, and Sarah should be claimed by Christian women although she may not always have been admirable. The injunction is remarkable, however, in naming a spiritual ancestor who is female rather than male.'[18]

Modesty

Head covering in the Christian case is not necessarily associated with modesty and can be interpreted as having a dual function. In the same way as the teaching regarding *hijab* may be read as being either oppressive or liberating, the scriptural passage relating to head covering in Christianity may be interpreted either as a means of placing women under masculine authority or may be understood, in the evangelical feminist context, as giving women a voice. The latter interpretation will be discussed below. Nevertheless head covering is not generally an issue in Protestantism in the West today in the way that it is in Islam, and Christian respondents and interviewees do not commonly dress in a way that is obviously emblematic of their religious commitment in the way that Islamic revivalist sisters do. Nevertheless, on my two visits to a Jesus Fellowship community in Sheffield, all the residents, both male and female and one friendly dog, were wearing bright red crosses around their necks. This is not related to modesty but certainly identifies them as members of Jesus Fellowship when they are in public. The extent to which there is or is not a modesty code associated with dress varies from group to group. My respondents and interviewees from Jesus Fellowship are the ones with a most recognizable dress code. That is because the women generally wear long skirts, no make-up and 'sensible' shoes.[19] A number of respondents, however, took my question on modesty to mean 'propriety', which is probably more appropriate in the Christian case in Britain today. Although some of the Christian respondents mentioned coming up against discrimination on the part of secularized society, they do not represent an obviously visible counter-culture. Nevertheless, in considering issues of religious discrimination, it is important that Christians should be taken into account.

Head covering

As mentioned above, the shift away from head covering for worship amongst Christian women appears to be largely a modern one. Further, in Catholicism, because of nuns' use of veiling, head covering has been popularly associated with celibacy. Therefore there is an association of the veil in Christian discourse with complete and continuing sexual abstinence. Head covering remains an issue in some house church groups and independent churches. As in the Muslim case, texts which are given a patriarchal interpretation and which even lend themselves to such interpretations can be framed differently and a feminist reading made.

Valerie Griffiths, a founder member of the biblical feminist organization Men Women and God, in an interview[20] made a radical reading of the Pauline passage. She pointed out that Paul in 1 Cor 11, clearly thought it permissible for women to prophesy, which she described as 'not just foretelling, but discerning the message of God to give his people'. Gilbert Bilezikian (1997), an evangelical writer who supports biblical feminism, gives a useful definition of prayer and prophecy (from a believer's viewpoint) which supports this view:

> Because they involve direct communication with God and from God, prayer and prophecy constitute the essence of worship. By prayer, the worshipper, along with the congregation, gains an entrance into the very presence of God – who then responds by giving His word to the congregation through the person prophesying.
> (Bilezikian 1997: 139)

Historically, prophecy can be read as a means of self-empowerment for some women (Bynum 1991; Mack 1992). No believer can argue with the voice of God and this can be used to counter oppressive readings of St Paul. According to Valerie Griffiths' reading, a woman is able to speak God's word. Previously I had focused only on head covering in the Christian context as a means of making women invisible and expressing subjugation to the authority of men and I had not seen that there is a way in which the head covering in the Christian groups could be read as permitting women to speak with a prophetic voice.

Christian responses: modesty

Because the Christian respondents do not generally stand out as being different in terms of their dress, there was less Christian response to the question: 'Have you had any problems, in secularized society, following the modesty codes of your religion? If yes please specify difficulties'? In fact, four of 43 Christian respondents thought the modesty code questions did not apply to Christians. Yet the extracts from the New Testament above are not dissimilar from the requirements for modesty in the Qur'an. It is interesting that the one leads to an elaborate dress code and division of spaces while the biblical requirement regarding dress is largely ignored yet other requirements, such as submission to masculine authority, are followed within the Christian revivalist and evangelical setting.

Six Christian respondents to the questionnaire did answer, however, that they experienced difficulties in relation to modesty codes and four of these were from Jesus Fellowship. The 'sensible' shoes, from my own observations after a number of visits to Jesus Fellowship houses as well as to a meeting of worship, are frequently Doc Martens. Worn with long skirts, this results in a mode of dress which although 'modest' and gendered, could only have emerged from the fashions of the 1980s and 1990s. Two Jesus Fellowship members wrote that they were ridiculed by non-Jesus Fellowship people for not wearing trousers. One of these extended the problem into a misunderstanding of her moral behaviour:

> In my faith, I dress modestly, don't drink, don't go to discos, don't go to movies, in that, my friends who are not Christians do not understand, think I'm stuffy and we don't have much in common as all I want to do is please God. All they want to do is please themselves. Even though I made it a point to keep in contact and see them, they didn't understand my faith.

A member of Pioneer Network, a woman in her early fifties who is in a church leadership role, wrote that in her previous work as a hospital manager: 'in relationship to behaviour at management conferences etc., I have sometimes felt ostracized by not joining in at every level socially and have had to work harder at finding positive areas to relate and retain rapport'. A 20-year-old member of Christians in York wrote that she too found herself mocked on account of her behaviour and her refusal to engage in 'drinking, drugs, [and] sexuality'.

All these women are perceived to be different because of their behaviour, and this creates boundaries between them and their secular friends or colleagues. These divisions are similar to the architectural separations in Islam, but these are invisible and interpersonal. There is a similarity here to the comment made by a Muslim respondent who found herself cut off from student life. In this case the code is a kind of invisible *hijab*. Although dress does not mark out the Christians as different, their behaviour may do so. The majority of Christian respondents, however, reported no problem in relation to their 'modesty codes'.

Covering in Christianity

As suggested in a previous chapter, the requirement by some Christian groups that women submit to masculine authority is drawn selectively from the teachings of St Paul. The principle that women through their submission should enhance the masculinity of the men is, although not initially apparent from a reading of Jesus Army/Jesus Fellowship literature, evident in an article in *Jesus Lifestyle*. Julie, a convert, describes her previous life: 'I wasn't just a feminist, I was sexist against males!' Julie relates how at a small meeting for new converts to Jesus Fellowship,

> A woman gave a talk on authority and submission. Her manner was gentle, womanly, peaceful – she carried a joy in just being herself. She talked about God's authority and the authority of the church 'submitting to one another in reverence for Christ'...God had given her a 'wisdom picture' in which she saw the women in the church as a picture of pressed flowers that were 'set in array' or beautifully displayed on card. The brothers in the church were the sturdy frame to protect the lovely picture and also make it more lovely by 'framing it'. The covering of the church was the glass on the top that protected the flowers from damage and dust. Covering and authority were not there to squash the flowers but to display and enhance their beauty.[21]

It is interesting that here women are envisaged as being displayed whilst in Islamic revival they are concealed by their dress. But the authority of the men in the restorationist Christian context becomes like a veil and is referred to as 'covering'. They are said to 'cover' the women with their authority. The term 'covering' in this frame of reference means 'watching over' or 'protecting'. The term is taken from the story of Japheth who covered Noah's nakedness (shame) (Genesis 9: 20–27). Walker writes that 'covering' is not to be understood in purely traditional religious terms. To be covered means that you submit your whole life – religious, social and economic – to your elders and apostles (Walker 1987: 209). This kind of covering then, like Islamic segregation in terms of spaces, relates to the social order. But because, in this case, the elders are always male, it is a hierarchical kind of 'covering', with the male 'covering' the female. Maria, a woman of about 60, who featured in the Everyman documentary on the Jesus Fellowship, was shown engaged in processing a mountain of laundry for the brothers and sisters. She refers to this 'covering' when she suggests: 'Freedom is knowing I'm looked after and cared for.'[22]

Walker (1987) and Davies (1986) see the house church as being overwhelmingly male-led. However, in more than a decade things can change. I interviewed Sally who is in church leadership in a Pioneer Network fellowship and there is also a respondent to the questionnaire who is in leadership within the same network. But this is far from typical.

Domestic arrangements frequently follow the pattern of the husband as head of the household, with wives submitting to their husbands and children to their parents (but especially the father) (Ephesians 5: 22–6:4) (Davies 1986: 61). Davies mentions that some house church meetings require a woman to wear a veil at worship. By doing so, the wife 'acknowledges by wearing the veil, even while worshipping, her submission to her husband' (ibid.: 68). This is in accord with Paul's recommendation in 1 Corinthians 11: 5. Here the woman is believed to be dishonouring her head by not wearing a veil when praying or prophesying. In the context of this passage 'her head' refers to her husband, and the husband's head is Christ (ibid.: 68).

This Pauline passage has, of course, been the core of much debate among biblical feminists who have argued, for instance, that the Greek word *kephale* has been misinterpreted to mean 'head' where the classical meaning is 'source' (Kroeger, in Hull 1989: 267 ff) or 'fountainhead' (Bilezikian 1997: 137). This argument is made in terms of the understanding of the day regarding reproduction, where the man was considered to be the source of the woman but 'seldom did "head" imply "chief" or "boss"' (Kroeger, Evans and Storkey 1995: 343; Kroeger in Hull 1989: 267ff). Counter-arguments have been made by evangelicals who believe their 'hierarchicalist' (masculist) position to be under threat (Piper and Grudem 1991).

Ann, an interviewee and a member of Christians in York, was the only Christian interviewee who had adopted head covering. She linked the issue of head covering in 1 Cor 11, not with modesty but with 'propriety in worship' and said that this is in relation to the issue of 'headship'. Headship interpreted from this viewpoint carries the hierarchical view of the relationship between Christ and the church, which is reflected in the relationship between men and women in marriage. Those hierarchicalists who wish to campaign for 'Recovering Biblical Manhood and Womanhood' argue that 'in the fall a major issue is that of role-reversal. It is not simply that Adam sinned: it is that he listened to his wife' (Scott 1994: 4).[23] From this perspective, that a woman is submissive to masculine leadership (not only in marriage but also in the context of the church) and covers her head for worship has implications regarding the redemption of men as well as women. This is because, according to this fundamentalist perspective, creation must be restored to its pre-fall order. According to this interpretation, the woman's 'head' is understood to be the husband whom she will 'shame' if she does not cover her head. Ann said that a lot of the women from her fellowship wear a scarf or a hat when they are praying or prophesying (which in terms of house church fellowships is unusual). Ann recounted how she had started to do this when praying with two student friends who covered their heads for prayer. She prayed on her own about whether she should cover her head too. At this point she thought she should not because she had understood, according to Martin Scott's (1992) book, that head covering in the New Testament was 'a cultural thing', that is, 'that the passage simply deals with the rightness of head-covering for the women of Corinth' (Scott 1994: 4). Ann said she asked God to show her clearly if she should cover her head for prayer. So when, two days later, on a train returning home for the summer vacation, she met a recent graduate who was engaged to one of her friends and who brought up the subject of head covering, Ann felt this was surely the answer to prayer. She asked him to explain the passage about head covering to her. He said, 'In Corinth there were a lot of prostitutes who apparently had shaved heads. In 1 Cor 2 Paul is comparing a woman who prays with her head uncovered to a prostitute. The word for "covered" is best translated as "veiled". The way Paul is arguing he isn't saying women should cover because of culture.' Strangely, this companion seems to be arguing that Paul's teaching does relate to the culture of the context. But Ann saw this meeting as providential and, because of the teaching in her particular fellowship concerning submission to male leadership, she adopted head covering for prayer.

The question 'Have you experienced any problems in relation to your religious choice and your ethnicity?' which elicited a number of answers concerning *hijab* from the Muslim respondents was answered in the affirmative by seven of the Christians. The vast majority (40 of 43) of the Christian respondents were white but five of the respondents used the question as an opportunity to write about their experiences of prejudice and the opposition of friends and family to their religious choices. I felt that (perhaps not surprisingly) these respondents had misunderstood my question and that this was connected to the problem of the invisibility of whiteness which is not generally seen as a 'raced' or ethnic identity (Ware 1992; Maynard 1994a: 21). There is, however, an increasing literature on the issue of white femininity as a construction of discourses which has helped to maintain racism (Ware 1992; Frankenburg 1993; Fine et al. 1997; Ferber 1998; Brown, Gilkes and Kaloski-Naylor 1999; Franks 2000).

Not all Christian respondents were blind to their whiteness. One respondent who described herself as 'Caucasian' wrote how she was ashamed of 'Western conceit and intolerance' and that she sees this as a problem of ethnicity and faith. Another respondent had experienced being 'the foreigner' with an 'alien religion' whilst a missionary in Japan and like the first five Christians who answered the ethnicity question, added her comment about the intolerance of society against committed Christians in the United Kingdom today. Another respondent wrote in response to the modesty code question that she had received 'a little persecution because of being a Christian' and another remarked how she had lost a job when her boss found out she was a member of Jesus Fellowship. The answers again showed that in a largely secularized society, although less visible than their Muslim counterparts, Christians can find themselves the object of discriminatory practices. These answers did show a degree of marginalization of some of the Christians within the work or home situation or socially in terms of rejection by their contemporaries. The social problem seems to arise particularly from their behaviour in terms of abstinence from alcohol and their restraint regarding sexual activity outside marriage.

Modesty and everyday life

The question 'How does following the modesty codes of your religion help you in everyday life?' elicited more answers from the Christian respondents than the previous 'modesty' question – 17 out of 43 Christian respondents in all. Of these, ten answers related either directly or loosely to dress and the other seven either directly or indirectly to behaviour.

The answers concerned with dress came from a variety of sources: four comments were from Jesus Fellowship members; three from Ichthus; two from Pioneer Network and one from Christians in York. Two of the answers from Jesus Fellowship members concerned with dress were related to an emphasis on gender difference in apparel. One respondent wrote: 'God says that men should look like men and women should look like women.' This becomes more explicable in relation to a belief in the need for a clarification of gender roles as a prerequisite for redemption. As described above, this relates to the idea that the 'creation order', which 'complementarian' or 'hierarchicalist' conservative Evangelicals believe was distorted by the fall, must, according to their belief, be re-established by a clear delineation of gender boundaries and the submission of women to masculine authority. Margaret, an interviewee from the Jesus Fellowship, explained how she had stopped wearing jeans when, one day, she had been mistaken, from behind, for an elder. As already indicated, in the Jesus Fellowship the elders are men. She had found this mortifying and has worn a skirt ever since. She described this in order to explain that there was not an explicit dress code in the Jesus Fellowship. Eight respondents wrote how they preferred to dress in a modest way that did not attract unwanted attention. One of these, a convert from Hinduism, gave a number of reasons for this. The first was the desire to avoid unwanted attention from men but the second echoes a statement made by Turner (1994) regarding the attractions of Islamic revivalist dress for purely economic reasons. She wrote: 'It avoids [my] needing to keep the latest trends and fashions' and 'enables me to find my identity'.

All the other respondents who referred to dress were concerned with pleasing God and/or not upsetting others and not drawing unwanted masculine attention and described how modesty in dress helped them achieve these ends. A member of Ichthus wrote: 'I believe it is pleasing to God and sensible to dress modestly though my church does not have a formal "modesty code".' Another respondent, a GP, wrote: 'The code relevant to me is to ensure I do not cause offence to my neighbour, so I dress conservatively at work where patients are of varying ethnicity, some devout Muslims, and I would not bathe topless!'

The comments about dress suggest an often unspoken dress code. For instance, Margaret, in response to my observation that none of the Jesus Fellowship sisters I had seen wore make-up, said: 'There is no rule about wearing make-up but I just got convinced about it. Then you find people accept you.' This indicates an implicit code which transmits itself by approval and acceptance. Regarding dress this interviewee showed concern, as did some of the Christian and Muslim respondents to the questionnaire, over a perceived inability on the part of men to control their own sexuality. She suggested: 'If women are dressed immodestly this is a problem because men are susceptible to what they see. They are more easily stumbled than women.' Frequently, for cultural or whatever other reasons, this proves to be the case, but the majority of feminists would have a problem with the idea that women should take responsibility not only for their own sexuality but also for the sexuality of men.

Different churches clearly have different dress codes. On my visit to the Pioneer People office to interview Martin Scott, the woman who greeted me at the door wore trousers as well as lipstick. At an interview with Sally, the church leader from Pioneer Network, Sally wore jeans and Doc Martens. She commented that when she goes to speak somewhere, 'I make sure I am acceptable'. This form of acceptability of dress no doubt changes from venue to venue, where she encounters groups which range from male evangelical ministers to the youth with whom she has a special ministry.

Comments which did not refer to dress (seven in all) related to behaviour which was described severally in terms of not swearing, abstinence from alcohol and not having a sexual relationship outside marriage. One respondent wrote how because of her faith she does not 'put people down'. Another respondent suggested that the moral code she keeps gives her a sense of purity and acceptability to God. Another commented that she felt she did 'stand out'. Two respondents said they felt more able to cope with the pressures of life and two others found that their moral code gave them boundaries and structure to their lives. The issue of limits to behaviour and guidance is an important one which finds echoes in answers to questions in other sections of the questionnaire. It is an issue which is discussed in the following chapter.

Head covering and modesty in two traditions

The ways in which women wear or do not wear head covering in the many faith communities which make up Christianity and Islam in Britain today differ according to culture and belief. Even within the revivalist communities there are many differences. In the Christian context head covering can be read in a number of ways. It may be understood as a sign of celibacy, as a sign of submission to masculine authority, or, in a more subversive reading, the teaching of St Paul on this issue may be understood as a sign that a woman has a right to prophesy and therefore to have the prophetic voice. Yet it is possible to make oppressive readings of head covering in both Christianity and Islam. Equally it is possible to make subversive readings of holy texts relating to head covering and to represent them in ways which offer forms of empowerment to women. This is significant in that patriarchal discourses may be subjected to feminist readings which overturn their meanings.

In the Christian case, the recent histories of Christianity in Britain and the United States mean that Christian practices have not been marginalized in the same way as Muslim practices. Nevertheless, in intra-Christian terms certain practices identified with Catholicism or Protestantism may be issues for polarization and, certainly, this remains the case in relation to Northern Ireland.

Although there are some similarities between the comments of the interviewees and respondents, there are many differences. Even though they might interpret modesty in a different way, the one thing that the majority of Muslim and Christian respondents would agree upon is the need for modesty. Like Islamic dress, modesty can be the cause of rejection by associates. It is a kind of invisible *hijab* which becomes apparent through relating. Similarities between informants from the two faith communities included a conviction of the importance of modesty in terms of behaviour, sexual constancy and no sex outside marriage. A number of Christian respondents shared a prohibition on alcohol with the Muslim respondents and a concern that modest dress should keep them safe from unwanted masculine attention as well as not tempt men into error. Further, there was a shared interest among some of the respondents concerning boundaries or guidance and the sense of order which living according to a modesty code brings. Interestingly, although I

have heard Muslim men suggest there is a great importance in expressing gender difference in dress[24] (as did two of the Christian respondents), none of the Muslim respondents mentioned the necessity for
clothing to reinforce gender boundaries.

6
Empowerment through Revivalisms: Some Gains and Losses

Empowerment

Historically, the much debated concept of power was largely assumed to have an existence independent of relationships. Michel Foucault (1979) changed this view by defining power as contextual and relational. From this viewpoint power relationships between individuals are constantly changing and what constitutes subversion in one situation becomes subservience in another, and vice versa. Self-empowerment, in terms of the taking of power for oneself or the bestowing of power, is subject to this same kind of situational framework. Empowerment in one situation and relationship may be dis-empowerment in another.

'Empowerment', a term frequently used in connection with social work, development and education is often modelled on autonomy (Rappaport 1987). In its most conservative use it may be limited to situations of absolute self-help (Onyx and Benton 1995: 51). Jo Rowlands draws on the Foucauldian model of power to demonstrate not only that power is relational, but also that oppression is internalized, and places 'internal barriers to women's exercise of power' (Rowlands 1998: 12). In doing so she comes up with a number of different kinds of empowerment which do not necessarily draw on self-sufficiency as a model. The internalization of control is demonstrated by Foucault (1977) in terms of disciplinary power which links power with surveillance. In *Discipline and Punish* he demonstrates this technology through the example of Bentham's panopticon prison, an architectural mechanization of social control. The guard in his central tower is able to view any of the cells at any time. The guard is obscured by shutters and so the prisoner is unable to know when he is object of the gaze. He therefore internalizes the surveillance, modifying his behaviour as if he were being watched at all times (Foucault 1977: 195–228). This model is easily transferable to the self-regulation of women in compliance with the internalized patriarchal gaze (Bartky 1988: 72). Thus women are disabled from the exercise of power by that interiorization of the patriarchal, panoptical gaze: a limitation which comes from within the self but which has its origins elsewhere. This psychological hobbling of women has a global significance for feminists as it presents itself in different ways in a multiplicity of contexts. A respect for and an attempt to understand the ways in which different women approach the resulting problems and the ways in which they attempt to re- empower themselves has significance for us all.

Rowlands explores the term 'empowerment' in relation to development discourse and she suggests that it has frequently been used in a context 'well rooted in the "dominant culture" of Western Capitalism' (Rowlands 1998: 11) in a meaning that has been associated with individualism, consumerism and autonomy. Rowlands suggests four kinds of power to which people might aspire. The first of these, 'power over', relates particularly to dominant hierarchical models, and in this context Rowlands suggests that empowerment for women means a masculine fear of loss or actual loss of power for men. Yet this is the most prevalent kind of power model and women, as well as men, are frequently holders of it. For instance, the mother holds it over the child, the doctor over the patient, and, however she shares her power, the power relation in that particular context, related to knowledge versus lack of knowledge, remains in place. In time, however, the power relation could reverse if, for instance, the patient becomes a consultant surgeon. Further, the power relation between them might be reversed in another situation. The other kinds of power which Rowlands suggests are 'power to'; 'power with' and 'power from within' (Rowlands 1998: 12).

The point of an analysis of power is to be found in the structural impossibility of escaping from power relationships of some kind. In order to bring about change in any particular context it is necessary to be able to make an analysis of the dynamics of power in that situation, a configuration of power held by a network of relationships which, according to the Foucauldian analysis, are likely to be multiple, diverse and, to some degree, fluid. I do not think that we should run away with the concept of the fluidity of power because these power relations still take place within structures where patriarchal relations dominate. Nevertheless, it is interesting that Rowlands engages with power in this differentiated way. A desegregated idea of power is far more useful in this particular context than the less nuanced notion of power versus submission and control. This is where an 'earthed' variety of poststructuralist analysis, which recognizes that choices are nevertheless constrained by a core of power relations that tend to remain fairly constant, is useful and can still lead to political action.

Rowlands looks at the way in which empowerment can be rooted in a person's self-awareness and be apparently independent of external relations. Especially important is the way in which it can be associated with cooperation with others and does not have to be based upon the given (white middle-class, able-bodied, masculine) model of autonomy.

By 'empowerment' I mean to gain 'agency', 'to be an actor' in the scheme of things, 'to exert power' of some kind and to feel oneself to be 'somebody' through a strategy of self-empowerment which does not, in the context of complementarian or Christian discourse, necessarily model itself upon autonomy – a concept which, I would argue, generally has its limits at many stages of the lifecycle of women (and men). In the literature empowerment is about advocacy, about giving women insight into their needs. In the discourse of complementarity, the structures within which women can operate are far more clearly delineated, so empowerment here is about reconstruction within clear limits and comes through imposing limits on existing male powers, as well as extracting entitlements. So I should expect the discourse to be distinct in that it focuses on the 'power within' and the 'power to' and occasionally 'power with' rather than 'power over' dimensions: 'generative rather than controlling power' (Rowlands 1998: 13).

The notion of power is important in this analysis. At any given time there will be a number of models of power operating in a person's life. Sally described how as a church leader she has authority over her husband in the context of the church but that she accepts the requirement to submit to him in terms of his having the 'casting vote' in the home and that in that context he has authority over her. So they share the power-over model whereupon the power ceases to be monolithic. When Sally described her ministry within the church she gave evidence of a 'power from within' and especially a 'power to' or power-sharing model. Sally commenced by saying: 'I think I'm quite a visionary leader.' This 'vision' suggests the 'power from within' paradigm: like prophecy, it is a knowing which comes from an inner conviction which does not apparently depend upon external influences. Sally continued:

> I've got a real desire to see other people develop and reach their potential ... to give them opportunity ... It's very much a giving away of power. It's about taking risks with people like 'A' who runs the rehab [drug rehabilitation] team. He has been off drugs for five years. It was his vision and he is heading it up with support at the same time.

Sally doesn't seem to have a problem with 'power to' or 'power with' in terms of sharing her power. She is interested in generative rather than controlling power. So within the hierarchical structure of Sally's church, there are all kinds of power dynamics operating. A model which can accommodate a multiplicity of different kinds of power and possible empowerment seems far more appropriate to the analysis of such a situation.

The issue of what is and what is not empowering for women has to be assessed from the standpoint of 'difference'. Many of my interviewees and respondents to the questionnaire contest a model of gender equality which is based on 'sameness' which requires women to compete on the same terms as men. They suggest that the autonomy which is requisite in order to participate in this kind of competition does not generally favour women in the different stages and conditions of their lives. This is rarely an insistence on the kind of biological/hormonal 'argument' posited by Shamsad Khan (1993) in his explanation of the requirement for two women witnesses in Islam but a judgement made with reference to the practicalities of child care and ageing in a society where women still take on the majority of responsibility for nurture and care and where women continue to be valued as objects. As has already been discussed, many women who join revivalist movements, especially in the case of Islam, see the 'equal but different model' as the way forward.

Rational choice theory

Rational choice is appropriate to a study of the religious choices of women in that women are regarded by many writers as receiving more positive social approval and support through participation in religion than men (Brasher 1998: 46). The economic imbalance, for instance, between the sexes in the United States, whereby women have less disposable wealth than men (Banner 1992)[1] means that 'women's ability to actualize themselves is more circumscribed than men's' and, following Iannaccone and Miles (1990), Brasher concludes from her study carried out in the United States that more women than men may turn to religious groups as a means of fulfilment. Most importantly, she suggests that 'religious groups offer them a more economically feasible way to achieve self-transformation and self-fulfilment than the culture in general does' (Brasher 1998: 47). Brasher, following Lofland and Stark (1965), writes how the main means of solving life's problems in the United States are politics, psychiatry and religion, and that religion is the least expensive of these (ibid.). The evidence I have collected has not convinced me that Brasher's suggestion that women turn to religion as a result of life problems, social or psychological distress is generally the case. I do, however, see societal pressures resulting in an economic drive and a requirement for support from a community as significant. Brasher points out that 'religious products' are offered free or at nominal charge and makes the point that 'The unpaid labor of women is a significant factor in religious groups being able to offer free or low-cost services' (ibid.). She writes how this creates a 'hermeneutical loop', a kind of parallel economy which services women but which keeps them in a lower pay-bracket. Significant to my analysis is Brasher's suggestion that a religion 'provides a place to reconstruct the self without the economic cost of consumerism' (ibid.). This fits with the evidence I have collected which suggests that women who join revivalist groups do so to become 'what they are not'. Unhappy with their experiences of secular Western or consumerist constructions of femininity, affiliation effectively allows them the possibility of becoming a new person. On a purely financial basis the cost of so radical a life-change within the secular marketplace, in terms of counselling, therapies, education and support required, would be prohibitive. But Brasher is keen to alert us to the fact that we should not consider monetary benefits alone. There are many other kinds of benefits, ranging from the material to the emotional and spiritual, and I have utilized the rational choice model in this more inclusive way. It is also the case that such a model contradicts the idea that women join such movements out of passive compliance to male demands.

Below I shall discuss the gains and losses, consequent on their religious allegiances, that my respondents reported in response to the questionnaire and in interviews. In order to ascertain the pros and cons I asked: 'Have you had to give up anything in order to practise your faith?' and 'If so, what have you had to give up?' Second, 'What have you gained through the practice of your religion?' I asked respondents to list the gains according to whether they regarded them as spiritual, intellectual, emotional, practical or material gains. Some respondents, especially a few of the Christians, made it plain that they found my question inappropriate. It is an inquiry which does not correspond with the respondents' feelings since they see religion as a holistic experience in which they as people change and gain a new consciousness rather than gaining something material or even specifically definable. So rational choice theory does not necessarily echo the voices of the respondents themselves. Nevertheless, the majority answered the questions, generously setting about splitting up the benefits they gained and in so doing providing interesting data. For analytical purposes it is worth making a categorization, albeit in a general way.

The Christian respondents

Conservative evangelical, independent or house church groups such as Jesus Fellowship and Christians in York, which require feminine submission not only in marriage but also to masculine leadership within the church, represent one end of the gender relations continuum, whilst Men Women and God, who often call themselves 'egalitarians', represent the other. Yet Christian respondents across the board have repeatedly mentioned, on the plus side, gaining 'confidence', a sense of 'identity', an 'extended family', a sense of security, and so on. But first I shall discuss what it was that the Christian respondents felt they had given up in order to practise their faith.

While Muslim respondents, apart from a few converts, reported having no sense of having given anything up in order to practise their faith, a number of Christians felt they had relinquished something. It is worth drawing attention to the fact that the sense of sacrifice was largely a Christian one and was especially associated with converts. In all, 25 of the Christian respondents replied that they had given something up.

The majority of the 43 Christian respondents to the questionnaire described themselves as converts, as did seven of the nine Christian interviewees. This prevalence of converts was also the case in Brasher's study (Brasher 1998: 31–5) and is largely due to a 'born-again' model of conversion which predominates amongst charismatic Christians and evangelicals. Although they may have come from a nominally Christian home, or indeed a practising Catholic or Anglican family, they regard themselves as becoming Christian in the exclusive sense of being 'born again' through the baptism of the Holy Spirit, and do not regard themselves as being Christians up to this point (Balmer 1989). As one respondent from Ichthus Fellowship described it: the transition 'from nominal Christian to a personal fulfilling relationship with Jesus was because I was overwhelmed by His love for me and His work on the cross.' Where other Christians might feel themselves to be in continual need of redemption from sin, born-again Christians regard themselves as 'saved' by that 'work on the cross'.

It may be that people who regard themselves as converts are more likely to feel that they have given up something. This is because they perceive themselves as having undergone a radical change which may demand alterations in 'life-style'. Their answers exhibited a number of repeated themes. Converts felt that they had constructed a new life for themselves which had involved the discarding of old ties and connections and even of free choice itself. But this is a choice to give up 'choice', perhaps because it has not, in some ways, lived up to its promise as a dominant concept in present-day Western consumerist society. Nevertheless, the choice to give up the concept of choice is made mainly in order to submit to God and this is seen as the greatest and most important choice of all.

The discipline of submission through sacrifice in the case of the Christians and through practices in the case of Muslims (for instance, in prayer five times a day) is a recurring theme among both Christians and Muslims. In this respect three Christians named their 'independence' as the thing they had relinquished. One of them, who said she gave up her 'independent will', was a conservative evangelical who takes a biblical feminist position. This giving up of independent will, in a Christian who is engaged in struggle over the position of women within her church, should be read in terms of the self-emptying (*kenosis*) required in order to serve God. As already mentioned, the bid for equality which biblical feminists make is to be 'equal to serve' (Hull 1989). The first two respondents who wrote of surrendering their independence were members of Jesus Fellowship. I find it interesting that members from both the groups I regard as being at either end of the complementarian/egalitarian continuum saw themselves as giving up their independence. This certainly does not fit with the 'power over' model of empowerment, but is more of an attempt to empty the self in order to become a channel of the spiritual 'power within'. But this can be conceived of only in terms of the power to serve, that is, 'power to' and 'power with'.

A number of others expressed the relinquishment of independence in different ways: for instance, one Ichthus Fellowship member wrote that she had given up 'My whole life!' and two members of Christians in York wrote that they had given up their past 'selfish way of life', whilst a member of the Pioneer Network said she had given up the 'pursuit of selfish ambition'. So if anything there is a giving up of the autonomy which the post-Christian feminist Daphne Hampson (1996) describes as being central to feminism and incompatible with Christianity. But it may be that my respondents do not see autonomy as a useful goal. Some respondents have given up their careers, their physical base and entire life-styles, as well as personal, physical or familial relationships, including emotional or key physical relationships. Two Christian respondents mentioned giving up a career: the first gave up acting, the second, who is a church leader in Pioneer Network, wrote that she 'recently gave up a career in hospital management as [I] felt it was necessary to give more time to my leadership role in the church'. Five Christians reported having given up different kinds of relationships, two of which were with male partners, whilst another respondent cited 'physical relationships', another some 'key relationships' and yet another had given up her two dogs in order to live in community.

Those who appear to give up the most in practical terms are those who convert from a different religious background. One convert who is a member of Jesus Fellowship and who was previously a Hindu wrote how she had given up her culture and that visiting her family was difficult. This kind of difficulty was also described by some Muslim interviewees who were white, Catholic converts to Islam. But converts from secular culture may also describe a yawning gap between their previous and present lives. One respondent, a member of Jesus Fellowship, wrote that she had forgone 'my previous life-styles, certain books, music, pictures, items, habits, education habits'. Although Jesus Fellowship has members living both in and out of community, the Jesus Fellowship respondents and interviewees live in community and this no doubt affects the degree to which their lives have changed. Only two Christian respondents mentioned having given up the style of clothing they had previously worn and both of these were members of Jesus Fellowship. Of these, one wrote that she had given up 'fashionable clothes' and the other 'trousers'.

Three of the Christian respondents said they had given up their homes, one to live in community, the other two for missionary work overseas. These last two, one from Ichthus Fellowship and one from Men Women and God, are now over retirement age; both have spent many years as missionaries abroad.

Where some had made sacrifices as a form of self-emptying, abandoning something that has been seen as hampering spiritual purity or preventing them from achieving their spiritual goals, for others the giving up consisted of more practical acts of purification such as abandoning specific 'sins'. Nine Christian respondents said they had given up smoking, drinking alcohol and/or drugs. Two Christian respondents wrote that they had given up 'sex before marriage' and two others wrote that they had given up 'sin', but did not elaborate.

Interestingly, one of the older Christian respondents had revised her position upon what it is that might constitute 'sin'. She had given up her acting career as well as smoking and drinking, but she 'later discerned that some of this was unnecessary and was a man-made rule'. This ability to revise one's position and still remain in a house church fellowship is an interesting one associated with 'thinking

Christians'. It does not conform to the stereotype of evangelicals and charismatics as 'fundamentalist', with beliefs set in concrete. This may also represent the kind of theological reassessment that becomes possible with the hindsight which maturity brings. It makes a dent in a stereotype of house church believers as unanimously bypassing theological speculation and draws attention to the fact that there is a range of positions held by different house church fellowships and their individual members.

The Muslim respondents

Where the majority of Christian respondents had described themselves as converts only five of the 30 Muslim respondents to the questionnaire and five of the nine interviewees described themselves as converts to Islam. All but one of these had previously been Roman Catholics. The majority of the Muslim respondents described themselves as having given up nothing for their faith but, as was the case for the Christians, it is the converts who had the sense of having given up the most. In fact, of the rest, reverts[2] to Islam and those who described themselves as having been Muslims all their lives, 11 answered that they had given up nothing for their faith, nine made no reply and four wrote that the question was 'not applicable'.

Of the converts who did have a sense of sacrifice in order to practise their faith, one said she had given up her 'previous life-style, that is, drugs, music, career'. As with the Christians, two wrote how they had given up alcohol, but also kinds of food which did not fit in with Islamic dietary requirements.

Three of the respondents who were converts mentioned the dress requirement of Islam which had meant giving up their previous mode of dress. A sister of 42 wrote in a similar vein to the Christian respondent who had revised her view when she commented: 'I gave up a lot of things in the beginning which I know now were unnecessary, for example – my name, my own dress sense, my identity, my culture, my family to a certain extent – sadly, types of food and enjoyment most of which I now understand was all a bit unnecessary'. Like the Christian respondent, she had later realized that, according to her changing understanding of her belief system, some of the sweeping changes she made to her life in the early years were somewhat superfluous. Perhaps the urge to make drastic changes and to give up many things in an early eager response to conversion mellows with time and age.

Converts: family and friends

Apart from one, none of the Muslims said they had given up relationships on account of their faith. The general lack of relinquishment is probably because of the low number of converts among the Muslim respondents to the questionnaire and because the influences which helped to bring about conversion of the Muslims sometimes came from their families or from close friends. Two interviewees had converted through their relationships with their husbands. In two cases these relationships had not lasted, but they had been introduced to Islam and both had remarried Muslim husbands. This contrasts with 31 Christian respondents who indicated that there had been a degree of external influence and the majority of these, 21 in all, suggested the influence came from Christian friends. This may account for a difference in that the relationships which influenced the converts to Islam were often closer: husbands, potential husbands or brothers. One Muslim respondent did, however, suggest the influence of friends in her conversion. She wrote that her acceptance of Islam was 'down to God' but that 'I did receive the pure message of Islam from two other Muslims whilst on holiday in Mexico with my husband'. She wrote: 'Their understanding of Islam greatly influenced my decision.' Neither she nor her husband were Muslims at that time and both converted.

Like the Christians who had converted to Christianity from another religious background, the two interviewees who were Irish converts to Islam experienced problems in relating to their families. It cannot be easy to give up the religious symbols of a lifetime whilst the family retains those symbols and values. Even though they were now married Muslims and had children, the Irish converts spoke of how their birth families still hoped they might turn away from Islam and return to the Catholic Church. There was also, for the Muslims, as indeed there is for some Protestants, a great deal they now considered shocking and idolatrous in the crucifixes and statues and devotion to the saints of their Catholic parents. Julie, who had two children, said that she finds it difficult to visit her mother's house in Northern Ireland. She described how her mother has a 'ginormous crucifix in the bedroom made by prisoners from Long Kesh and a giant-size portrait of Jesus in another room. It is difficult to go back with the children. There are too many images about.' It will be seen below that some converts to Islam regard Islam as a refuge of logic away from what they regard as the irrationality of their previous beliefs.

In summary, it is interesting to contrast what the Muslims do not say with what the Christians do. Amongst the Muslims there is little sense of having given things up and no Muslim mentioned giving up her life or her will. The things they gave up were mainly practical – certain foods, alcohol, gambling and, in one case, 'sex during Ramadan'. Sex had a low profile, although modesty was mentioned by three converts as a requirement of Islam. In both Christian and Muslim cases, it is the converts who have a sense of giving up their old way of life, habits and connections. For Muslims, there is a greater emphasis on the *Ummah* (the Muslim community as a whole) and upon the family as the basic unit of Islam. Most of them did not have non-Muslim friends. Although they support each other through networks and organizations, Muslim women are not obliged to go to the mosque for Friday prayer and, increasingly, young Muslims who are revivalists and converts to Islam find it difficult to find a mosque to which they feel able to belong. The Christian house church and charismatic movement depend largely on communal modes of worship and a sense of group identity which, in dispersed communities, often forms a kind of family substitute.

The gains

The following section relates to accounts respondents gave regarding their sense of spiritual, intellectual, emotional, practical and material benefits received through their religious affiliations. Although it is apparent that the importance to respondents and interviewees of spiritual gains took precedence over the material, I cannot avoid addressing the spiritual and material gains together. This is because the responses highlight differences in understanding regarding what is a rightful kind of gain and indeed what, for example, a 'material' gain might be. For instance, five of the younger, unmarried Muslims saw the provision which the Qur'an makes for a woman in marriage in terms of 'independence of wealth' and in placing the responsibility for financial provision for the family upon the husband, as a material gain. Yet this is a future gain, not a current one. But perhaps the expectation of future provision is in itself a present-day gain in that it takes the anxiety out of anticipation of the future. Lack of financial anxiety may be counted as a material as well as an emotional advantage.

As mentioned above, some respondents, mainly among the Christians, clearly regarded my question as being inapplicable and verging on the improper. For instance, one conservative evangelical wrote: 'Inadequate question – not about gaining something – about identity'. Another wrote: 'I cannot quantify in boxes like this. I'm a Christian because I believe in truth, not because of the idea of reward.' This apparent frustration with the question by conservative evangelicals may perhaps be traced to a reaction against the strand of the Gospel of Prosperity which at times finds its way into the house church movement from the United States. I think it also reflects the romanticism of liberal theology which creeps, unnoticed, into conservative evangelicalism. Materialism is despised: one becomes a Christian to serve and to give.

Spiritual gains

'Fulfilled', 'calm', 'confident', 'secure', 'inner peace', 'happiness' and 'contentment' are words and phrases that recur throughout the answers of both the 25 Muslim respondents and the 36 Christian respondents who described spiritual gains. Confidence was also given as a material gain by one of the Muslim respondents. By spiritual gains I mean those that are abstract and intangible and yet at the core of the belief. The answers appear to be along these lines. They give a picture of calm security, a self-assurance that comes with the sense, as described by one Muslim, of a 'deep belief and confidence and security in the total submission of oneself to God – that whatever is meant for you will never pass you and what is not for you will never be yours regardless of effort'. The respondent is located within firm limits. She is freed from anxiety because God will give her that which is best for her. Another Muslim respondent wrote in the same vein: 'When you fully appreciate that God is in full control, life takes on new meaning. You are secure in your belief that providing you are following God then God will only want the best for you.'

The serenity which results from a direct relationship between God and the believer, is also mentioned by 18 of the Christian respondents. For them, the emphasis is on a living and interactive relationship with God/Jesus/Holy Spirit. As one Christian respondent wrote: 'I feel Jesus around me and the Spirit fills the inner voids of my life.' There is more emphasis on a 'felt' and personal relationship with an internalized God amongst the Christian respondents, of God as a friend who responds to an individual's particular requests, for instance as expressed in the words of an Ichthus Fellowship member: 'I now have an awareness of God that I didn't have before. I can talk to him at all times on anything and see my prayers being answered.' Where Muslims and fundamentalist Christians believe revelation to be complete with their respective holy books, charismatics believe that God continues to reveal himself through the Holy Spirit. Sixteen of the Christians mentioned this personal, living relationship with God/Jesus/Holy Spirit. A Muslim respondent mentioned the link with the Creator through the Qur'an in terms of guidance where 'All questions, such as why am I here, where am I going, etc. are answered. This gives an internal feeling of satisfaction.' Another Muslim respondent wrote that she found security in the idea that 'Worship of God is not confined to when things are going wrong or when one goes to the mosque: God and his worship are incorporated in your daily routine of life and are just as "important" as other aspects of life, not a once a week affair.' Another wrote that she was 'aware of God and a lot happier'. Muslims and Christians alike declared themselves secure and confident in their relationship with God. This perhaps conforms to the 'power from within' model suggested by Rowlands. Six of the Christians wrote that they had gained the Fruits or the Gifts of the Holy Spirit, such as speaking in tongues or discernment. This is in contrast to the more cognitive kinds of spiritual gains described by the Muslims. For instance, one respondent wrote that she found in Islam 'an articulation of the spiritual that is logical, comprehensive, balanced and clear'. She is one of the five converts from Catholicism who, through questionnaires or interviews, have communicated the degree to which they find Islam to be 'logical' in contrast to Catholicism.

Intellectual gains

Respondents were asked to describe any intellectual gains. I wished to discover if respondents had any sense of increased knowledge or wisdom, enhanced ability to think logically or greater competency to understand the world. To some extent Muslims have, as seen in the previous section, described some spiritual gains in these terms. I also used the term 'intellectual' in an attempt to identify whether the respondents felt their thinking and analytical skills had been stimulated. I wanted to discover if there is more beyond the received idea of religious revivalists as unthinking recipients of ideology than the stereotype allows. Many respondents (26 of the Muslims and 31 of the Christians) described themselves as having gained intellectually from their faith. Muslim interviewees especially emphasized the importance in Islam of learning and gaining knowledge. Eleven of the Muslims wrote how Islam actively urges the believer to gain knowledge. One respondent wrote that Islam imparts 'the vision to seek knowledge from the cradle to the grave'. For the Muslims, the form this study may take includes private study based upon the Qur'an, frequently in translation into English, and study groups organized by, for instance, Young Muslims UK or the GCSE group for young Muslim women discussed earlier. There are also meetings, films, talks and exhibitions held regularly by the student Islamic societies of the various universities. One interviewee, Zainab, explained how although as a child she had attended Qur'an classes at the *madrasa* where she learned to recite the Qur'an in Arabic, it was not until her brother introduced her to an English translation of the Qur'an that she found new and relevant meaning for herself and chose to return wholeheartedly to Islam. The vast majority of the Muslim respondents and interviewees do not have Arabic as their first language. Christian respondents, on the other hand, would learn through Bible study groups and attendance at meetings in their respective fellowships and cell groups.[3] Christian and Muslim respondents recorded a range of intellectual gains from wisdom and understanding and a general stimulation to learn, to specific academic achievements or a particular gain in knowledge of the Bible or the Qu'ran.

Where the Muslims tended to use and be at home with the word 'knowledge' (ten), the Christians tended to use the words or phrases 'understanding' (six), 'intellectual stimulation' (five) or 'wisdom' (two). This may reflect the Muslims belief that the Qur'an offers clear proof and guidance, while the Christian faith is bound up with the mystery of death and resurrection, ideas which require the believer to make a leap of faith.

Two Christians and one Muslim claimed to have had practical or academic success through the practice of their faith. Two Christian respondents used the term 'stretching' as in: 'Constantly [intellectually] stretching even in the "motherhood phase" as needing to answer and explore theology'. Three of the younger Muslims wrote that their faith made them interested in contemporary issues in the world. There was no parallel statement among the Christians. Christian 'knowledge' was expressed in terms of knowing God and knowing the self and there was less apparent concern about gaining knowledge of the world in which we live.

Five Christians made 'meaning of life' statements such as 'I now understand why we are here' and two Muslims made similar statements, but emphasized the comprehensive nature of the knowledge gained, for instance: 'the Qur'an encompasses all aspects, be it spiritual, scientific, intellectual. . . . It again and again tells us human beings to question our existence, purpose and destination.' The Muslim statements give a sense of a direct relationship with knowledge and guidance through the Qur'an whereas the Christian acquisition of knowledge appears to be more social and communal through attendance at Bible study groups and having the opportunity to teach others. Seven Christians mentioned Bible study or Bible knowledge as an intellectual gain. This was the only context in which the Christian respondents used the term 'knowledge'. Seven Christian respondents mentioned interaction with others in terms of teaching, following courses of study or attending study groups. For instance, one respondent wrote that she was intellectually stimulated by 'sharing with "older" (this means older in faith rather than in age) Christians, I get challenged here'. Three Christians wrote they had enjoyed having the opportunity to teach. Again, here is the emphasis upon service as being the real goal. Four Muslim and one Christian respondents wrote that their faith had caused them to wish to study or to learn about other cultures and religions.

Overall, the Muslim view of intellectual gain was broader in the sense of encompassing all kinds of knowledge. There was no division between sacred and profane knowledge with only the sacred being worth having. This may well be because of their view of the Qur'an as containing all knowledge and as revealing (and reflecting) the order of the created universe.

Emotional gains

With regard to emotional gains, respondents' statements ranged from those demonstrating a wish to control emotionalism in themselves and those showing a positive reaction to emotions and which defined the ability to express emotion as a strength or a healing process. These are two extremes to be found within the responses. What is interesting in terms of Rowlands' analysis of kinds of empowerment is that faith for my informants seems to deliver both 'control over' and 'freedom to'. In reporting 'control over' emotions there is an example of the 'power over' which I had not initially expected to find. In this case it is 'power over' the self. This could be interpreted as an example of the Foucauldian internalization of the patriarchal gaze demanding conformity to a masculine model of contained emotions. Yet there is clear pleasure for some respondents in this sense of control, especially where they have had a previous sense of their emotions controlling them. This same pleasure is reported as 'self-discipline' by some of the respondents regarding practical gains in the section below. My respondents who write of self-discipline do not regard it as oppressive: on the contrary, it is seen as a source of liberation from the tyranny of unfettered emotion.

Homa Omid has pointed out how Ali Shariati, an ideologue of the Iranian revolution, wrote about the necessity to understand such a concept and not to confuse freedom and liberty. She wrote how liberty represents 'the absence of constraints' but freedom is something richer which is won 'through struggles and hardship and wisdom and growth'[4] (Omid 1994: 153–4). Early in second-wave feminism some feminists had encountered this kind of problem. In *The Tyranny of Structurelessness* (1970), distributed in the United States, Freeman pointed out that there was 'no such thing as a "structureless group" and that covert power relations were rife beneath the mask of structurelessness' (Freeman n.d.: 3). This is akin to the idea of liberty versus freedom, that untamed liberty requires some kind of internal structure in order to prove satisfactory. It explains how it is that the structures of the churches and of Islam might appeal to those like my first Muslim interviewee, Laura, who had experienced a 'free school' education and found it wanting. Those who have experienced the tyranny that 'liberty' in the form of structurelessness can offer may feel inclined to seek out guidance and boundaries so that they may learn to control their emotions rather than having their emotions dominate them.

Twenty-six of the 30 Muslim respondents and 37 of the 43 Christian respondents reported emotional gains. Four of the 30 Muslims who responded to this part of the question, like their Christian counterparts, wrote that they had peace of mind. Five Muslims mentioned control of negative emotions as making them 'stronger', 'happy' or able to cope with difficult situations or 'more mature and confident'. Another respondent wrote: 'I find the practice of my religion provides me with the necessary skills and ability to be able to cope with emotional situations.' A further four Muslim respondents mentioned 'emotional balance' in terms of being 'less emotional', gaining 'emotional strength' or emotional self-knowledge'. So amongst the Muslims there was an emphasis on happiness or peace of mind coming through control of the emotions in terms of an ability to discipline the self and not to be tempted to be led by emotional needs.

Emotional well-being was also important to the Christians but they seemed to experience it differently. Seven of the Christians explicitly mentioned that they had found 'emotional healing', six wrote that they had gained emotional stability and five emotional release. This emphasis upon emotional release is at the opposite end of the continuum to the 'control over' model of dealing with emotions. It is perhaps more in keeping with psychotherapeutic practice than with the model of self-control. One Jesus Fellowship member wrote: 'I find that with the Holy Spirit, I am able to express myself more, being healed in my emotions and am freed from fears. . . . I can be myself and [I am] not afraid of what others might say. I laugh and cry a lot, [a] great release of tensions.' Another, a member of Ichthus wrote: 'I feel its okay to cry. I couldn't let my feelings go [before], but its fine to show emotions.'

Many Christians wrote about a rich sense of belonging as an emotional gain. Five of these mentioned a gain of 'family' and friends and seven mentioned a sense of love as a gain, three of these in terms of their sense of being unconditionally loved by Jesus/God or the Holy Spirit. Six Christians also reported that they had found peace of mind and two described a loss of fear.

The emphasis on expressing emotion and losing fear through love and connectedness fits snugly with the model of positive mental

health to be gained through reaching out to others in an interdepend-
ent way ('power with') as described in Baker Miller (1988), a manner
of relating which she identifies with 'subordinates' but which nevertheless leads, in terms of connectedness, to positive mental health.
The healing which takes place is 'power from within', in this case the
power within being the Holy Spirit.

Eleven Christians wrote that they had gained a sense of security.
Two Muslims wrote that their sense of God's justice meant that they
had confidence that all would be well for them in the end or that
they had gained a sense of confidence. This is perhaps similar to
the sense of security described by the Christians and in keeping
with the sense of security described in the section on spiritual gains.

The main difference between the two groups of respondents was
that Muslims seemed to gain by having their emotions more under
control or by being 'less emotional', whereas the Christians gained
from having emotional release or healing through emotional expression. The 'Toronto Blessing' in some new Christian churches often
took the form of a kind of healing and was frequently described in
therapeutic terms. The Muslims seem to have acquired 'power over'
their emotions and the Christians 'power to' and 'power with' as well
as 'power from within'. Two Muslim interviewees did, however, mention their own healing experiences. Both were converts to Islam.
Linda spoke of how she had gone through difficult times with her
first husband who was a drug dealer and how, after having her first
child and leaving her husband, she had lived in poverty and ill
health. Her conversion to Islam changed her life in every way. She
regained her health, wealth and well-being. Another Muslim participant, Rabia, in a supplementary interview, described suffering from
depression, and that she had exchanged taking anti-depressants five
times a day for praying five times a day. She ascribed the sense of
control she had gained in her life to Islamic practices and prayer.

Practical gains

By practical gains I mean those that facilitate the smooth running of
life: the everyday ways in which faith might help to oil the cogs of
personal existence. The Muslims had a very strong sense of the
applications of their religion to everyday life and interpreted them
in terms of structures and frameworks of self-management and as the
means of exerting control not only over themselves but over time

and the everyday organization of the self. This follows the description of the ability Islam gave the respondents to take control over their emotional life and represents a cultivation of the self and the environment. The responses of the Christians were more relational in terms of being about the practical ways in which their faith enabled them to receive and give help and friendship, and the sense of community and family they obtained from being part of a Christian fellowship. There is a greater sense of autonomy in the practical gains of the Muslims, although they too mentioned societal factors. Five mentioned how the woman's role in the family was practical in that it maintained family structures and relationships within the family and between relatives. So they saw woman's role not only as pivotal to family life (and family life as pivotal to Islam) but also saw this as extremely practical for the good of society and for themselves. This view locates them at the centre, rather than at the periphery, of Islam. For Muslims, the theme of self-discipline entered largely into the practical gains in terms of personal organization as well as in family and societal structuring. Twenty-six of the 30 Muslims described practical gains. Eight Muslims mentioned how they had obtained organizational skills in terms of time-keeping, punctuality and self-discipline which had come from praying five times a day and other Islamic practices.

Four Muslims mentioned advice and guidance in terms of the Qur'an as a means of organizing their life. Like Ali Shariati, two Muslim respondents described how this guidance offered them freedom. One wrote: 'Islam allows me complete freedom to study, work and participate in society.' It may be difficult to see how being constrained by self-discipline or being dictated to by the Qur'an could be defined as freedom. Yet the chapter on rights addresses the fact that women are given specific entitlements within Islam which they find liberating. Many women who are Muslims do not know of their rights but those who pursue knowledge through an Islamic education, to which they have an entitlement, are in a better position to claim their rights. For instance, a woman in Islam has the right to marry whom she wishes. This helps women to resist in situations where they are being pressed into an unwanted or enforced marriage. Islam in this case is empowering because it allows the respondent to make her case, backed up by the Qur'an. She is assisted by meeting other Muslims who seek to overturn cultural interpretations of Islam, such as the members of Young Muslims UK, who work to oppose enforced marriages. The example of 'Aziza (see chapter 4), the Bedouin woman who claimed an annulment of an enforced marriage, is one which illustrates the way in which Islam can offer women freedom which they do not otherwise have. In the chapter on modesty some Muslim women described wearing the *hijab* in terms of having the liberty to move freely in society without being regarded as a sexual object.

This view of freedom is not uncontested; self-discipline and the ability to control the self may be perceived as internalized oppression by some, but it is experienced by some of my respondents as an improvement in the quality of life and as a means of being free from influences which had caused them to be unhappy and to feel out of control. This was particularly the case for converts who had formerly felt themselves to by tyrannized by consumerist culture, drugs or alcohol and the sexual exploitation of women. Like power, this kind of freedom is contextual. This freedom should be measured against cultural backgrounds, both Western and Eastern, which might not facilitate in their particular case the freedoms of which these women now speak.

A member each of the Muslim and the Christian groups of respondents mentioned how they had been given help with looking after their children, whilst two more (one from each group) spoke of how they felt their beliefs helped them to be better mothers. Thirty-one Christians in all responded to this 'practical gains' section of the questionnaire in the affirmative. Thirteen wrote how they had acquired an extended 'family', community or friends, the theme of relatedness and belonging which had also emerged as an important emotional gain for Christians in the previous section. Two more, as in the previous section, wrote that they no longer had fear – one of these in terms of 'no longer fear of men' and the other in terms of 'no stress, worry or fear'. Nine of the Christians also mentioned help and support of a practical kind. Being part of a believing community empowers the individual by offering resources which would not be available to them outside the communal base. This is especially the case where people, through reasons of marriage or work, find themselves geographically distant from their families. Debbie, one of my interviewees, described how she and her husband had, after graduating, initially been offered a home in order to move to the area to join the church fellowship. Now they have young children and are living far from their parents, they are offered practical support and encouragement by the substitute family of their church. The community empowers in the 'power to' and 'power with' way.

One Christian who is a church leader in Pioneer Network said that she had gained the ability to speak in public. It is interesting that she had found her voice through Christianity, rather than the opposite, which is the tendency, when a literal reading is made of the writing of St. Paul 1 Cor 14: 34–35.[5] This is in keeping with suggestions in the chapter about rights and how women can gain a voice through Pentecostalism in terms of the prophetic voice. This respondent is, however, a woman who has taken on church leadership which has given her the opportunity to learn the skill that many women lack.

Respondents made a wide range of practical gains following their religious commitment. These ranged from the ability to structure their life and environment and exert a sense of control to an experience of freedom, finding a voice and better access to resources such as help with child care and re-skilling. The benefits which come from association are multiple. Religious meetings are one of the few venues where women may be welcomed on their own and where divorced women and single parents might make acquaintances and find assistance.

Material gains

In making an analysis of the answers participants gave to the material gains question it was evident that it is difficult to separate particular material benefits from spiritual, emotional and practical advantages. This is because an increased sense of well-being and peacefulness, greater self-organization, better time-keeping and companionship as well as a sense of identity are likely to result in material benefits. Although the question was answered in the affirmative by 15 Christians and 14 Muslims who wrote that they had gained materially through their religious affiliation, there were some respondents who thought the question was not applicable to the issue of faith. Of the 14 Muslims who wrote that they had gained materially through the practice of their religion, five of the younger unmarried Muslims (above) saw the Qur'anic provision for women in marriage as a future material gain. This was perceived in terms of their own 'independence of wealth' and the requirement of the husband to provide for the family. A married respondent described how she had gained 'a good husband and financial support' when she was a single parent. Five other Muslim respondents reported a sense of emotional ease over finance which could also be considered a gain. Two other Muslim respondents wrote that to gain material things was permissible in Islam as long as one paid *Zakat* (a form of giving to charity which is one of the Five Pillars of Islam). Two of my interviewees who are converts to Islam described how it was permissible within Islam to do good works in order to receive a reward. This reward is of course a spiritual one and not a financial one, but perhaps these poles are not so easily separated. Paradise in Islam is described in terms which suggest comfort and prosperity and gives the impression that reward is not frowned upon in Islam (Qur'an 3: 14–15). The description of Paradise is such as to 'entice the readers towards the afterlife' (Wadud-Muhsin 1992: 52–9). The promise of 'gardens with rivers flowing beneath' must have been deeply alluring to the desert Arabs of the seventh century CE. Linda pointed out that this expectation of a reward in Paradise on the part of the giver frees the person in need to receive the gift without guilt or embarrassment. She explained how when, as a single parent, she was in financial distress, a sister offered her some money which she felt reluctant to accept. The sister pointed out that if Linda did not take the gift she would be preventing the donor from receiving her reward. This relieved Linda of embarrassment and allowed her to accept the gift. Another interviewee suggested: 'There is no reclusive idea in Islam. You take a pot of soup to a sick person because they are your neighbour and because of the idea of reward.'

Some of the Christian respondents had benefited materially in the most necessary of ways: two had gained a home, one a lone parent with two sons, the other a student. Two Christian interviewees had also gained assistance with housing. Members of Christian communities seem to help each other a great deal in this way: one interviewee, had been temporarily housed in order to move and another was offered assistance with purchasing a house. Five Christians said they had gained materially in terms of financial help when needed, one respondent having received cheques from church members for the replacement of a car which had been stolen. Seven Christian respondents felt that God provides for them in their daily needs. Three Christians described friends as a material gain. So although there was a sense of the idea of financial or material gain in relation to faith being improper amongst some of the Christians, many had a sense of material well-being and assistance through their belief and their faith community. This echoes the findings of Brasher (1998) in terms of the cost-effectiveness of religious goods and services. Some of the benefits which my informants describe may be counted in financial terms, but others represent the kind of goods which it is impossible to buy.

Two Muslim respondents, like five of the Christians, said they were less materialistic or not materialistic because of their faith. One Muslim, a convert, wrote: 'One does not expect to gain materially except what is ordained for you – materialism is one of the main reasons in society one turns to Islam.' Amongst some of the Christians the sense of being less materialistic was seen as something to celebrate. One Jesus Fellowship member wrote: 'I'm less materialistic – yeah!!' Certainly if one's need to be a conspicuous consumer decreases the sense of well-being must increase and one's pocket can benefit as well. One Muslim wrote: 'The fact that most people wear simple clothes... such that there is a sort of uniformity means less money and time spent on deciding what to wear.' Similarly, a Christian respondent wrote that a material gain for her was her 'need to not put materialistic things before other things'. This spells financial well-being in terms of release from preoccupation with lack of money. Another Christian, an Ichthus member, wrote: 'I used to buy expensive clothing and keep a very nice home. These things don't matter any more.' So a simplification of needs is also an improvement in material prosperity.

Although some respondents felt that the association with material gain and faith was inappropriate, the majority of respondents did not seem to feel inhibited about discussing their sense of improved material and therefore emotional prosperity. But it is also the case that lack of want makes for a greater sense of well-being even if it is the result of a simplification of life-style, choice of dress and a redefinition of needs. Further, material gain may take the form of an expected future good as in the case of the anticipated provision by the husband and the expected independence of wealth within a Muslim marriage. But clearly a number of respondents gained in terms of financial gifts and other forms of highly tangible assistance when they were most in need through the mediation of their associates and co-believers. Although women clearly do not join religious movements for material benefits, these benefits cannot be ignored.

Kinds of empowerment

I have found more evidence of the 'power over' model of empowerment among my respondents through their religious affiliation than I had expected. Perhaps the exercise, to some degree, of the 'power over' model is an inevitability in a competitive society which continues to be based on patriarchal relations. It is also partially explained as a strand of the diversity of kinds of power to be found in any given situation. Interestingly, the reports of the acquisition of self-discipline suggest that for some there is gain in terms of 'power over' the self. Indeed the sense of self-control the Muslims gained was emphatic and the consequent sense of freedom was a recurring theme. This difference between the self-monitoring of the Muslims and the self-expression of the Christians is marked and significant in attempting to understand the differences in their approaches. Although it could be argued that the Muslim emphasis on self-control is merely a sign of internalized oppression, the pleasure the respondents feel in having a sense of control over their lives is evident.

What light does the foregoing material throw on why women might join revivalist movements? Clearly there are a number of benefits to be drawn from such an association. These range from the spiritual to the material, but they are by no means mutually exclusive. Many of the gains described point to a decrease in anxiety. This comes from two contradictory ways of dealing with control. The tendency among the Muslims is to take control of their lives, but the Christians have a tendency to relinquish that control and depend upon the 'power within'. The Muslim way is through defining and implementing 'limits' and following the guidance of the Qur'an and for the Christians it is through their interactive relationship with their Maker. A sense of quality of life and a sense of identity come from the experience of a special relationship with God, and from the very tangible affiliation with other believers as well as from the religious practices both individual and communal. Some of the benefits are highly practical in terms of financial assistance and help with housing. Through their affiliation, the respondents who are converts have been able to become new beings and construct new lives. Some respondents have a sense of gaining love and experience freedom from fear.

The benefits include the practical meeting of needs that women have, which are different for women from diverse backgrounds at different times in their lives. Some have made the extraordinary choice to abandon choice by 'giving up independent will'. They have chosen to abandon choice because they have tried it and it did not work for them. But, ultimately, the respondents have been telling me that it does not matter what they gain or lose. At times, the same faith can provide totally contradictory rewards. Yet there is a consistency in that what is important is identity and the ability to construct a life experience. That is what empowerment is.

Conclusion

Revivalisms exhibit a range of models of gender relations ranging from the requirement for stereotypically submissive women to one which exhorts women to struggle for their Islamic rights in the Muslim case or their 'equality to serve' in the Christian evangelical feminist instance. In all cases these paradigms are claimed to spell justice and equality between women and men. In none of these instances along the continuum of degrees of submission to God and sometimes to men are they contesting patriarchal relations head on. But since the demise of radical feminism most Western feminisms, including academic feminism, are of this reformist kind.

Although the models of religious choice outlined at the end of chapters 1 and 6 share a degree of applicability, they are not all equally useful. What the participants do have in common is a sense of empowerment and enrichment from their religious choices. In making an evaluation I have employed the theoretical concepts of empowerment and rational choice, both of which have given some helpful indicators for assessing women's choices.

In looking at why some women elect to join religious groups which are considered by some to be anti-women, a rational choice framework treats women as agents and not as passive victims. They are assumed to be working in their own best interests and, in the case of religious choices, the interests they are taking account of are understood to be wider than those which are purely financial. For participants there are gains and losses involved in affiliation with revivalist groups but in terms of losses, converts to either tradition feel this to be more keenly the case. This is not surprising in that they have had to relinquish more in terms of culture, friendships and other relationships and make a complete reorganization of lifestyle. This transformation, the ability to become a new person, is of course one of the attractions of revivalist religion.

Participants in this study find forms of empowerment in a degree of obedience, submission or self-abnegation. As I have indicated in chapter 3, the respondents and interviewees generally regard the 'obedience' or submission to be before God and not necessarily to men. This is especially the case for the Muslim respondents. But generally, apart from the biblical feminists, both Christian and Muslim participants accepted varying degrees of submission to masculine authority in marriage and, in some Christian instances, to masculine religious leadership as a concomitant of their submission to God.

Both Islamic activists for women's rights and evangelical feminists contest patriarchy within their religious traditions, but they still largely appear to regard marriage as a holy state. Nevertheless, many of the participants have become radicalized over the years. This is because it is not easy to accommodate patriarchy even if one sets out to do so. Yet even if among the non-feminists there is not an overt feminist agenda there is a kind of empowerment strategy which can be traced within the choices of the majority of respondents and interviewees. They are delineating spaces for themselves within patriarchal structures and are using the opportunities that delineation of gender roles allows them to their advantage. For Muslim women, as we have already seen, there are entitlements to be claimed if they know how and live within a culture which accepts these rights to be the case.

A shared outcome is a contention that, in the context of existing patriarchal structures and prevailing religious constraints, participants are exercising their religious rights and responsibilities and are thereby extracting entitlements that they find empowering. Using a complex process of reconstruction and reinterpretation, they are moulding their lives and the men in their lives to conform to important moral standards which offer them ethical authority and intellectual respect. Clearly, the form of empowerment achieved can be viewed only as a *kind* of empowerment within the constrained choices available to them within patriarchal structures.

Biblical feminists like Islamic activists for women's rights are often rejected as non-feminist by secular feminists. Neither Islamic nor biblical feminists look to secular sources for their inspiration, yet it is probable that secular feminism has been influential by making education available to many women, who then have raised expectations and enhanced skills for study. How one defines feminism is a task which has always been problematic because of difficulties related to ownership of the definition, especially in the face of difference. This makes Parvin Paidar's minimalist definition of feminism as 'aiming to increase women's rights, opportunities and choices within any ideology or context' (Paidar 1995: xi) all the more relevant. Paidar offers a more cross-cultural and inter/extra-faith interpretation. For the purposes of this study I find this definition accommodates an inclusive view of feminism which is able to embrace women from different cultures and systems of belief and which does not seek to lay constraints upon the kinds of specific improvements feminists should seek.

Both Muslims and Christians see the need to have structures and constraints which facilitate their functioning as women, as mothers, as wives. Because they do not hanker after the autonomous model of empowerment they find the connectedness which they gain from being part of a believing community empowering. In many ways their notion of empowerment comes from abandoning open choice. This is where they are distinct from the majority of Western secular feminists, who are willing and able to respond to difference but who must have the option of choosing.

Notes

1. Revivalisms and feminisms

1. As with the Wahhabi movement in Arabia, which, inspired by the teachings of Ibn Taymiyya (d. 728), rose up against the corruption of religion in the 12th/18th century.
2. In Sunni Islam during the tenth century AD, 'the gate of *ijtihad* was closed' with the establishment of the four great schools of legal interpretation. The Shi'ites too at first prohibited *ijtihad*, taking it to be synonymous with *bida* (religious innovation) but it was reinstated in AD 1325 (see Mortimer 1982: 301).
3. Fuad Nahdi, 'Conversation with Anisa Abd El Fattah', *Q-News*, Vol. 3, No. 29, 14–21 (October 1994), 4–5.
4. Roger Forster, in an interview with Noel Stanton, 'Men of Vision and Action', *Jesus Life* (second quarter, 1998), 14.
5. *Jerusalem Bible* (London: Darton, Longman & Todd, 1974).
6. *Modern Jesus Army Street Paper*, No. 41 (first quarter, 1996), 8. Jesus Fellowship Website http://www.jesus.org.uk 20 May 1998.
7. Young Muslims UK Website: http://www.idiscover.co.uk/ymuknet/ 1 July 1996.
8. A Muslim women's organization based in Brent, North London.
9. Fuad Nahdi, 'Drugs and Muslims in Harlesdon', *Q-News* (May 1998), 26–9.
10. Paul Vallely and Andrew Brown, *Independent*, Cover Story, 'The Best Place to be a Muslim' (6 December 1995), 2–4.
11. CAIR (Council on American-Islamic Relations), Washington DC, 12 June 2000.
12. *Newsweek*, 'International Religion: The New Islam' (16 March 1998).
13. Ibid.
14. Intentionally started by a few missionary members of a larger fellowship.
15. Malise Ruthven, 'Hallelujah for the Sceptic', *Independent*, (13 July 1995).
16. Ibid.
17. 'Men of Vision and Action', No. 24. Bryn Jones is interviewed by Noel Stanton, *Jesus Lifestyle*, No. 24 (second quarter 1993), 12–14.
18. Qur'an 21: 30, 51: 47.
19. For instance: Qur'an 22: 5; 23: 14.
20. Alexis Carrel, *Man and the Unknown* (London: Hamish Hamilton, 1935) is cited by Sayyid Qutb, *al-Islam wa Mushkilat al-Hadara*, 6th edition (Beirut and Cairo: Dar al-Shuruq 1980/1400) pp. 132–5, in Choueiri (1990: 143).
21. Ibrahim Abusharif, 'Brain Wane', *Q-News*, Vol.: 3, No. 29, 14–21 (October 1994), 6–7.

22. See Roland Barthes 'Death of the Author', in *IMAGE-MUSIC-TEXT* (Glasgow: Collins-Fontuna, 1977).
23. In Keith Thomas, *Religion and the Decline of Magic* (London: Weidenfeld and Nicolson, 1971), pp. 568–69.
24. Patricia Gundry cites Julia O'Faolain and Lauro Martines (eds.), *Not in God's Image* (New York: Harper and Row, 1973) p. 130 in Gundry (1980: 48).
25. D. Martin, *Luthers Werke* (Weimar: Kritische Gesamtausgabe, 1883), 17, 1, 25, in Wiesner (1990, p. 127).
26. Fiona MacDonald, 'Jesus Army Wants You', *Independent* (29 April 1995), 16–22.
27. See Dr Syed Mutawalli ad-Darsh, 'What You Ought to Know', *Q-News*, No. 285 (February 1998), 27. A gay Muslim reader is advised to remain celibate and not to marry.
28. Qassim Amin, *Tahrir al-Mar'a* (The Liberation of Women) (Cairo, 1899), in Ahmed (1992).
29. CBE website: http://www.cbeinternational.org.
30. The writers are drawing upon 1 Pet. 2:9; Rev. 1:5–6.
31. Interview with Valerie Griffiths 1 May 1997.

2. Reflexive methodology

1. Julia Kristeva (1974) might be regarded as a forerunner of what has come to be called postfeminism.
2. This is a false dichotomy as there are 'secular feminists' who are believers of different kinds. I use the term merely to indicate feminists who claim a secular rather than a biblical or Islamic source for their feminism. The differentiation is necessary in order to discuss the issue.
3. See Hampson (1990) for a detailed outline of this position.
4. See Clifford and Marcus (1986 p. 7) in Stacey (1988: 25).
5. Christians for Biblical Equality http://www.cbeinternational.org (7 April 2000).
6. From an interview with Valerie Griffiths at her home, 30 April 1997.
7. Fiona MacDonald, 'Jesus Army Wants You', *Independent* (29 April 1995), 16–22.
8. Issued by the Jesus Fellowship Central offices, Nether Heyford, Northampton NN7 3LB.
9. *Qur'an – The Final Testament*, Universal Unity, PO Box 15067, Fremont, CA 94539.
10. International Community of Submitters, Masjid Tucson, PO Box 434776, Tucson, AZ 85733–3478; United Submitters International Society, Box 335–916 West Broadway, Vancouver, B. C. V5ZIK7.
11. Based upon 24: 31 and 33: 59 of the Qur'an.
12. In order to get his arithmetic to work, Khalifa had to omit 9: 128–9 of the Qur'an (which he objected to on doctrinal grounds).
13. Yasmin, Internet Islamic Forum 27 December 1995.

14. Mosque visit, 13 February 1998.
15. MacDonald, 'Jesus Army Wants You', 16–22.
16. Dingwall (1977: x) in Homan (1991: 119).
17. Belson (1975: x) in ibid.
18. See Myfanwy Franks, 'Crossing the Borders of Whiteness? White Muslim Women who Wear the *Hijab* in Britain Today', *Ethnic & Racial Studies*, 23 (5) (September 2000).
19. This is the title of a book by D. Riesman, *The Lonely Crowd: A Study of the Changing American Character* (New Haven: Yale University Press 1950). It is a title which expresses the postmodern condition of extreme individualism so that a crowd consists of isolated individuals, together in body only.
20. Subsequent interviewing experience has led me to adopt the use of a mini-disc recorder which picks up the quietest voice and renders it audible.
21. A broader account was given in a paper by the author entitled 'Caught in the Crossfire: A Case of Mistaken Identity among Religious Revivalists and Secularists', presented at the BASR Conference, Sterling University, September 1999.
22. 'First Sex', Channel 4 television, 26 July 1994.

3. Marriage, obedience and feminine submission

1. NSRV.
2. See, for instance, Wadud-Muhsin (1993: 71).
3. Pickthall translation.
4. The qualifying statements were: 1) A woman should be obedient to her husband in all things; 2) A woman should be obedient to her husband when he is right in his judgement; 3) A woman should use some degree of flexibility in deciding when to be obedient; 4) Other. Please specify.
5. Respondent's own exclamation mark.
6. Jeffrey Weiss, 'Baptist Proposal Asks Husbands to Lead Families', *Dallas Morning News*, 12 May 1998. Later acceptance of the proposal was reported on BBC News 10/6/98. Link for the story on CNN's website: http://www.cnn.com/US/9806/10/ southern.baptists.ap 11 June 1998.
7. URL: http://www.cbmw.org/ 22 June 2000.
8. Interview with Catherine Clark Kroeger, London 4 July 1998.
9. E-mail interview with Karen, 7 June 1999.
10. Piper and Grudem, (1991); see URL: http://www.cbmw.org 1 July 1998.
11. David Pawson, *Leadership is Male* (Guildford: Eagle, 1997).
12. *Jesus Life*, No. 41 (1997).

4. Rights and responsibilities

1. URL: http//www.moslem.org/essay.htm 23 January 2000.
2. Matthew 23: 25–29 (NRSV).
3. St Paul's Epistle to Galatians, 4:9 (NRSV).

4. This is in a context where for most Christians some regulations, for example, the food laws in Acts 15: 20, have been de-emphasized.
5. CNN website, 'The text of the new section of the Southern Baptist Convention's statement of Baptist Faith and Message', from SBCNet URL: http://www.sbcnet.org/bfm0.htm 11 June 1998.
6. NRSV translation.
7. See Shamsad M. Khan (1993).
8. This is deduced from the fact that the verse opens with mention of loans: 'O ye who believe! When ye contract a debt for a fixed term, record it in writing.' Surah 2: 282 Pickthall translation.
9. Internet Islamic Forum, 21 December 1995.
10. The contributor was there to evangelize.
11. Visit to Young Muslims UK Coreworkers Meeting, Islamic Foundation, Markham, Leics on 9 March 1996.
12. *Jesus Life*, No. 44 (second quarter, 1998), 24.
13. Respondent's written emphasis.
14. Noel Stanton talking to Roger Forster, in 'Men of Vision and Action', *Jesus Life*, No. 44 (second quarter 1998), 12.
15. My emphasis.
16. Sue Geophilous gave a paper entitled 'A Theology of Survival: Women and Domestic Violence', in which she drew attention to this situation at The First AUDTERS National Postgraduate Conference held at SOAS, 16–18 April 1998.
17. Yasmin, Internet Islamic Forum, 18 December 1995.
18. For instance to the Qur'anic interpretations of Muhammad Abduh and Rashid Rida, the latter founding the journal called *Manar*.
19. Mary Ali and Anjum Ali, quoted in Muslim Parliament Home Page URL: http://www.ummah.org.uk/mp/ 1 July 1996.
20. Yasmin, Internet Islamic Forum, subject 17 December 1995.
21. Khadija C, Internet Islamic Forum, 17 December 1995.
22. Fuad Nahdi, 'Conversation with Anisa El Fatah', *Q-News*, Vol. 3 No. 29 (14–21 October 1994), 5.
23. Khadija C, Internet Islamic Forum, referred to the Ahmed Ali translation: *Al-Qur'an, a Contemporary Translation*, (Princeton, NJ: Princeton University Press, 1993 [1984]).
24. From Griffith (1984: 159).
25. Reported on BBC News 10 June 1998. Link for the story on CNN's website: http://www.cnn.com/US/9806/10/southern.baptists.ap 11 June 1998.

5. Modesty codes and the veil

1. Pickthall translation.
2. Pickthall translation.
3. Selma Douglas, 'What about the Men's *Hijab*?' *Q-News* (7–13 July 1995), 7.
4. Michel Foucault, 'The History of Sexuality: An Interview', trans. G Bennington, in *Oxford Literary Review*, Vol. 4, No. 2 (1980), 13.

5. Karima Umar, 'Islamic Dress: the Total Experience', wittily describes how she finds herself buying a lot of 'Girl Scout Cookies' because she asks herself, 'What impression do I (as a visible Muslim) make on this child?' *Q-News*, No. 171 (7–13 July 1995), 6–7.
6. 'First Sex', Channel 4, 26 July 1994.
7. Nilufer Göle is referring to Pierre Boundieu, *Distinction* (Cambridge, Mass: Harvard University Press, 1984).
8. 'Victorian Hostility Prevails against Hijab', *Q-News*, No. 290 (May 1998), 9.
9. Rakeem al Shabazz, *Q-News*, No. 291 (June 1998), 5.
10. 'Victorian Hostility Prevails against Hijab'.
11. Haleh Afshar, Women's Hour, BBC Radio 4, 20 August 1998.
12. *Islamophobia: A Challenge For Us All* (London: The Runnymede Trust, 1997).
13. Shagufta Yqub, 'Ameena Mohammed: Boxing and Kicking the Habit', *Q-News*, No. 293 (August 1998), 30–1.
14. Ibid.
15. URL:http://so146.essex.ac.uk/users/rafiam/women4.html 11 January 1996.
16. Sarah Joseph, 'The Phenomena of Conversions to Islam: Victorian Converts' *Trends* Vol. 7, 5 (n.d.), 6–9.
17. Kroeger (forthcoming).
18. Ibid.
19. An observation made by Fiona Macdonald, 'Jesus Army Wants You', *Independent*, Features (29 April 1995), 16–22.
20. Interview with Valerie Griffiths at her home 1 May 1997.
21. Under the caption 'Jesus Christ Changed my Life', *Jesus Lifestyle*, No. 22 (fourth quarter 1992), 25.
22. 'Brothers in Arms', Everyman, BBC1 2 June 1996.
23. Martin Scott is making a critique of the argument put forward in Piper and Grudem (1991: 110).
24. Abdul-Haqq Baker, head of Brixton Mosque (London) suggested that to remove the beard is to become 'effeminate' as 'the beard is the one main characteristic of the man' at a talk for Islamic Awareness Week, University of Leeds, 14 November 1996.

6. Empowerment through revivalisms: some gains and losses

1. Lois Banner, *Women in Modern America: A Brief History*, 3rd edition. (Fort Worth: Harcourt Brace 1995 [1974]), in Brasher (1998: 47).
2. I here use the term 'revert' to denote those born into Muslim homes and who, for a time, moved away from Islam, only to return with renewed vigour. Some Muslims use the term in the same way as I am using 'convert'. I use both terms in order to differentiate for the purpose of making an analysis.

3. Regular fellowship meetings held in people's homes.
4. Eqbal, *Alameh Az Didegaheh Zendeh Yadeh Dr. Ali Shariati*, in living memory of Dr. Shariati *Kayham* (24 July 1991) in Omid (1994, pp. 153–4).
5. 'As in all the churches of the saints, women should be silent in the churches. For they are not permitted to speak, but should be subordinate, as the law also says. If there is anything they desire to know, let them ask their husbands at home. For it is shameful for a woman to speak in church.'

Bibliography

Afkhami, M. *Faith and Freedom: Women's Human Rights in the Muslim World* (London and New York: I. B. Tauris, 1995).

Afshar, H. 'Fundamentalism and its Female Apologists', in R. Prendergast and H. W. Singer (eds.), *Development Perspectives for the 1990's* (Basingstoke: Macmillan – now Palgrave, 1991), 303–18.

Afshar, H. 'Islam: Empowering or Repressive to Women?', in M. King (ed.), *God's Law versus State Law* (London: Grey Seal, 1995), 54–61.

Afshar, H. 'Why Fundamentalism? Iranian Women and their Support for Islam', *Women: A Cultural Review*, Vol. 6, No. 1 (Summer 1995a), 18–34.

Afshar, H. 'Islam and Feminism, Legal and Literary Perspectives', in M. Yamani (ed.), *Feminism and Islam, Legal and Literary Perspectives* (Reading: Ithica Press, 1996), 197–216.

Afshar, H. *Islam and Feminism: An Iranian Case Study* (Basingstoke: Macmillan – now Palgrave, 1998).

Afshar, H. and Maynard, M. (eds), *The Dynamics of 'Race' and Gender* (London and Bristol, PA: Taylor and Francis, 1994).

Ahmad, K. 'The Nature of Islamic Resurgence', in J. L. Esposito (ed.), *Voices of Resurgent Islam* (New York and Oxford: Oxford University Press 1983), 218–29.

Ahmed, L. 'Early Feminist Movements in Turkey and Egypt', in F. Hussain, (ed.), *Muslim Women* (London and Sydney: Croom Helm, 1984), 111–26.

Ahmed, L. *Women and Gender in Islam* (New Haven and London: Yale University Press, 1992).

Al-Azmeh, A. 'Islamist Revivalism and Western Ideologies', *History Workshop Journal*, No. 32 (1991), 44–53.

Alexander, S. and Taylor, B., 'In Defence of "Patriarchy"', *New Statesman* (1 February 1980).

Amin, Q. *Tahrir al-Mar'a* in L. Ahmed, *Women and Gender in Islam* (New Haven and London: Yale University Press, 1992).

Anderson, K. and Jack, D. C. 'Learning to Listen: Interview Techniques and Analyses', in S. Gluck and D. Patai (eds), *Women's Words* (New York and London: Routledge, 1991), 11–26.

Anwar, G. 'Muslim Feminist Discourses', *Concilium* 1 (1996), 55–61.

Arat, Y. 'Islamic Fundamentalism and Women in Turkey', *Muslim World*, Vol. LXXX (1990), 17–23.

Armstrong, K. *The Gospel According to Woman: Christianity's Creation of the Sex War in the West* (London and Sydney: Pan, 1987).

Ask, K. and Tjomsland, M. (eds), *Women and Islamization* (Oxford: Berg, 1998).

Ayella, M. '"They Must Be Crazy": Some of the Difficulties in Researching "Cults"', in C. M. Renzetti and R. M Lee (eds), *Researching Sensitive Topics* (Newbury Park and London: Sage, 1993), 108–24.

Balmer, R. *Mine Eyes Have Seen the Glory: A Journey into Evangelical Subculture in America* (Oxford: Oxford University Press, 1989).

Balmer, R. 'American Fundamentalism: The Ideal of Femininity', in J. S. Hawley (ed.), *Fundamentalism and Gender* (Oxford: Oxford University Press, 1994), 47–62.

Banner, L. *Women in Modern America: A Brief History*, 3rd edn (Fort Worth: Harcourt Brace 1995 [1974]).

Barr, J. *Fundamentalism* (London: SCM Press, 1977).

Barthes, R. *Image-Music-Text*, trans. S. Heath (Glasgow: Collins-Fontana, 1977).

Bartky, S. L. 'Foucault, Femininity and the Modernization of Patriarchal Power', in I. Diamond and I. Quinby (eds), *Feminism and Foucault* (Boston, Mass: Northeastern University Press, 1988), 61–86.

Barton, S. W. *The Bengali Muslims of Bradford, Leeds* (University of Leeds, Department of Theology and Religious Studies 1986).

Batson, C. Daniel, Choenrade, P. and Ventis, W. L. *Religion and the Individual: A Social-Psychological Perspective*, second edition (New York: Oxford University Press, 1993).

Becker, G. S. *The Economic Approach to Human Behavior* (Chicago: University of Chicago Press, 1976).

Belson, W. A. *Juvenile Theft: The Causal Factor* (New York: Harper and Row, 1975).

Bendroth, M. L. 'Fundamentalism and Femininity: Points of Encounter between Religious Conservatism and Women', *Church History*, Vol. 61 (1992), 221–33.

Berger, P. L. *The Sacred Canopy* (New York and London: Anchor Books, Doubleday, 1967).

Berktay, F. 'Looking from the "Other" Side', in J. de Groot and M. Maynard (eds), *Women's Studies in the 1990s: Doing Things Differently*, (Basingstoke: Macmillan – now Palgrave, 1993), 110–31.

Bhavnani, K. 'Complexity, Activism, Optimism: An Interview with Angela Y. Davis', *Feminist Review*, No. 31 (Spring 1989), 66–81.

Bilezikian, G. *Beyond Sex Roles: What the Bible Says About Woman's Place in Church and Family* (Grand Rapids, Michigan: Baker Book House, [1985] 1997).

Bordo, S. 'Feminism, Postmodernism, and Gender Skepticism', in L. J. Nicholson, (ed.), *Feminism/Postmodernism* (London: Routledge, 1990), 133–56.

Borland, K. '"That's Not What I Said": Interpretive Conflict in Oral Narrative Research' in S. B. Gluck and D. Patai (eds), *Women's Words* (New York and London: Routledge, 1991), 63–76.

Brasher, B. E. *Godly Women: Fundamentalism and Female Power* (New Brunswick, New Jersey and London: Rutgers University Press, 1998).

Brenner, S. 'Reconstructing Self and Society: Javenese Muslim Women and "the Veil"', *American Ethnologist*, Vol. 23(4) (1996), 673–97.

Brierley, P. and Hiscock, V. (eds) *UK Christian Handbook* (London: Christian Research Association, 1994/95).

Brierley, P. and Wraight, H. *UK Christian Handbook* (London: Christian Research Association, 1996/7).

Brierley, P. (ed.). *The UK Handbook of Religions Trends No. 2: 2000/2001 Millennium Edition* (London: Christian Research, 1999).

Brown, H., Gilkes, M. and Kaloski-Naylor, A. (eds), *White? Women: Critical Perspectives on Race and Gender* (York: Raw Nerve Books, 1999).

Bucaille, M. *The Qur'an and Modern Science* (Birmingham: UK Islamic Mission Dawah Centre, 1993).

Bulbeck, C. *Living Feminism: The Impact of the Women's Movement on Three Generations of Australian Women* (Cambridge: Cambridge University Press, 1997).

Butler, J. *Gender Trouble: Feminism and the Subversion of Identity* (New York: Routledge, 1990).

Bynum, C. Walker, *Jesus as Mother: Studies in the Spirituality of the High Middle Ages* (Berkeley: University of California Press, 1982).

Bynum, C. Walker, *Fragmentation and Redemption: Essays on Gender and the Human Body in Medieval Religion* (New York: Zone Books, 1991).

Carby, H. 'White Woman Listen! Feminism and the Boundaries of Sisterhood', in *The Empire Strikes Back* (London: Hutchinson in association with Centre for Contemporary Cultural Studies, 1982), 212–35.

Carrel, A. *Men and the Unknown* (London: Hamish Hamilton, 1935).

Chaudhry, M. S. *Women's Rights in Islam* (Lahore: Sh. Muhammad Ashraf, 1991).

Chesler, P. *Sacred Bond: Motherhood under Siege* (London: Virago, 1990).

Chevreau, G. *Catch the Fire: The Toronto Blessing – An Experience of Renewal and Revival* (London: Marshall Pickering, 1994).

Choueiri, Y. M. *Islamic Fundamentalism* (London: Pinter, 1990).

Clifford, J and Marcus, G. E. *Writing Culture: The Poetics and Politics of Ethnography* (Berkeley: University of California Press, 1986).

Coakley, S. 'Kenosis and Subversion', in Daphne Hampson (ed.), *Swallowing a Fishbone? Feminist Theologians Debate Christianity* (London: SPCK, 1996), 82–111.

Coffey, A. and Atkinson, P. *Making Sense of Qualitative Data* (Thousand Oaks, London and Delhi: Sage, 1996).

Connolly, C. 'Washing Our Linen: One Year of Women against Fundamentalism', *Feminist Review*, No. 37 (Spring 1991), 68–77.

Cooey, P. M, Eakin, W. R. and McDaniel, J. B. (eds), *After Patriarchy: Feminist Transformations of the World Religions* (Maryknoll: Orbis, 1991).

Cornwall, M. 'Faith Development of Men and Women over the Lifespan', in S. Bahl and E. Peterson (eds), *Ageing and the Family* (Lexington, Mass: Lexington Books/D. C. Heath, 1989), 115–39.

Cotton, I. *The Hallelujah Revolution* (London: Little, Brown, 1995).

Cotton, I. 'The Hallelujah Chorus', *The Guardian Weekend* (25 November 1995), 34–41.

Dalley, S. *Myths of Mesopotamia: Creation, the Flood, Gilgamesh, and Others*, trans. S. Dally (Oxford: Oxford University Press, 1989).

Daly M. *Beyond God the Father* (Boston: Beacon; and London: Women's Press [1973] 1986).

Daly, M. *Gyn/Ecology* (Boston: Beacon; and London: Women's Press [1978] 1984).

Davidman, L. *Tradition in a Rootless World: Women Turn to Orthodox Judaism* (Berkeley: University of California Press, 1991).

Davies, W. R. *Rocking the Boat: The Challenge of the House Church* (Basingstoke: Marshall Pickering, 1986).

Davis, A. *Women, Race and Class* (London: The Women's Press 1982).

De Groot, J. and Maynard, M. (eds) *Women's Studies in the 1990s: Doing Things Differently?* (Basingstoke: Macmillan – now Palgrave, 1993).

Diamond, I. and Quinby, L. (eds), *Feminism and Foucault* (Boston, Mass: Northeastern University Press, 1988).

Dingwall, R. *The Social Organisation of Health Visitor Training* (London: Croom Helm, 1977).

Douglas, Ann *The Feminization of American Culture* (New York: Knopf, 1977).

Duelli Klein, R. 'How To Do What We Want To Do: Thoughts about Feminist Methodology', in G. Bowles and R. Duelli Klein (eds), *Theories of Women's Studies* (London: Routledge and Kegan Paul, 1983).

Du Bois, B. 'Passionate Scholarship: Notes on Values, Knowing and Method in Feminist Social Science' in G. Bowles and R. Duelli Klein (eds), *Theories of Women's Studies* (London: Routledge and Kegan Paul, 1983), 105–16.

Dworkin, A. *Right-Wing Women* (London: The Women's Press, [1979] 1988).

Edwards, R. 'Connecting Method and Epistemology: A White Woman Interviewing Black Women', *Women's Studies International Forum*, Vol. 13, No. 5 (1990), 477–90.

Elster, J. *Rational Choice* (Oxford: Blackwell, 1986).

Enayat, H. *Modern Islamic Political Thought* (Basingstoke and London: Macmillan – now Palgrave, 1982).

Esposito, J. L. *Voices of Resurgent Islam* (New York and Oxford: Oxford University Press, 1983).

Esposito, J. L. *Islam. The Straight Path* (New York and Oxford: Oxford University Press, 1991).

Faludi, S. *Backlash* (London: Chatto and Windus, 1991).

Ferber, A. L. *White Man Falling: Race, Gender, and White Supremacy* (Lanham, Md.: Rowman and Littlefield, 1998 [?]).

Festinger, L., Riecken, H. W. and Schachter, S. *When Prophecy Fails* (Minneapolis: University of Minnesota Press, 1956).

Finch, J. 'Feminist Research and Social Policy', in M. Maclean and D. Groves (eds), *Women's Issues in Social Policy* (London and New York: Routledge, 1991), 194–204.

Fine, M., Weis, L., Powell, L. C. and Mun Wong, L. (eds), *Off White: Readings on Race, Power and Society* (New York and London: Routledge, 1997).

Fiorenza, E. Schussler, *In Memory of Her: A Feminist Theological Reconstruction of Christian Origins*, (London: SCM, 1984).

Foucault, M. *Discipline and Punish*, trans. A. Sheridan (London: Allen Lane, 1977).

Foucault, M. *The History of Sexuality*, Vol. 1 (London: Penguin, [1979] 1990).

Foucault, M. 'Truth, Power, Self: An Interview with Michel Foucault, October 25th 1982', in H. Gutman and P. H. Hutton, *Technologies of Self* (Amhurst: University of Massachusetts Press, 1982), 11.

Frankenberg, R. *White Women, Race Matters* (University of Minnesota Press and London: Routledge, 1993).

Franks, M. 'Crossing the Borders of Whiteness? White Muslim Women Who Wear the H*ijab* in Britain Today', *Ethnic and Racial Studies*, Vol. 23 (5) (September 2000), 917–29.

Freeman, J. *The Tyranny of Structurelessness* (Kingston-upon-Thames: The Anarchist Workers Association, n.d. also issued as a pamphlet by Agitprop, 1972).

Game, A. *Undoing the Social* (Milton Keynes: Open University Press, 1991).

Geaves, R. A. 'The Reproduction of *Jamaat-i Islami* in Britain', *Islam and Christian–Muslim Relations*, Vol. 6, No.2 (December 1995), 187–210.

Gerami, S. *Women and Fundamentalism: Islam and Christianity* (New York and London: Garland Publishing Inc., 1996).

Gergen, K.J and Gergen, M. M. 'Toward Reflexive Methodologies', in F. Steier (ed.), *Research and Reflexivity* (London, Newbury Park and New Delhi: Sage, 1991), 76–95.

Ginsburg, F. 'The Case of Mistaken Identity: Problems in Representing Women on the Right', in R. Hertz (ed.), *Reflexivity and Voice* (Thousand Oaks: Sage, 1997), 283–99.

Gluck, S. B. and Patai, D. (eds), *Women's Words: The Feminist Practice of Oral History* (New York and London: Routledge, 1991).

Gohari, M. J. *Taliban: Ascent to Power* (Oxford: Oxford Logos Society, 1999).

Göle, N. *The Forbidden Modern: Civilization and Veiling* (Ann Arbor: The University of Michigan Press, 1996).

Gordon, D. F. 'Getting Close by Staying Distant: Fieldwork with Proselytizing Groups', *Qualitative Sociology*, No. 10 (3) (1987), 267–87.

Graham, H. 'Do Her Answers Fit His Question? Women and the Survey Method', in E. Gamarnikow, D. Morgan, J. Purvis and D. Taylor (eds), *The Public and the Private* (London: Heinemann, 1983).

Gram-Hanssen, K. 'Objectivity in the Description of Nature: Between Social Construction and Essentialism', in N. Lykke and R. Braidotti (eds), *Between Monsters, Goddesses and Cyborgs* (London and New Jersey: Zed Books, 1996), 88–102.

Grant, J. *White Woman's Christ and Black Woman's Jesus: Feminist Christology and Womanist Response* (Atlanta, Ga: Scholars Press, 1989).

Grant, J. 'The Sin of Servanthood: And the Deliverance of Discipleship', in Emilie M. Townes (ed.), *A Troubling in My Soul: Womanist Perspectives on Evil and Suffering* (Maryknoll: Orbis, 1995).

Griffith, E. *In Her Own Right: The Life of Elizabeth Cady Stanton* (Oxford: Oxford University Press, 1984).

El Guindi, F. *Veil: Modesty, Privacy and Resistance* (Oxford: Berg, 1999).

Gundry, P. *Heirs Together: Mutual Submission in Marriage* (Ministry Resources Library, Grand Rapids: Zondervan Publishing House 1980).

Haddad Y. Y. 'Sayyid Qutb: Ideologue of Islamic Revival', in J. Esposcto (ed.), *Voices of Resurgent Islam* (New York and Oxford: Oxford University Press, (1983), 67–98.

Hampson, D. *Theology and Feminism* (Oxford: Blackwell, 1990).

Hampson, D. *Swallowing a Fishbone* (London: SPCK, 1996).

Hardesty, N. A. *Women Called to Witness: Evangelical Feminism in the Nineteenth Century* (Nashville: Abingdon Press, 1984).

Harding, S. Introduction: 'Is There a Feminist Method?', in S. Harding (ed.), *Feminism and Methodology* (Indiana University Press and Milton Keynes: Open University Press, 1987), 1–14.

Hartsock, N. 'Rethinking Modernism', *Cultural Critique*, Vol. 7 (1987), 187–206.

Hassan, R. 'Muslim Women and Post-Patriarchal Islam', in P. Cooey, W. R. Eakin and J. B. McDaniel (eds), *After Patriarchy* (Maryknoll: Orbis, 1991), 39–64.

Hawley, J. S. *Fundamentalism and Gender* (Oxford: Oxford University Press, 1994).

Heelas, P. *The New Age Movement* (Oxford: Blackwell, 1996).

Hoff, J. 'Gender as a Postmodern Category of Paralysis', *Women's History Review*, Vol. 3, No. 2 (1994), 149–68.

Hollway, W. '"I Just Wanted to Kill a Woman". Why?: The Ripper and Male Sexuality', *Feminist Review*, No. 9 (October 1981), 33–40.

Homan, R. *The Ethics of Social Research* (London and New York: Longman, 1991).

Hull, G. Gaebelein. *Equal to Serve: Women and Men in the Church and Home* (London: Scripture Union, 1989).

Humphreys, L. *Tearoom Trade: Impersonal Sex in Public Places* (Chicago: Aldine, 1975).

Huntington, S. P. 'The Clash of Civilizations?, *Foreign Affairs*, Vol. 72, No. 3 (1993), 22–50.

Iannaccone, L. 'Rational Choice: Framework for the Scientific Study of Religion', in L. Young (ed.), *Rational Choice Theory and Religion: Summary and Assessment* (New York: Routledge, 1995).

Iannaccone, L. and Miles, C. 'Dealing with Social Change: The Mormon Church's Response to Change in Women's Roles', *Social Forces*, Vol. 68, No. 4 (1990), 1231–50.

Jorgenson, D. L. *Participant Observation: A Methodology for Human Studies* (Newbury Park, London and New Delhi: Sage, 1989).

Kabbani, R. 'A Holy Revolution', *Spare Rib* (December 1992/January (1993), 35–41.

Kandiyoti, D. *Women, Islam and the State* (Basingstoke and London: Macmillan – now Palgrave, 1991).

Kandiyoti, D. 'Beyond Beijing: Obstacles and Prospects for the Middle East', in *Beyond Beijing* (Syracuse, University Press, 1997).

Karam, Azza, M. *Women, Islamisms and the State: Contemporary Feminisms in Egypt* (Basingstoke: Macmillan – now Palgrave, 1998).

Kelly, L. Burton, S. and Regan, L. 'Researching Women^ Lives or Studying Women^ Oppression? Reflections on What Constitutes Feminist Research', in M. Maynard and J. Purvis (eds), *New Frontiers in Women's Studies* (London and Bristol, PA: Taylor and Francis, 1996), 27–48.

Khan, S. M. *Why Two Women Witnesses?* (London: Ta-Ha Publishers Ltd, 1993).

Kian, A. 'Women and Politics in Post-Islamist Iran: the Gender-Conscious Drive to Change', *British Journal of Middle Easter Studies*, Vol. 24 (1) (1997), 75–96.

Kose, A. 'Native British Converts to Islam: Who Are They?, Why Do They Convert?', *The American Journal of Islamic Social Sciences*, Vol. 12, No. 3 (Fall 1995), 347–59.

Kristeva, J. 'La femme, ce n'est jamais ça' *Tel Quel*, 59 (Automne 1974), 19–24 .

Kroeger, C. Clark, Evans, M. and Storkey, E. *The Women's Study New Testament: based on the NRSV* (London: Marshall Pickering, 1995).

Kroeger, C. Clark. *Women's Bible Commentary* (InterVarsity Press, forthcoming).

Land, H. and Rose, H. 'Compulsory Altruism for Some or an Altruistic Society for All?', in P. Bean, J. Ferris and D. Whynes (eds), *In Defence of Welfare* (London and New York: 1985), 74–95.

Lewis, P. *Islamic Britain* (London and New York: I. B. Tauris, 1994).

Loades, A. (ed.), *Feminist Theology: A Reader* (London: SPCK, 1990).

Lofland, J. *Doomsday Cult* (Englewood Cliffs, NJ: Prentice- Hall, 1966).

Lofland, J. and Stark, P. 'Becoming a World Saver: A Theory of Conversion to a Deviant Perspective', *American Sociological Review*, Vol. 30 (1965), 862–75.

Lorber, J. and Farrell, S. *The Social Construction of Gender* (Thousand Oaks: Sage, 1991).

Luff, D. 'Dialogue across the Divides: "Moments of Rapport" and Power in Feminist Research with anti-Feminist Women', *Sociology* Vol. 33, No. 4 (November 1999), 687–704.

Lyon, W. 'Islam and Islamic Women in Britain', *WOMAN: A Cultural Review* Vol. 6, No. 1 (Summer 1995), 46–56.

Lyotard, J.-F., *The Postmodern Condition: A Report on Knowledge*, trans. G. Bennington and B. Massumi (Manchester: Manchester University Press, 1984).

McCarthy Brown, K. 'Fundamentalism and the Control of Women' in J. S. Hawley (ed.), *Fundamentalism and Gender* (Oxford: Oxford University Press, 1994), 175–201.

McCrickard, J. 'Born-Again Moon: Fundamentalism in Christianity and the Feminist Spirituality Movement', *Feminist Review*, No. 37 (Spring 1991), 59–67.

McClintock Fulkerson, M. 'Changing the Subject', *Literature and Theology*, Vol. 10, No. 2 (June 1996).

McRobbie, A. 'The Politics of Feminist Research: Between Talk, Text and Action', *Feminist Review*, Vol. 12 (1982), 46–57.

Mack, P. *Visionary Women: Ecstatic Prophesy in Seventeenth-Century England* (Berkeley, Los Angeles and London: University of California Press, 1992).

MacRobert, I. *The Black Roots and White Racism of Early Pentecostalism in the USA* (Basingstoke: Macmillan – now Palgrave, 1988).

Makhlouf, C. *Changing Veils: Women and Modernisation in North Yemen* (London: Croom Helm, 1979).

Malet, K. 'Headless Women? The Role of Single Women in the Contemporary Evangelical Church' (MA dissertation, University of York, Centre for Women's Studies, 1998).

Mascia-Lees, F., Sharpe, P. and Ballerino-Cohen, C. 'The Postmodernist Turn in Anthropology: Cautions from a Feminist Perspective', *Signs*, Vol. 15, No. 11 (1989), 7–33.

Maynard, M. 'Methods, Practice and Epistemology: The Debate about Feminism and Research', in M. Maynard and J. Purvis (eds), *Researching Women's Lives from a Feminist Perspective* (London and Bristol, PA: Taylor and Francis, 1994), 10–27.

Maynard, M. '"Race", Gender and the Concept of "Difference" in Feminist Thought', in H. Afshar and M. Maynard, (eds) *The Dynamics of 'Race' and Gender* (London and Bristol, PA: Taylor and Francis, 1994a).

Maynard, M. and Purvis, J. (eds), *New Frontiers in Women^ Studies: Knowledge, Identity and Nationalism* (London and Bristol, PA: Taylor and Francis, 1996).

Mellor, P. A. and Shilling, C. 'Reflexive Modernity and the Religious Body', *Religion*, Vol. 24 (1994), 23–42.

Mellor, P. A. and Shilling, C. *Re-forming the Body: Religion, Community and Modernity* (London, Thousand Oaks and New Delhi: Sage, 1997).

Mernissi, F. *Women and Islam: An Historical and Theological Enquiry*, trans. Mary Jo Lakeland (Oxford: Blackwell, 1991).

Mernissi, F. *The Veil and the Male Elite* (New York: Addison-Wesley, 1991a).

Mernissi, F. *The Forgotten Queens of Islam*, trans. Mary Jo Lakeland (Cambridge: Polity Press, 1994).

Mernissi, F. 'Arab Women's Rights and the Muslim State in the Twenty-first Century: Reflections on Islam as Religion and State' in M. Afkhami (ed.), *Faith and Freedom* (London and New York: I. B. Tauris, 1995), 33–50.

Miller, J. Baker, *Toward a New Psychology of Women* (Harmondsworth: Penguin, [1976] 1988).

Mirza, K. and Nielson, J. S. *The Silent Cry: Second Generation Bradford Muslim Women Speak*. Series: Muslims in Europe (Birmingham: Centre for the Study of Islam and Christian Muslim Relations, Selly Oak Colleges, 1989).

Moghissi, H. *Feminism and Islamic Fundamentalism: The Limits of Postmodern Analysis* (London and New York: Zed Books, 1999).

Moi, T. *Sexual/Textual Politics* (London and New York: Routledge, 1985).

Morgan, M. *The Total Woman* (New York: Pocket Books, 1975).

Mortimer, E. *Faith and Power: The Politics of Islam* (New York: Vintage, 1982).

Mulvey, L. 'Visual Pleasure and Narrative Cinema', *Screen*, Vol. 16, No. 3 (1975), 1–20.

Najmabadi, A. 'Hazards of Modernity and Morality: Women, State and Ideology in Contemporary Iran', in D. Kandiyoti (ed.), *Women, Islam & the State* (Basingstoke: Macmillan – now Palgrave, 1991), 48–76.

Nielson, J. *Muslims in Western Europe*. Islamic Surveys (Edinburgh: Edinburgh University Press, 1992).

North, C. 'Crushing the Bones: The Attraction of Christian Fundamentalism for Women', in *Women against Fundamentalism*, No. 8 (1996), 19–20.

Oakley, A. 'Interviewing Women: A Contradiction in Terms', in H. Roberts (ed.), *Doing Feminist Research* (London: Routledge & Kegan Paul, 1981), 30–61.

Oakley, A. *Subject Women* (London: Fontana Paperbacks, 1982).

Oakley, A. *Social Support and Motherhood* (Oxford: Blackwell, 1993).

Odeh, L. A. 'Post-colonial Feminism and the Veil: Thinking the Difference', *Feminist Review*, No. 43 (Spring 1993), 26–37.

Omid, H. *Islam & The Post-Revolutionary State in Iran* (Basingstoke, Macmillan – now Palgrave, 1994).

Onyx, J. and Benton, P. 'Empowerment and Ageing: Toward Honoured Places for Crones and Sages', in G. Craig and M. Mayo (eds), *Community Empowerment* (London and New Jersey: Zed Books, 1995).

Ozorak, E. W. 'The Power but not the Glory: How Women Empower Themselves Through Religion', *Journal for the Scientific Study of Religion*, Vol. 35 (1) (1996), 17–29.

Page, R. 'Elizabeth Cady Stanton's *The Women's Bible*', in A. Loades (ed.), *Feminist Theology: A Reader* (London: SPCK, 1990), 16–21.

Paidar, P. *Women and the Political Process in Twentieth-Century Iran* (Cambridge: Cambridge University Press 1995).

Pateman, C. 'The Patriarchal Welfare State', in L. McDowell and R. Pringle (eds), *Defining Women* (Cambridge and London: Polity Press, 1992), 223–45.

Pawson, D. *Leadership is Male* (Guildford: Eagle, 1997).

Percy, M. *Words, Wonders and Power: Understanding Contemporary Christian Fundamentalism and Revivalism* (London: SPCK, 1996).

Phoenix, A. 'Practising Feminist Research: The Intersection of Gender and "Race" in the Research Process', in M. Maynard and J. Purvis (eds), *Researching Women's Lives from a Feminist Perspective* (London and Bristol, PA: Taylor and Francis, 1994), 49–71.

Phoenix, A. 'Dealing with Difference: The Recursive and the New', *Ethnic and Racial Studies*, Vol. 21, No. 5 (September 1998), 859–80.

Piper, J. and Grudem, W. *Recovering Biblical Manhood and Womanhood: A Response to Evangelical Feminism* (Wheaton, Illinois: Crossway Books, 1991).

Poland, F. 'Breaking the Rules: Assessing the Assessment of a Girls' Project', in L. Stanley (ed.), *Feminist Praxis* (London and New York: Routledge, 1990), 159–71.

Poston, L. *Islamic Da'wah in the West: Muslim Missionary Activity and the Dynamics of Conversion to Islam* (New York and Oxford: Oxford University Press, 1992).

Pride, M. *The Way Home: Beyond Feminism, Back to Reality* (Westchester, Illinois: Crossway Books 1985).

Puar, J. 'Identity, Racism and Culture: Second Generation Sikh Women and Oppositionally Active "Whiteness"', in M. Maynard and J. Purvis (eds), *New Frontiers in Women's Studies: Knowledge, Identity and Nationalism* (London and Bristol, PA: Taylor and Francis, 1996), 127–50.

Rahman, F. *Islam* (Chicago: University of Chicago Press, 1979).

Rappaport, J. 'Terms of Empowerment/Examples of Prevention: Toward a Theory for Community Psychology', *American Journal of Community Psychology*, Vol. 15, No. 2 (1987), 121–48.

Renzetti, C. M. and Lee, R. M. (eds), *Researching Sensitive Topics* (Newbury Park and London: Sage, 1993).

Richardson, J. T. 'Experiencing Research on New Religions and Cults: Practical and Ethical Considerations', in W. B. Shaffir and P. A. Stebbins (eds), *Experiencing Fieldwork: An Inside View of Qualitative Research* (Newbury Park and London: Sage, 1991), 62–71.

Riesman, D. *The Lonely Crowd: A Study of the Changing American Character* (New Haven: Yale University Press, [1950] 1993).

Riviere, J. 'Womanliness as Masquerade', in V. Burgin, J. Donald and C. Kaplan (eds), *Formations of Fantasy* (London: Methuen, 1986).

Rose, S. *Keeping Them out of the Hands of Satan: Evangelical Schooling in America* (New York and London: Routledge, 1988).

Roseneil, S. 'Postmodern Feminist Politics', *The European Journal of Women's Studies*, Vol. 6 (1999), 161–82.

Rosenhan, D. L. 'On Being Sane in Insane Places', *Science* Vol. 179 (19 January 1973), 250–8.

Rowbotham, S. *Hidden from History: Three Hundred Years of Women's Oppression and the Fight Against It* (London: Pluto Press, 1973), 74, 77.

Rowbotham, S. 'The Trouble with "Patriarchy"', *New Statesman*, 21/28 (December 1979), 970–1.

Rowlands, J. 'A Word of the Times', in H. Afshar (ed.), *Women and Empowerment* (Basingstoke: Macmillan – now Palgrave, 1998), 11–34.

Ruether, R. R. 'The Liberation of Christology from Patriarchy' in A. Loades (ed.), *Feminist Theology: A Reader* (London: SPCK, 1990), 138–57.

Russell, L. M. and Clarkson, J. S. (eds), *Dictionary of Feminist Theologies* (London: John Knox Press, 1996).

Ruthren, M. 'Hallelujan for the Sceptic', *Independent* (13 July 1995).

Sabbah, F. A. *Woman in the Muslim Unconscious*, trans. Mary Jo Lakeland (New York, Oxford and Beijing: Pergamon Press, 1984).

Saiffullah Khan, V. 'The Pakistanis: Mirpuri Villagers at Home in Bradford', in J.L Watson (ed.), *Between Two Cultures: Migrants and Minorities in Britain* (Oxford: Blackwell, 1977), 57–89.

Saivings, V. 'The Human Situation: a Feminine View', *Journal of Religion*, Vol. 40 (1960), 100–12.

Scanzoni, L. and Hardesty, N. *All We're Meant to Be* (Waco, Texas: Word Books, 1974).

Scott, M. *The Role and Ministry of Women* (Esher, Surrey: Word (UK) Ltd./ Pioneer, 1992).

Scott, M. *Women in Leadership: Issues and Essays* (Cobham, Surrey: Pioneer People, 1994).

Shaaban, B. 'The Muted Voices of Women Interpreters' in M. Afkhami (ed.), *Faith and Freedom* (London and New York: I. B. Tauris, 1995), 61–77.

Shaham, R. (1993) 'A Woman's Place: A Confrontation with Bedouin Custom in the Shari'a Court', *Journal of the American Oriental Society*, Vol. 113 (1993), 192–7.

Shepard, W. 'Fundamentalism, Christian and Islamic', *Religion*, Vol. 17 (1987), 355–78.

Sölle, D. *Thinking about God* (London: SCM Press, 1991).

Spradely, J. P. *The Ethnographic Interview* (New York, Chicago and London: Holt, Rinehart and Winston, 1979).

Stacey, J. 'Can There be a Feminist Ethnography?', *Women's Studies International Forum*, Vol. 11, No. 1 (1988), 21–7.

Stacey, J. 'Imagining Feminist Ethnography: A Response to Elizabeth E. Wheatley', *Women's Studies International Forum*, Vol. 17, No. 4 (1994), 417–19.

Stanley, L. and Wise, S. *Breaking Out: Feminist Consciousness and Feminist Research* (London: Routledge and Kegan Paul, [1983] 1993).

Stanley, L. and Wise, S. *Feminist Praxis: Research, Theory and Epistemology in Feminist Sociology* (London: Routledge, 1990).

Stanton, E. Cady. *The Women's Bible* (Edinburgh: Polygon, [1898] 1985).

Stapleton, R. Carter. *The Gift of Inner Healing* (Waco, Texas: Word Books, 1976).

Storkey, E. *What's Right with Feminism* (London: SPCK, 1985).

Stowasser, B. F. *Women in the Qur'an, Traditions and Interpretations* (New York and Oxford: Oxford University Press, 1984).

Townes, E. M. *A Troubling in My Soul: Womanist Perspectives on Evil and Suffering* (Maryknoll: Orbis Books, 1995).

Trible, P. 'Feminist Hermeneutics and Biblical Studies', in A. Loades (ed.), *Feminist Theology: A Reader* (London: SPCK, 1990), 23–9.

Trible, P. *Texts of Terror: Literary-Feminist Readings of Biblical Narratives* (Philadelphia: Fortress Press, 1984).

Tucker, R.A and Liefeld, W. L. *Daughters of the Church* (Grand Rapids: Zondervan Publishing House, 1987).

Turner, B. S. *Orientalism, Postmodernism and Globalism* (London and New York: Routledge, 1994).

Van Leeuwen, M. S. *Gender and Grace* (Illimois: Inter Varsity Press, 1990).

Wadud-Muhsin, A. *Qur'an and Woman* (Kuala Lumpur: Penerbit Fajar Bakti Sdn. Bhd., 1992).

Walker, A. *Restoring the Kingdom: The Radical Christianity of the House Church Movement* (London: Hodder and Stoughton, 1985).

Walker, A. 'Fundamentalism and Modernity: The Restoration Movement in Britain' in L. Caplan (ed.), *Studies in Religious Fundamentalism* (London: Macmillan – now Palgrave, 1987), 196–210.

Ware, V. *Beyond the Pale: White Women, Racism and History* (London: Verso, 1992).

Warner, S. R. 'Work in Progress toward a New Paradigm in the Sociology of Religion', *American Journal of Sociology*, Vol. 98 (1993), 1044–93.

Warnock Fernea, E. *In Search of Islamic Feminisms: One Woman's Global Journey* (New York, London, Toronto, Sydney and Auckland: Doubleday, 1998).

Werbner, P. and Modood, T. (eds), *Debating Cultural Hybridity: Multi-Cultural Identities and the Politics of anti-Racism* (London: Zed Books 1997).

Wichroski, M. A. 'Breaking Silence: Some Fieldwork Strategies in Cloistered and Non-Cloistered Communities', *Qualitative Sociology*, Vol. 19, No. 1 (1996), 265–81.

Wheatley, E. E. 'How Can We Engender Ethnography with a Feminist Imagination?' A Rejoinder to Judith Stacey, *Women's Studies International Forum* Vol. 17, No. 4 (1994), 403–16.

Wheatley, E. E. 'Dances with Feminists: Truth, Dares, and Ethnographic Stares', *Women's Studies International Forum*, Vol. 17, No. 4 (1994), 421–3.

Wiesner, M. 'Luther and Women: 'The Death of Two Marys' in A. Loades (ed.), *Feminist Theology: A Reader* (London: SPCK, 1990), 123–37.

Williams, D. S. *Sisters in the Wilderness: The Challenge of Womanist God-Talk* (Maryknoll: Orbis, 1993).

Williams, D. S. 'A Womanist Perspective on Sin', in Emilie M. Townes (ed.), *A Troubling in My Soul* (Maryknoll: Orbis, 1995), 130–49.

Wolffe, J. 'Fragmented Universality: Islam and Muslims', in G. Parsons (ed.), *The Growth of Religious Diversity: Britain from 1945* (London: Routledge, in association with Oxford University Press, 1993), 133–72.

Yegenoglu, M. *Colonial Fantasies: Towards a Feminist Reading of Orientalism* (Cambridge, New York and Melbourne: Cambridge University Press, 1998).

Young, L. (ed.), *Rational Choice Theory and Religion: Summary and Assessment* (New York: Routledge, 1995).

Index

academic feminism 44–5
access to revivalist groups 54–6, 61
Adam and Eve, interpretations
    of 29
adultery, punishment for 109
Afshar, Haleh 5
Ahl al-Qur'an (People of the
    Qur'an) 29, 52, 104
Ahmed, Leila 25–6
Algeria 134
altruism, compulsory 46
Amin, Qassim, *The Liberation of
    Women* (1899) 26
An-Nisa Society 14
anthropology, socio-cultural 73
anti-feminism 5–6
    among Christian groups 125
Anwar, Ghazal 28, 120
Apocalypse 13
Arabs, pre-Islamic 108–9
Arat, Yesim 135
authority
    and 'covering'
        interpretation 150–3
    male 22, 24, 78–9, 186
    as protection 91–2
    see also leadership
autonomy 33
    and empowerment 159, 160, 161,
        162
    negation of 105, 166
Azuza Mission 13

Badawi, Dr Zaki 140
Balmer, Randall 80
Baptist churches 50
Baptist Faith and Mission
    Statement 85–6, 107
Barker, Eileen 62
Barnhouse, Donald Grey 23–4, 90

Bartky, Sandra 3
benefits 183–4
    Christian perception of 164–5
    emotional gains 175–7
    intellectual gains 172–4
    material 35, 164, 170–1, 180–3
    practical gains 177–80
    spiritual 164, 171–2
    welfare 114
Bible 18, 78, 90
    see also New Testament
Bible study groups 173, 174
biblical feminism 6, 29–34, 186–7
    and concept of equality 106, 107
    and prophecy 148
    view of submission 90, 146
    and women's rights 116
black women 39, 146
    and concept of equality 106–7
Borland, Katherine 71
Bradford, Muslim immigrant
        community 14, 16
Brasher, Brenda 77, 87, 163–4, 165
Brethren in Christ Church 50
Bucaille, Maurice, *The Bible, the
        Qur'an and Science* 20
Bulbeck, Chilla 69–70

Campbell, John, Jesus
        Fellowship 55, 60
caring, women's role in 45–6
celibacy
    as option for women 22, 23
    and submission to
        leadership 87–8
    veil associated with 147
chador, responses to 138
charismatic movement 10, 12,
        17–19, 172
    and concept of renewal 107, 165

child-rearing, support in   87,
    179–80
childbirth   23, 86
choice   1, 163–4, 183–4
    and life-style losses   165–8
    see also benefits; rational choice
        theory
Christian fundamentalism   23–4,
    90–1
    rejection of science   21
Christian revivalism   9, 11, 12–13
    charismatic   17–19
    see also house church fellowships
Christianity
    and concept of rights   105, 107–8,
        114–16, 124–5
    expansionism   132
    and improvement of women's
        status   109
    'muscular'   91
    and rights through religious
        affiliation   115–16
    tradition of head covering   145,
        147–8, 151–2
    see also Bible
Christians
    born-again   54, 165
    interviewees   63
    non-stereotypical views   97–9
    perceptions of gains and
        losses   164–8, 170–83
    responses to question of obedience
        in marriage   84–9
    submission to male leadership   90
Christians for Biblical Equality   30,
    49
Christologies, feminist   32, 33
church attendance   18
Church of England, use of
    'obedience'   80
Church of God, Cleveland,
    Tennessee   93
class
    and choice of veil   133
    and concept of equality   106–7
    of interviewees   38

colonial feminism   26
community living   51, 167, 179
complementarity   27, 30, 120
conservative evangelicalism   10, 30,
    31, 164, 171
consultation
    mutual (Christian view)   85
    mutual (*shura*)   80, 82, 95–6
control   183
    masculine   22
    social   130, 138, 160
conversion, as aim of Christian
    revivalists   19
converts to Christianity, 'born
    again'   54, 165
converts to Islam   54, 55, 63, 169–70
    African-American   15–16
    changes made by   168–9
    racial abuse towards   137, 141
    and wearing of *hijab*   137, 141,
        143–4
Cotton, Ian   17–18, 19, 50
Council on Biblical Manhood and
    Womenhood (CBMW)   4
Covenant Ministries   49
covering
    Christian interpretation of   150–3
    see also head covering; *hijab*
creation myth, Sumerian   4
crosses, emblematic   147
cult, use of term   54, 56
cultural hybridity   16
culture
    and faith   16–17
    and interpretation of
        Islam   111–12, 120–1, 122–3
    as loss   167
custom, and religion   16–17

Darwinism, rejection of   21
data collection   37–8, 43
Davis, Angela   39
decision-making
    by men   78
    women excluded from   127, 144
deconstructionism   38–9

difference 1, 35, 39
  and equality 121
  and shared voice 4–5
divorce
  and custody of children 114
  guilt-free 105, 117
  legal rights 113, 117, 126
  and remarriage 117, 118
domesticity, conflict with
    liberty 120–4
dress
  hostility towards Islamic 137,
    138, 140, 143–4
  interpretation of Qur'anic ruling
    on 119
  Islamic revivalist 53, 132–3
  modest 148–9, 153–5
  reform 133
  see also head covering; *hijab*
Dworkin, Andrea 5, 121

e-mail
  correspondence on 55–6
  interviews 38, 48
economic imbalance 163
economic independence 29, 104–5,
  120
ecstatic practices 10, 12–13
  Sufism 12
  'Toronto Blessing' 12–13, 177
education, women's right to 105,
  117, 187
egalitarianism 106
  see also complementarity
Egypt
  feminism in 25–6
  Islamic 'fundamentalism' 14,
    130–1
  wearing of *hijab* 133, 134
emblems 147
empiricism, feminist 43–4
employment
  legal rights 113, 114
  see also work
empowerment 29, 159–63, 186, 187
  and emotional gains 175

kinds of 183–4
  in self-abnegation 94
  and types of power 160–1, 183–4
Enlightenment, the, and concept of
    rights 25, 103, 124
equality
  in biblical feminism 30
  in Christian interpretations
    106–7
  and difference 121
  Enlightenment view of 25
  feminist concepts of 27
essentialism 21
ethnography 45–8, 73–4
Evangelical Alliance 49
Evangelical Theology 32
evangelicalism 31
  submission in marriage 85–9
  see also conservative
    evangelicalism

faith 173
  biblical feminism and 30
  and culture 16–17
Faludi, Susan, *Backlash* 5
families
  converts' relations with 169–70
  extended 112, 170, 178, 179
family, as basic unit of Islamic
    society 59, 170, 178
feminine submission
  in New Testament 146
  in Protestant
    fundamentalism 23–4
  see also obedience; submission
femininity
  as social construction 3, 42–3
  sublime model of 22
feminism 2, 34, 40, 187
  academic 44–5
  in Arab world 133
  and autonomy 33, 105–6, 166
  backlash against 5–6
  conflict between freedom and
    domesticity 120, 124
  Islamic rejection of term 34, 123

feminism (*cont*)
   and legal rights 113
   as man-hating 25, 113
   recruitist 74
   see also Islamic feminism; Muslim
      feminism; women's rights
feminist research 39, 44–5
feminist standpoint 43–4, 47
feminist theology 28, 29–34
   rejectionist 33
finance, personal 1, 121, 125
   legal rights 113, 114
   rights in divorce 118
   rights within marriage 118, 121,
      126, 170–1, 180–1
Fiorenza, Elisabeth Schussler, *In
   Memory of Her* 32–3
Fiqh (jurisprudence) 28
fitra, concept of 20–1
Forster, Roger, *Jesus Life* 13
Foucault, Michel 67, 130, 131
freedom
   conflict with domesticity 120, 124
   spiritual 79
   within Islam 178–9
fundamentalism
   and 'feminization' of religion
      90–1
   and 'Other' 9–11
   positive impacts of 77
   use of term 5, 10

gains *see* benefits
Game, Ann 42
gatekeepers
   and access to groups 54–5, 61
   selection of interviewees 63
gender
   dismantled 38
   dress differences 154, 157
   relations 21, 185
gender equality, in biblical
   feminism 30, 106
gender scepticism 2, 3
generational differences, among
   British Muslims 15, 16–17

Genesis, 3:16 (on pain) 86
Gerami, Shahin 77
Ginsburg, Faye 73–4
glossolalia, phenomenon of 12
God
   feminine images of 33
   spiritual links with 171–2, 183
   submission to 24
Göle, Nilufer 37, 72, 134
Gordon, D. F. 69
Gospel of Prosperity (US) 171
Grant, Jacquelyn 106–7
Great Britain
   hijab (veiling) in 135–44
   house church movement 17
   Muslim communities 14–15,
      51–2
   occupation of Egypt 25–6
   protection of rights 104
Griffiths, Valerie 49, 148
Gundry, Patricia 22, 92–3, 109

Hadith (sayings of the Prophet)
   interpretation of 28, 122, 123
   rejection of 29, 52, 104, 118
Hagar's story (Genesis) 32, 146
hair, braided 146
hajib (separation) 128–9
Hampson, Daphne 105–6, 166
Harding, Sandra 41, 43
Hassan, Riffat 118
head covering
   in Christian tradition 145, 147–8,
      151–2
   St Paul's injunction on 31, 145,
      152
   see also dress; *hijab*; modesty;
      veiling
healing 177
hierarchies 38, 150–2
hijab (veil or covering) 29, 66,
   127–8
   benefits of 59, 133–4, 139–40,
      143–4
   in Britain 135–44
   as exclusionary 131–2

rejected by Submitters 52
  as symbol of defiance 131
  as symbol of Islamic revival 27,
    132–5
Holy Spirit, revelation of 78, 172
homosexuality 23
house church fellowships 9, 10, 18
house church movement 17–18,
    49–50
  Gospel of Prosperity 171
  male leadership 24, 90, 151
  and remarriage of divorcees 117
  social programmes 19, 107, 125
  views of obedience in
    marriage 97–9

Ichthus Christian Fellowship 13,
    18, 19, 154, 165
  social projects 19
Ichthus Fellowship 49–50
  and women's rights 115
idolatry 80
ijtihad (independent reasoning) 12,
    27
independent church movement 24,
    107
India, colonial 29
Indigenous Women's Theology
    (Native American) 32
inheritance
  Muslim women's rights of 29,
    105, 109, 117
  pre-Islamic traditions 108–9
Internet
  Islamic groups' use of 52
  Jesus Fellowship use of 50, 51
  participant observation on 48
  proselytization on 14
Internet groups 4
interpretative conflict 71
interviewees 63–4
  perception of submission 87–8
interviews 64–5
  conduct of 65–7
  group 65
  interpretative conflict 71

mixed methods 74–6
power relations 67–72, 74–5
transcripts and editing 69
use of tape recorders 64–5
Iran
  Islamic 'fundamentalism' 14
  reform under Reza Shah 133
Iran, Islamic Republic of 33
Isis, cult of 146
Islam
  codification 28–9
  cultural interpretation of 16–17,
    111–12, 120–1, 122–3
  'fundamentalism' 5, 14, 130–1
  gender balance in 91
  meaning of word 52
  medieval 22, 28
  modernist feminism 26
  modesty and head covering
    in 127–8, 129–35
  particular rights for women 104–5
  progressive readings of 28–9
  as religion for women 119–20
  revivalism in 11–12
  tradition of renewal (*tajdid*) 10,
    12
  Zakat (charitable giving) 181
  see also Muslim feminism;
    Muslims; Qur'an; Shi'i; Sunni
Islamic feminism 6, 26–7, 186–7
  compared with biblical
    feminism 118
  and complementarity
    principle 30–1, 118
Islamic Foundation, Leicester 52,
    55, 104
  weekend workshop 58–9
Islamic revivalism 9, 20–2
  in Britain 14–15, 135–44
  and concept of *fitra* 20–1
  modesty and headcovering 127–8
  in United States 15–16
  use of *hijab* 132–5
  see also hijab
Islamists, non-feminist 27
Islamophobia, Report 140

Jamaat i-Islami   15
Java, Islamic dress in   134, 136
Jesus Army   92
    work with homeless   60
Jesus Fellowship   14, 49, 50–1, 75,
        147
    and celibacy   23
    community living   51, 167
    and economic equality   115
    male and female roles   93, 164
    ministry to young men   91–2
    modesty in dress   149, 154, 155
    New Creation headquarters
        (Northampton)   54, 60
    Sheffield branch   60
Jordan   134
Judaic law   105
Judaism   87
    women's rights in   108

Kabbani, Rana   29, 120, 123
Karam, Azza   130–1
Khalifa, Rashad   52
knowledge
    Christian use of term   174
    in Qur'an   173, 174

law
    and rights   108
    rights under British   112–14
leadership
    concept of   88–9
    men and church   78, 87, 101
    and power   161–2
    in Protestant revivalism   24
    and submission   90–4, 100–1
    see also authority
Leeds University, 'Islamic Awareness
    Week'   59, 136, 144
liberation theology   32
lived experience   3, 7
    acknowledgment of   21–2
    of marriage   87
losses, Christian perception of
    165–8
Luff, Donna   37, 68, 74

Luther, Martin, and role of
    women   22, 23

McClintock Fulkerson, Mary   93–4
male gaze   3, 139–40
Manchester, Muslims in [West
    Didsbury]   16
marriage   92–3
    'biblical   92–3
    Christian views of obedience
        in   84–9
    as holy state   86, 186
    Islamic view of   29, 86
    Muslim view of obedience in
        82–4
    obedience in   79–80, 81–9
    Protestant view of   22–3, 86
    right to marry freely   112, 117,
        126
    rights within   113, 117, 126
    shura (mutual consultation) in   82
    submission in evangelical   85–9
    submission in   77–9, 95–6
Married Women's Property Act
    (1870)   29, 120
masculinity, reinforcement of   24,
    90–1
materialism   171, 182
men
    as church leaders   78, 87, 101, 186
    membership of Christian revivalist
        groups   58
    reclaiming Christianity for   91
    responsibilities as husband
        117–18
    responsibility for decisions   88–9
    submission to God   82, 89, 95–6,
        100, 123
Men Women and God, and women's
    rights   115
Men Women and God (conservative
    evangelicals)   10–11, 30, 49,
    164
    biblical feminism of   6, 30
    and obedience in marriage   84
Methodists, early   13

methodology 37–8
  and ethnography 45–8
Middle Ages
  feminine images of God 33
  sublime femininity 22
Middle East 77
millennialism 13–14
  1990s 19
  and concept of rights 107, 125
Millerites (United States) 13–14
miracles 17
modesty
  in behaviour 149, 155
  in Christian tradition 146–7,
    148–9, 153, 156–7
  Qur'anic requirement of 128–9,
    130, 156–7
Morgan, Marabel, *The Total
    Woman* 24
motherhood 5, 117–18
  legal rights 113, 126
  reaffirmation of 77
Mujerista Theology (Latina) (US) 32
'muscular Christianity' 91
Muslim feminism 26, 27, 28–9
Muslims
  in Britain 14–15, 51–2
  as enemy of West 55
  interviewees 63–4
  non-stereotypical views 95–7
  perception of women's
    rights 116–17
  perceptions of gains and
    losses 168–9, 170–83
  responses to question of obedience
    in marriage 82–4, 96
  second-generation British 54

Nahdi, Fuad 14, 15
natural law
  and complementarity 27
  Qur'an and 20, 21
New Creation Community,
    Northampton (Jesus
    Fellowship) 54, 60
New Testament 4, 109

nuns
  interpretation of vows 84
  use of veiling 147

Oakley, A. 67, 69
obedience, use of term 62, 78, 83–4
objectification 42–3, 75
  sexual 1, 134
objectivity 41–2
Odeh, Lama Abu 132–4
Omid, Homa 175
oppression
  internalized 3, 159
  Islamic dress portrayed as 140–1
Other, fundamentalism as 9–11

Paidar, Parvin 187
Pakistan, cultural interpretation of
    Islam 16–17, 120
participant observation 38, 56–61
patriarchal relations 6, 9, 186
  and violence 4
patriarchy, and interpretation of
    tradition 23, 24, 112
Pecan fellowship 19
Pentacostal movement 10, 18, 93,
    107
  ecstatic practices 12
pessimism, and millenialism 13–14
Phoenix, Ann 37, 67–9
Pioneer Network 18, 49–50, 155
  and male leadership 151
  modest behaviour 149
Pioneer People (Surrey) 49, 61, 75
  policy on women's role 98–9
postmodernist theory 2, 21, 38,
    40–1
poststructuralist analysis 2–4, 21,
    40, 161
power
  Foucauldian analysis of 67,
    159–60
  see also empowerment
power relations 40
  in interviews 65–6, 74–5
  and structure 175–6

prayer, Christian   18, 61
Promise Keepers (US)   91
prophecy, women's permission
      to   31, 148
proselytization, on Internet   14
protection
   provided by male authority   91–2
   veiling as sign of   130
Protestantism, and role of
      women   22–3

Queer Theology   32
questionnaires   61–3
   question on gains and losses   164
   question on obedience in
         marriage   81–9
   question on rights   104, 112–14
   respondents   63–4
   snowball   37–8, 43, 48–9
Qur'an   78
   beating of women
         (Surah 4:34)   4, 122–3
   dress and decorum
         requirement   128, 129
   interpretation, by men   11–12, 28,
         112, 119
   naturalness of   20, 21
   and science   20
   as source of knowledge   173, 174
   on submission of women   79
   tafsir (interpretation)   83, 85,
         122–3
   on women acting as witnesses
         110
   women's interpretation of   28, 29,
         120, 122–3
   women's rights in   6, 104, 110–11

racism   137, 141, 153
rational choice theory   34–5, 103,
      163–4, 185
religion
   renewal of interest in   34–5
   and social custom   16–17
   women as members   6, 31
religiosity, feminist   44

researcher(s)
   and participant observation
         56–61
   power in interviews   65, 67–72
   role of   47, 73–4
resistance, *hijab* as signifying   128,
      135
respondents
   Christian   48, 49–51
   Muslim   48, 49, 51–4
responsibilities, towards
      children   113–14, 162–3
reverts to Islam   53–4, 168
revivalism   2, 11–13
   as authentic version of
         religion   111
   gender relations in   9
   reasons for joining   34–5
   use of term   10–11, 62
   in the West   14–17
revivalists, and secularists   72–3
rewards   106, 181–2
rights   103–4
   Christian view of   105, 107–8,
         114–16, 124–5
   in early societies   108–9
   and equality   106–7
   in Qur'an   6, 104–5
   superiority of God-given over
         human law   116–17
   through religious affiliation
         115–17
   under British law   104, 112–14
Roman Catholicism   42, 111
   head covering tradition   145,
         147
Roman Catholics, converts to
      Islam   63
Rowlands, Jo   159, 160–1

sacrifice   166, 167
St Paul   105, 150
   injunction on head covering   31,
         145, 152
   on submission to male
         authority   24, 79, 100, 106

St Peter, on submission of wives   86, 146

science, and the Qur'an   20

Scott, Martin, Pioneer People   55, 60

segregation
   hajib (separation)   128–9, 136
   in Islam   127–8, 144
   as social control   130

self, power over   175, 176, 177, 178, 183

self-abnegation/self-emptying (*kenosis*)   34, 79, 105–6, 166
   as means of empowerment   93–4

servant, concept of   107

sex, extramarital   23

sexuality   1, 22, 134

Shakers   13

Shariah (Islamic law)   28, 52, 104
   as superior to customary law 111–12

Sheffield, Jesus Fellowship community house   60

Shi'i, clerical leadership   11

shura (Islamic principle of mutual consultation)   80

sin   31, 167

single women, view of submission   87, 96, 97–8, 99

social control   160
   veiling and segregation as   130, 138

social justice   19, 106–7, 115

social responsibility   125

Southern Baptist Convention, and submission in marriage   85–6, 107

speaking in tongues   12, 13

spiritual goals   97

'Spring Harvest' charismatic meeting (1978)   17

Stacey, Judith   45, 47–8

Stanley, Liz   44, 45

Stanton, Elizabeth Cady   125
   The Women's Bible (1898)   30

Stanton, Noel   50

status, enhancement of   115

structure, need for   67, 175–6, 187

submission
   complexity of issue   99–101
   concept of   79–81, 186
   dangers of unconditional   86–7
   and leadership   90–4, 100–1
   in marriage   77–9, 81–9
   mutual   82–3
   as self-emptying   79
   'tie-breaker' idea of   89
   to male church leadership   78, 87
   unconditional   99–100
   use of term   62, 84

Submitters, International Community of (Islamic group)   29, 52–3, 104, 110–11
   and claim to women's rights 118–20
   and social responsibility   125

suffering   97

Sufism   12, 17

Sunnah (example of the Prophet)   28, 52, 104, 109, 119

Sunni Islam   11
   ijtihad (independent reasoning)   12, 27

support, practical   87, 179–80, 182–3

surveillance   159–60

tafrita, ritual of   131–2

tafsir (interpretation of Qur'an)   83, 85, 122–3

Taliban, Afghanistan   138

theodicy   97

'Toronto Blessing'   12–13, 177

Turkey, dress reform   133, 134

Unification Church   62

United States   125, 163
   conservative evangelicalism   10
   feminist theology   32
   Muslims in   15–16, 55
   Protestant fundamentalism   90–1
   Southern Baptist Convention   85–6

universities, Islamic societies   53, 55

Van Leeuwen, Mary Stewart   86–7
veiling
    in ancient world   129–30
    degrees of   134–5
    as social control   130, 138
    see also hijab
Vineyard Fellowship   18, 50
violence
    images of   4
    towards wives   86–7

Wadud-Muhsin, Amina   109, 110, 130
Welsh Revivals   13
Wheatley, Elizabeth   47–8
Wichroski, Mary Anne   83–4
witch hunts   22
witness, women forbidden to act
    as   22–3, 109–10
Womanist Theology (African-American)   32, 146
women
    attempts to define   39
    'biological destiny'   21
    as church members   6, 31, 90–1
    compulsory altruism   46
    differentiated from wives   90

prophetic ministry of   31
    as Qur'anic scholars   120, 122
    religiosity   44
    right-wing   5–6
    support in child-rearing   87, 179–80
    vulnerable   91
women's rights   123
    importance of   125
    in Qur'an   6, 104–5
    in religious traditions   25
    within revivalism   10
    see also feminism; rights
work
    right not to   5, 117–18, 121
    right to   5
    see also employment
working-class women, shared
    interests   39

Yemen   131–2
York, Christian revivalist
    meeting   58, 151, 164
Young Muslims UK (YMUK)   15, 51–2, 75, 104, 173
    and interpretation of Islam   178–9
    sisters' work group   58–9
    website   14

Zoroastrianism   29